BELIEFS AND BELIEVERS
Teleclass Study Guide

John K. Simmons, Ph. D.
Professor of Philosophy and Religious Studies
Department of Philosophy and Religious Studies
College of Arts and Sciences
Western Illinois University
Macomb, Illinois 61455

Produced by:

Governors State University
University Park, Illinois

KENDALL/HUNT PUBLISHING COMPANY
4050 Westmark Drive   Dubuque, Iowa 52002

ACKNOWLEDGEMENTS

The producers wish to express their thanks to the following individuals without whom the production of this teleclass would not have been possible.

Teleclass Students:

Anita Anderson
Phyllis Beckman
Nancy Bonnevier
Barbara Campbell
Janet Cowser
Warren Daubenspeck
Yvonne Daubenspeck
Suzanne Detlahn
Elmer Eisenberg
Jamie English
Geoff Eysenbach
Virginia Eysenbach
Sharon L. Gibson

Chris Goldenstein
Lynne Hostetter
Robert Hostetter
Helen E. Hughes
Larry Larson
Mary L. McGinnity
Elaine MacKenzie
Virginia Parker
Barbara Sherman
Annette Sullivan
Susan J. R. Vorwerk
Valeria R. Wolff

And the faculty and staff of the:

Division of Humanities and Social Sciences
Dr. Sonny Goldenstein, Chairperson
College of Arts and Sciences
Dr. Roger K. Oden, Dean
Governors State University

Table of Contents

Introduction to the Second Edition

I am very happy to introduce to you the *second edition* of "Beliefs and Believers." "Beliefs and Believers" offers you an opportunity to explore religion and religions in an open-minded, unbiased fashion. As the title suggests, you are exposed to real people, real believers who help you understand what it is they believe, why they believe it, and how their beliefs guide personal and collective behavior within their respective communities.

Instructors and administrators who have used the original edition of the teleclass for years and found it to be exactly what they need in an introductory course in the humanities or social sciences might wonder why we would tinker with success; "if it ain't broke, don't fix it!" There is much truth in that venerable cliché. However, I hope to assure you that we have kept the best of the original version – lively class sessions, provocative guests, world experts, and *teachable* subject matter – and combined it with sparkling new production techniques, a truly global perspective in terms of interviews with *real* believers, scintillating student discussions, and a greatly enhanced thematic and organizational approach to the already *learner-friendly/teacher-friendly* course concepts. I thought it would be interesting to share some background on the creation and evolution of the *Beliefs and Believers* teleclass while expressing my excitement in having the opportunity to create a new offering of this already successful teleclass.

Beliefs and Believers: A Short History of the Teleclass, or, "Why Does This Class *Work?!*"

Beliefs and Believers was born in the "educational trenches" during my first years as a teacher at Western Illinois University (WIU). Perhaps that is why it *works* in so many different higher education settings. WIU is a typical mid-sized state university, with approximately 13,000 students, many of them the first in their family to explore higher education. I arrived at WIU in the fall of 1987, a newly-minted Ph.D. from a highly-touted research program, in love with my discipline, and possessed by the erroneous notion that everyone naturally cared about religious studies and had an instinctive feel for the humanities. Wrong! It only took a few lectures in my over-crowded, lower-division classes to realize that WIU students looked upon religious studies as a kind of *metabolic impediment* to their "more practical" educational goals.

That harsh realization provided the inspiration spark that ignited the *Beliefs and Believers* prototype. While theory and concepts are important, students were bored to death in classes that consisted only of lectures. I realized that I had to bring "religious studies alive," and what better way to do it than to bring *real believers*, via video, into the classroom. On my own, with my department's camcorder, I roamed about Illinois making rough interview tapes with Hindus, Buddhists, Christian fundamentalists, pagan-priestesses and just about any other religious person who would put up with me. Those "home grown" tapes made all the difference in the classroom. Suddenly, my students were paying attention. And, more importantly, they were learning.

My new approach was barely a year old when, in 1989, I was most fortunate to come out on top of an Illinois state university system-wide teleclass competition. This creative idea, spawned by Dr. David Ainsworth of Governors State University, was to produce teleclasses that could then be used throughout the Illinois university system, spreading the educational talent around, so to speak. Under Dr. Ainsworth's expert guidance as executive producer, we completed the first edition of *Beliefs and Believers* during the Spring 1990 semester.

Since 1990, I have taught *Beliefs and Believers* every semester to my practical, down-to-earth WIU students. Now imagine, for a moment, the veritable plethora of new insights that might emerge in an eight year period of teaching, drawn from student discussions, the reworking of key themes and concepts, and the inevitable emergence of new perceptions on how to organize and present video material. Then imagine the opportunity to travel half way around the world to obtain video material in order to fulfill the essential *Beliefs and Believers* pedagogical goal; affording students, through video interviews, the opportunity to meet real believers in our educational quest to understand religious activity.

For me, it was an opportunity of a life time, and a GSU video crew of five plus myself set off on a preproduction journey that would find us interviewing a Muslim Sufi sheik in Israel, a provocative woman channeler teaching Gnostic yoga under the majesty of Washington's Mt. Rainier, a Coptic Orthodox Christian monk absorbing the silence of the Egyptian desert, a Taoist priest honoring the ancestors in San Francisco, Chicago-based Imam W. Deen Muhammad, world leader of African American Islam, as well as witches, pagan-priestesses, fundamentalist Christians, and many, many other fascinating believers who spoke eloquently and passionately about their belief systems and the impact of religion on their respective communities.

I look forward to having you accompany me and the teleclass students into the fascinating world of believers and their beliefs. Please feel free to share your comments, reactions, and insights with me. I learn as much from my "distant" students as I do from my classroom students.

Welcome aboard!! Enjoy the ride!

Professor John K. Simmons

Department of Philosophy and Religious Studies
Western Illinois University
Macomb, IL 61455

J-SIMMONS@wiu.edu

Course Description

"Beliefs and Believers" is an exploration into the nature and function of belief structures or "worldviews." These worldviews exist in formal organized entities such as traditional religions or as political and personal ideologies, such as feminism or environmentalism. Worldviews do not exist in a vacuum. The dynamic, living relationship between a religious organization or worldview and its immediate cultural environment provides a "living laboratory" for the study of beliefs and believers. In this course, representatives from a wide variety of religious and secular perspectives will help you develop an understanding of what they believe and why they believe it. You will gain some initial exposure to the religious systems of major world religions – Hinduism, Buddhism, Taoism, Confucianism, Judaism, Christianity, Islam – as well as systems of belief which are outside the scope of what are deemed to be mainstream religious institutions, such as new age religions, neo-paganism, and "civil religion." I hope that by developing your skills of worldview analysis you may then begin to apply them in your own encounters with different belief systems.

Rationale

Traditionally, a plurality of religions and secular worldviews in any given society has resulted in tensions — sometimes leading to violence. What is needed is a religiously literate nation, one where citizens have learned to respond to religious differences, not with fear and violence, but with interest and understanding. The object of the course is to engage the subject of religious diversity in a non-threatening but thought-provoking manner, so that you will learn to be better informed about the place of religion and the need for religious tolerance in a pluralistic society.

Expected Student Outcomes

At the end of this course you should be able to:

Identify major religions and worldviews and describe them according to the following dimensions - mythic, experiential, doctrinal, ritualistic, ethical and social.

Class Outline

The videotapes are conducted in lecture/discussion style, supplemented with previously video-taped interviews and documentaries. Religious diversity in the United States is discussed according to six dimensions - experiential, mythic, ritual, doctrinal, ethical, and social. There are 24 one-hour videotapes, beginning with two introductory sessions on the nature of religion and on the conditions under which religious diversity has flourished in the United States. The six dimensions of religion are then discussed in detail.

The experiential dimension explores types of religious experience, meditation, mysticism East and West, and features Buddhism, the Apostolic Church of God, and New Age bookstores.

The mythic dimension explores the power of myth as "paradigmatic narrative," functions of myth, types of myths, and "civil religious" myths.

The ritual dimension explores varieties and functions of ritual, symbols and symbolic expression on both religious and secular levels.

The doctrinal dimension explores the functions of doctrine, the "dark" side of religion, and authoritative answers about the unexplainable.

The ethical dimension includes discussion of the relationship between belief and behavior, a cross-cultural look at religion-based ethical stances, and religious fanaticism.

The social dimension explores the relationship between religion and politics, the nature of sects, cults, churches, and denominations, Protestant roots of America, new religious movements, New Age religious quests, environmentalism, and feminism.

The final class session consists of a summary and review of the major themes discovered in the course. Class discussion focuses on the extent to which the course has changed the class participants' perceptions on religion and religious diversity.

How to Use This Course

Use the Study Guide as just that, a guide for your study of this course. In the guide I comment on each lesson in turn adding background material which will make the videotapes more meaningful. I then comment on the videotape discussion, and I suggest that you read this section *before* you watch the videotape, as an "advance organizer" for your thoughts. I also suggest review questions for you to reflect on. And at the end of each chapter, I list some references in case you would like to do some further research in various areas.

So, please, help yourself to a successful learning experience by following the instructions in the guide for each lesson, and watch the tapes in sequence.

Good luck, and may you too find that you have had a "vibrant, exciting" experience as you learn about "Beliefs and Believers."

BELIEFS AND BELIEVERS
Class 1 – Introduction: What Is Religion?

Introduction

Reflection: *Think about what the term "religion" means to you. Jot down a quick definition of the term. When you finish viewing the tape, go back and compare your definition with those expressed by students in the class. In addition, please reflect on why you have chosen to take this course and what you expected to gain from this educational adventure. How do your objectives and goals compare to those of the students in the class?*

What is religion? If asked to define the term, the average person might say something like, "Going to church, believing in God or reading the Bible." But religion is more than what goes on in those unusually shaped buildings that occupy prime real estate in the towns and cities of the United States. And religion is more than the predominantly Christian experience that characterizes religious life in this country.

From the earliest times, religion has provided human beings with a sense of purpose, meaning, order, belonging, psychological well-being and destiny. It has been a major, if not *the* major determinant of human behavior since the dawn of human consciousness.

Human beings are *reality creators*. Whether one wishes to say that human beings create world views or respond creatively to some transcendent reality, human religious consciousness can nevertheless be viewed as the womb from which culture and civilization emerge. Because values expressed religiously cause people to behave socially in certain ways, religion is inextricably linked to the quest for power, the political process. Is it any wonder that at the center of the vast majority of the world's wars and conflicts a religious dispute can be found? On the other hand, religions throughout history have provided the inspiration for that which is most beautiful, most sublime in human culture.

The very fact that religion has had and continues to have such a profound impact on human experience raises two key issues that we will grapple with throughout the semester. One is the pervasiveness of religion and the other is the diversity of religious expression. Of course in "Beliefs and Believers," when we use the term "religion," we are not speaking only of traditional religions such as Islam, Buddhism, Judaism, Hinduism, Christianity, Taoism, etc., but also of secular political ideologies such as Communism or ecological perspectives as promoted by groups such as Greenpeace. The point is that people act according to their *worldview*. This is the term we will use in this class to refer in a general sense to the colorfully creative ways in which human beings have related and continue to relate to the world around them.

Overall, as you view Class 1 keep in mind that when dealing with a subject like religion, it is best to keep definitions open-ended. No doubt your own definition of religion will change as we continue on our journey into this fascinating world. Students often want to know the right answer so that they feel comfortable at test time. But to get the most out of this class, don't be afraid to *live with the material* for a while before formulating your own ideas on exactly what the material means or how it relates to our exploration of "beliefs and believers."

1

Class 1

Key Class Themes

This lesson focuses on the following themes:

1. Benefits of taking a class in religious studies
2. Characteristics of religious studies
3. What is religion?
4. Identity and Relationship
5. Pervasiveness of religious experience
6. Boundary questions and rites of passage
7. Power of religion vs. truth of religion

Videotape Synopsis

- Class discussion
    Benefits of taking a course in religious studies
- Video interview with Professor Ninian Smart, University of California, Santa Barbara
- Class discussion
- Video interview with Professor Martin Marty, University of Chicago
- Class discussion
    Religious diversity
- Lecture/Graphics on Characteristics of Religious Studies
- Lecture/Graphics on Approaches to the study of religion
- Lecture/Graphics on What is religion?

Videotape Commentary

I suggest you read this section before you watch the videotape. You will find that it will help you organize your thoughts so that when you watch the tape it will be more meaningful. When you have finished viewing the tape, you may want to read this section again.

Class Discussion

What might a student gain by taking "Beliefs and Believers?"

There is the old adage that if you want to get along at a social gathering, never discuss sex, politics, or religion. Well, as we all know, sex and politics tend to be *primary* topics of discussion whenever any group of people get together to socialize. Religion, however, still carries something of a stigma and is studiously avoided as a topic of conversation. Perhaps it is because people consider religion to be a private affair. Perhaps it's because the topic tends to generate so many disagreements. Or perhaps it's because religion touches the most profound existential questions that challenge all human beings, and consequently never lends itself to light conversation. The sociologist Thomas O'Dea once described religion as the human response to three disturbing features of human existence: uncertainty, powerlessness, and scarcity. Obviously these topics do not go over well with the cocktail party set!

However, there are definite benefits in overcoming our squeamishness regarding religion, and once recognized, any open minded person should be more than willing to jump into what is certain to be a stimulating conversation. And that, of course, is the primary purpose of "Beliefs and Believers." We open our first class with a most appropriate question to the students? Why are they taking this course, and what do they expect to get out of this unique intellectual journey? Their responses along with our interview with Professor

2

Ninian Smart reveal some very good reasons why it is especially important, even crucial, to study religion in our present day and age.

Janet opens the discussion with an excellent point. Studying the religions of the world will make us more compassionate towards peoples around the world who may live in a very different cultural setting from our own. How true! When difference is encountered, be it a person, place or thing, ignorance generates fear, and fear in turn quickly dissipates into hatred and violence. Before a person can care about other human beings or feel compassion for them, one needs to understand them, and that includes understanding the most fundamental beliefs that provide a framework for how these people see the world.

As our beautiful, blue Earth shrinks due to the explosion in mass-communication and transportation technologies, there is a practical reason for developing what we will call *worldview analysis skills.* Whether your chosen profession might be business, medicine, education, the arts, international relations, law or politics, you are certain to encounter colleagues and co-workers who are religiously diverse. Knowing how to appreciate and respect their religious perspective and also having the skills to explain your own religious path (or lack thereof) without becoming defensive will make you a much better communicator and facilitate whatever your shared professional goal might be.

Larry offers an interesting analogy comparing "truth in language" with "truth in religion." So often the topic of religion is avoided because people feel that their chosen set of answers to life's profound questions is the one and only truth. To study another religion is a) useless because this different set of answers must be delusional or b) dangerous in that it may undermine the believer's faith in his or her chosen worldview. Following Larry's analogy, would any thinking person from, say, the United States claim that learning to speak Chinese would have a damaging effect on her or his English skills? Of course not! In fact, most people who learn another language note that their communication skills, writing and speaking, improve in the language of their birth.

Suzanne contributes to this discussion by offering an insight she garnered from a Native American, James Yellowbanks. He said, "You don't have to turn into someone else in order to appreciate someone else." This is very good advice, indeed, for students embarking on a semester-length investigation of religion. Walking a mile in someone's moccasins before you judge them, another Native American proverb, does not mean you get to keep the moccasins! Just as learning another language improves one's overall language skills, studying different religions can only work positively to help us deepen our own faith or formulate our own spiritual beliefs or philosophy of life.

Video Interview with Professor Ninian Smart, University of California, Santa Barbara

We put the same question, "What are the benefits of studying other religions?" to one of the *bona fide* world experts in the field of religious studies, Professor Ninian Smart. Professor Smart has spent a lifetime studying religions and religious peoples from around the world, so his perspective is well worth pondering. Interestingly enough, his answers almost mirror the insights shared by the students in our opening discussion.

He remarks that every civilized person should know about the world's religions. He adds that what we are about to do, study other religions, often challenges people's assumptions about religion. In studying religions that have emerged in other cultures, we can deepen our understanding of our own culture. Again, we are speaking about the benefit of overcoming cultural ignorance. How are we to understand Mexican or Vietnamese culture without appreciating how, in each instance, Roman Catholic or Buddhist ideas have informed cultural understandings about politics, economics, selfhood, nature, family, life and death?

In turn, how can we genuinely understand the history and culture of the United States without considering how Protestant Christian ideas influenced cultural creations in the early colonial period. Or again how can we comprehend our culture without considering how millennial fervor coupled with evangelical enthusiasm inspired the pioneers to extend the nascent nation's boundaries westward or, in more recent times, how the rise of the New Religious Right corresponded with the country's general *moral malaise*? Indeed, studying the religions of other cultures makes one more attuned to how the complex fabric of our own culture is woven with assumptions about identity and relationship that are fundamentally religious in nature.

We also asked Professor Smart to shed some light on one of the basic misconceptions students bring to their first religious studies class. Quite understandably, the uninitiated confuse religious studies with theology. As Professor Smart points out, theology is primarily concerned with establishing religion's *truth*. The academic study of religion is concerned with the *power* of religious activity. As Chris astutely notes in our post-interview discussion, the power we speak of here is the power of *behavior*. Other students observe that we see that power in magnificent art, architecture, and music but also in horrific violence and hatred done in the name of religion. In any event, theologians teach religion. Professors of Religious Studies teach *about religion*, and as you will come to see as we move through the semester, there is a huge difference between these two approaches.

The Place for Religious Studies

During the class lecture/graphics section, we will go over in more detail the characteristics of religious studies. But since this is our first class, it may be helpful to expand our discussion on the difference between religious studies, what we are doing in "Beliefs and Believers," and studying religion within a faith community.

If you have never encountered the academic study of religion, and you are a person from a traditional religious background, the difference between the two endeavors should quickly become evident. First, no one is telling you what to believe. No one is telling you what the *truth* is about life. And no one is speaking to you from within a particular faith community, be it Roman Catholic, Methodist, Nation of Islam, Buddhist, or Scientology. We are interested in understanding and describing different phenomena that we encounter in our exploration of worldviews; we are not interested in establishing which one presents the *correct* view of reality.

Second, while no one would think of inhibiting your own spiritual growth or denying you the chance to express your perspective on reality or the dimensions of your chosen worldview, it is simply not the aim of this class to nurture or deepen your faith. Indeed, it may happen, but it is not a class objective or goal. Should you wish to do so, feel free to pray during exams! The point is that we are here to learn about different worldviews, not to be religious in the sense that one might experience "renewed faith" on a church retreat. Though we will certainly encounter *true believers* in this class, no one is out to convert you or convince you that any one worldview does or does not present *ultimate truth*.

Third, when you gather to study religion from a faith community perspective, say, at a Bible study group, you bring with you a number of agreed upon presuppositions about the nature of reality. Examples are "God created human beings and the world, Jesus is my savior, so I'm going to go to heaven when I die," and so on. In the academic study of religion, we suspend or bracket our own religious views in order to come to the most balanced, authentic understanding of another perspective. Going back to our Native American proverb, that does not mean a Christian has to give up Christianity in order to grasp Buddhist principles. It simply means that we will try to approach worldviews with an open mind.

Video Interview with Professor Martin Marty, University of Chicago

As mentioned, another practical objective of "Beliefs and Believers" is to develop a genuine appreciation for religious diversity. An obvious reason is that most of us will continue to live in the United States, and this society is characterized by religious pluralism. "Pluralism" is a term which roughly means a number of different worldviews existing reasonably peacefully within the same society. In our quest to understand religious pluralism as it shapes American society, we turn to the premier scholar in American religious history, Professor Martin Marty. You might reflect on the following study questions prompted by Professor Marty's comments:

1. In the 21st century, will we see more or less religious pluralism in American society?

2. From the perspective of religious pluralism, how is American society different from what it was at the time of the founding of the nation?

3. How has the immigration of other peoples from other parts of the world affected religious pluralism in the United States?

4. In terms of religious diversity, is a midwest state such as Illinois, where Professor Marty resides, representative of other parts of the United States?

Following the interview, two opposing points are made in class discussion. Suzanne describes growing up in an inter-religious family. For her, appreciating religious diversity comes from a life time of watching first her parents then her own family learn to genuinely appreciate and have respect for the different religious perspectives present in the family setting. Making accommodations for differences in religious holidays, ritual practices or sets of answers to profound life questions is for Suzanne, simply a way of life.

On the contrary, Jamie provides us with an always welcome reality check. Religion, indeed, wields power and in the hands of the psychologically or emotionally challenged charismatic leader, all manner of evil can break loose. Believers can be stripped of their wealth, their hope, their purpose and their free will when they are broken under the power of a dysfunctional leader who, nevertheless, is skilled at controlling people through the power of religious ideas. Though later in the course when we discuss sects and cults, we might want to qualify his use of the term "dangerous cults" in describing these sorts of groups, the fact is that he is right. Developing worldview analysis skills also means achieving a level of critical analysis which will allow you to differentiate between what is genuine and authentic in religion and what, unfortunately, is fraudulent even dangerous. Religion, like politics, is about power. Just as the most altruistic and compassionate goals of a political system can be corrupted by a maniacal leader, so in religion what is sublime and beautiful can, in the wrong hands, become demonic.

Graphics / Lecture

The graphics on the characteristics of religious studies are fairly self-explanatory. What is being outlined for you is the methodological approach scholars use in the discipline of religious studies. And these will be the methods we will rely on throughout the semester. Regarding the "approaches to religion," if it is not obvious to you now, soon you will see that the *social/practical* approach delineates the intellectual journey we will be taking in "Beliefs and Believers."

I would, however, like to add a few additional comments on the following two sets of graphics, "What is Religion?" and "Pervasiveness of Religious Experience." In my traditional classroom setting at Western Illinois University when I begin the "Beliefs and Believers" course each semester, I tell my students that there is an ongoing homework assignment in this class; it will never be collected, it will never be graded, but failure to follow-up on this assignment can make the difference between success and failure in the course. That assignment is as follows: learn to see in the world around you what we discuss in class. It may take you a few classes to catch my drift, but when you learn to see the world through *religious studies glasses*, some new and remarkable insights will become your extra credit for taking this course. I guarantee that the class themes we discuss are pervasive in the world around us. Countless students have come back the day after we've discussed, say, ritual activity, and with a gleam of new understanding in their eyes tell me about how they never realized this or that activity, so commonplace in their experience, was a perfect example of a key class theme.

Your first assignment of this sort is to *see* how identity and relationship touch on virtually every human activity. When you wake up tomorrow morning, try to be conscious of how many of your thoughts and moment-to-moment decisions revolve around themes of who you are and what your relationship is to the people, activities and purposes that fill up your day. Is it any wonder that something as fundamental and powerful as religion would be intimately involved in defining identity and guiding relationships?

Students who have gotten the most out of this class feel compelled to begin an informal journal from the first day. Why don't you try it? For your first entry, jot down several examples you observe of the human preoccupation with identity or relationship. Or if you happen to be attending a religious service over the week, see how many examples of this same fundamental process you can detect in the sermon, ritual activity, symbols and attitudes of the believers who share the service with you.

Pervasiveness of religious experience is another key class theme to put to the *observer's test*. Students seem to struggle with this word "pervasive," but by using it I am purposely making a bold statement: No matter how non-religious you might be, at some time due to some event, you will experience the religious impulse whether it be a need to find meaning in a tragic occurrence such as a cataclysmic nature event, or a way to express thankfulness for an extraordinary event such as the birth of a child or a way to try to explain the often inexplicable challenges and changes of everyday human existence. Religion traditionally has provided ways to help humans make sense of their lives by providing answers to profound life questions, guiding ethical behavior and offering solace and comfort in the face of our shared mortality.

For the sake of clarity on this key point, allow me to again put before you the basic ideas in a simple outline form. Think back on your own life experience, and put the *pervasiveness of religion* theory to your own personal test.

Pervasiveness of Religious Experience

1. Boundary questions = questions concerning identity, relationship, meaning, purpose, etc.
2. Rites of Passage = major life events: birth, death, suffering, adulthood, marriage, love, tragedy, etc. = rites of passage generate boundary questions.
3. Most people are forced to ask boundary questions, at least during rites of passage.
4. Religions provide answers to boundary questions experienced during rites of passage.
5. Since all human beings go through rites of passage, religion in pervasive in human experience.

As the last piece of advice to end our first study guide chapter, don't just swallow our key class themes hook, line and sinker. Think for yourself. Put these ideas to the test. There are no easy answers in the wonderful world of religion, just an endless stream of provocative questions that must constantly be tested against real life experience.

Welcome aboard!

Videotape Graphics

 At this stage we suggest you watch the videotape. The graphics you will see on the screen are reproduced below to save you the trouble of copying them down. You might like to add your own comments as you watch the tape.

Religious Studies

Characteristics
– multidisciplinary
  - Cultural Studies
  - American Studies
– descriptive (phenomenological)
– polymethodic
– multicultural, comparative
– worldview analysis (open-ended)

Religious Studies

Methodology
observe, describe, compare, contrast cultural phenomena especially as it pertains to religions and religious movements

---

Approaches to Religion

– historical / cultural
– social / practical
– philosophical / theological
– personal

What Is Religion?

Religion = identity
       and
      relationship

Belief

Relate

What Is Religion?

Religion deals with answers to identity-forming questions:

Selfhood – "Who am I?"
Meaning – "Why am I?"
Purpose – "What do I do?"

What Is Religion?
Religion is relationship-guiding or defining; how do we relate to the Other?

Class 1

What Is Religion?

The Other can be many things:
– God
– nature
– other human beings – *compassionate*
– other cultures
– death, suffering, change
– rites of passage – *Birth, marriage* *Boundary?*

Pervasiveness of Religious Experience

Boundary questions =
identity, meaning, purpose, etc.

Touches all humans + all cultures

Pervasiveness of Religious Experience

Rites of passage =
birth, death, suffering, adulthood, marriage,
love, tragedy, etc. =
generate boundary questions

Pervasiveness of Religious Experience
All people ask boundary questions at least
during *Rites of Passage*

Pervasiveness of Religious Experience

Religions provide answers to *boundary questions*
experienced during rites of passage =
pervasiveness of religion

Review Questions

Answering the following questions will help you review key class themes and prepare for the examinations.

1. Is it necessary to have a clear definition of "religion" in order to study it?

2. How does the academic study of religion differ from theology or studying religion within a distinct faith community?

3. What are the benefits that might come from studying other religions?

4. What do we mean by "the pervasiveness of religious experience?"

5. What does Professor Martin Marty mean by "religious pluralism?" Will the United States continue to become more religiously diverse in the 21st century? (Also see the review questions for the Marty interview above.)

Sources and Further Readings

Livingston, James C. *Anatomy of the Sacred: An Introduction to Religion*, 3rd edition. Upper Saddle River, NJ: Prentice Hall, 1998.

Marty, Martin. *Pilgrims in Their Own Land*. NY: Penguin, 1984.

Schmidt, Roger. *Exploring Religion*, 2nd edition. Belmont, CA: Wadsworth, 1988.

BELIEFS AND BELIEVERS
Class 2 – Six Dimensions of World Views

Introduction

Reflection: *Think back on any experience you might have had attending a religious event? What kinds of activities occurred? Can you describe them and perhaps identify them as a dimension of religion? Also, please reflect on the holy. What makes some experiences sacred, extraordinary or beyond everyday existence? Where do human beings acquire their sacred symbols used in all religious activity?*

Where Do Religions *Come From?*

In Class 2, an interesting question arises: If no one had ever conceived (or responded to the revelation) of Christianity, Buddhism and Islam and so on, would not some other kind of "religion" have had to emerge to guide human beings through life's many challenges and changes? Though the answers to the most profound life questions regarding identity, meaning, purpose and destiny have been as diverse as the cultural expressions in which they arose, the fact is that all human beings must stand against the whirlwind of joy and suffering, hope and despair, life and death, wonder and horror which is the stuff of human existence. If nothing else, our mortality is the commonality that binds us together and forces us to formulate *religious answers* to the sometimes overwhelming demands of our shared human condition. Once again, we are at a *key class theme: the pervasiveness of religion.* Whether or not a person belongs to an identifiable religious organization, he or she must confront what we will come to call *boundary questions.* Another *question to live with* arises: Is the impulse to find answers to these questions ultimately a religious impulse even if it drives scientific or secular inquiry?

In this class, we will explore the *six dimensions of worldviews* which provide the overall structure for "Beliefs and Believers." Before you view the videotape, we need to underscore some key points. First, dividing worldviews up into six dimensions is not like cutting a pie into nice, neat pieces. In fact, as you will hopefully come to realize by the end of this class, all the dimensions are interrelated; thus, it is virtually impossible to separate one out from the others. So why do it at all? We have arbitrarily chosen these six dimensions so that you can begin to develop a structure, a framework, a grid that you can *lay down* on the different worldviews you encounter in order to better understand how a particular worldview *works* for the believers who adhere to it.

A rather crude analogy might be found in an automotive class. If you want to learn how a car works, you begin by analyzing the various components of the engine, transmission, braking system, etc., so that, in the end, you have mastered the overall function of the vehicle. All the components of the car are equally necessary, none is more important than another, and without all of them working smoothly together, you have a useless pile of junk. Of course, here, when speaking of worldviews, the analogy breaks down. A religion with a broken ritual dimension, for instance, is not hauled out to the junk yard. The point is that we have chosen this system of worldview analysis for educational purposes. Always remember that a true believer, in the practice of his or her chosen worldview, would never systematically break down religion in this manner.

The Six Dimensions of Worldviews

"Never judge a man 'til you have walked a mile in his moccasins" goes an ancient Native American proverb. This is certainly good advice, especially when trying to come to a genuine understanding and appreciation for a different religion or worldview. But a follow-up question arises: "How do we go about getting into those moccasins and heading down the trail on that mile walk?"

In pondering this question, Professor Ninian Smart, the world renowned expert in religious studies we met in Class 1, came up with the six dimensions of worldviews. "Beliefs and Believers" is based on Professor Smart's useful model for analyzing a diversity of religions and worldviews. While in the introductory mode, we would like to take a moment to introduce you to Smart's six dimensions so that we can put on those moccasins and head out on what is sure to be a fascinating journey.

1. The Experiential Dimension

What does it mean to "feel the presence of God?" Or to experience *the Holy?* Or to be "one with the universe?" What compels people, even non-believers, to enter into reverent silence during an encounter with one of Europe's great cathedrals, the pyramids in Egypt or a Buddhist temple in Japan? Religious experience, as we will see, is difficult to describe but, nonetheless, a powerful and important part of human experience. It is a portal that allows us to move from the everyday, ordinary experience into a new, extraordinary level of consciousness. "Who am I?" "Where did I come from?" "Where will I go when I die?" "What is the purpose of life?" Whenever and wherever people have pondered these deep, searching questions, the experiential dimension emerges. Thus, this dimension, a pervasive part of human experience, is also the source of the world's great religions.

2. The Mythic Dimension

What is a myth? Most people would answer "a false story, a fable, something fantastic, outside the bounds of reality." In the field of religious studies, however, the term is used in a very different – and correct – manner. Myths are profoundly true stories within the worldview of a believer. They may not be provable through the scientific method, and they may defy common sense or logic, but, nevertheless, they are *real* in that they guide the behavior of believers. Great religious leaders like the Buddha, Muhammad, or Jesus ignited the sparks of religious experience in their followers. Their followers, in turn, felt called upon to describe the life and works of their teachers in powerful narratives that cross the boundary between historical fact and faith. Myths provide models that guide human behavior within a given faith community – and, thus, are an important link between belief, believer, and behavior.

3. The Ritual Dimension

Ritual is what believers DO! From the point of view of the student, it is where "moccasin-walking" becomes the most exciting and most colorful. Rituals provide believers with a symbolic mode of communication designed to propel them out of ordinary experience and into extraordinary realities. As we will see, rituals are often based on the myths contained in a given worldview. Believers feel called upon to do what their great leaders did. Thus, Christians celebrate the ritual of the Last Supper (the Eucharist) just as Jesus did almost 2,000 years ago. And in participating in this unique, myth-based ritual, a devout Christian is brought back into authentic Christian experience

Taken together, we might think of the Experiential, Mythic and Ritual dimensions as an inward turning force in religions. Profound life questions arise and call for answers in the experiential dimension. A charismatic leader provides answers to those questions expressed in great deeds and inspired teachings. In the mythic dimension, those words and deeds are described, usually in sacred texts but sometimes in oral tradition. For believers, the key events in the mythic dimension are acted out in rituals which, in turn, transform ordinary experience into uniquely extraordinary experience (see diagram below).

Religious Experience

Ritual ← Myth

4. The Doctrinal Dimension

The doctrinal dimension cuts to the very heart of the course in that it is about what people believe. In fact, when the question "What is your religion?" arises, people are usually asking, "What do you believe, what are the set of answers you have accepted to life's profound questions?" While religion is more than just a set of answers, we will find that religious doctrines have a profound effect on the behavior of believers within a given religious community. In bringing order or focus to the colorful, symbolic world of myth and ritual, religious doctrines offer believers *authoritative proof* that their religious reality and everyday reality are one and the same. This is the positive side of the doctrinal dimension. However, when two very different descriptions of reality collide, world history tells us that the doctrinal dimension can stir believers to commit the most bloody atrocities in the name of their belief.

5. The Ethical Dimension

As people believe, so they will behave. Simply put, doctrine is to ethics as belief is to behavior. The ethical dimension, religious or secular, provides human beings with guidelines for *proper patterns of action*. The ethical dimension is relational. Whether expressed as laws, moral commandments, custom, or a system of values, it is the ethical dimension that guides us towards *proper* relationships with God (or Being), each other, nature, and culture. Ethics instill a sense of obligation and responsibility and provide mechanisms for redemption when there is a breakdown in ideal relational patterns. The Ten Commandments in Hebrew scripture, the Beatitudes in Christian scripture or the Eight Fold Path in Buddhism are classic examples of the ethical dimension. Of course, different doctrines may call for different ethical standards. Thus, ethical issues such as abortion, suicide, euthanasia, or sexual orientation are furiously debated by factions who approach these issues from different religious or secular perspectives.

6. The Social Dimension

Were it not for the social dimension, there would really be no reason to study religions except out of intellectual curiosity. But because human beings have chosen to gather together in communities to protect and propagate their religious perspectives, it is in the social dimension that the raw power of religious belief and behavior is made manifest. Just as the experiential, mythic, and ritual dimensions can be seen as inward turning forces in religion, the doctrinal and ethical dimensions turn outward, ultimately impacting on the social dimension in more ways than you might imagine (see diagram below). As stated in the rationale for this course, we live in a society with an enormous variety of worldviews. When we study the social dimension, we investigate how those worldviews are institutionalized in society. How do religious organizations interact with other institutions in society? Can we find neutral terms to describe different organizational patterns defined in terms such as *church, denomination, sect,* and *cult?* Why are some religions considered conventional while others are deemed non-conventional? And, ultimately, our exploration of the social dimension will provide some answers to a key course question: "How can we learn to appreciate a religious perspective that is different from our own?"

The Relationship of the Six Dimensions

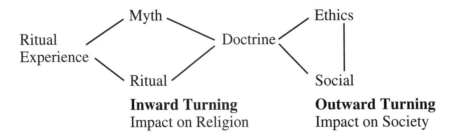

In Class 2, we will go into further discussion of the six dimensions of worldviews. In addition to providing an effective structure for the course, these dimensions will help you go *moccasin-walking* during our encounters with different religions in "Beliefs and Believers" and, hopefully, long after you have completed this course. Enjoy the journey!

Key Class Themes

This lesson focuses on the following themes:

1. What is Religion?
2. The Six Dimensions of Worldviews
3. The Source of Religious Symbols
4. The Sacred and the Holy
5. The Sacred and the Profane
6. Hierophany
7. Axis Mundi

Videotape Synopsis

- Interview with Rev. Cecil Williams at Glide Memorial Methodist Church
- Class discussion
- Mt. Beatitudes roll-in
- Graphics/lecture - Six Dimensions of Worldviews
- Class discussion
- Acra roll-in
- Graphics/Lecture - The Sacred and the Holy

Videotape Commentary

I suggest you read this section before you watch the videotape. You will find that it will help you organize your thoughts so that when you watch the tape it will be more meaningful. When you have finished viewing the tape, you may want to read this section again.

Interview with Rev. Cecil Williams at Glide Memorial Methodist Church, San Francisco

Creating a teleclass is always an adventure. And you have to possess some of the adventurer's optimistic "go for it" attitude in order to *make things happen* in gathering the video material for a course like "Beliefs and Believers." Such is the case with our interview with Reverend Cecil Williams. I won't belabor you with the details of every roll-in we produced for the class, but the Williams story is a classic example of a great interview emerging out of total chaos!

I had no connection at all to the Glide Memorial Methodist Church or to Reverend Williams but, based on his reputation, I decided to call the church two months before our San Francisco video excursion to set up an interview. Typically, I was bounced around to a number of employees until someone finally set up what I thought was a confirmed interview. We arrived well before the 9:30 a.m. Sunday service on the day the interview was scheduled and given the immediate circumstances, the timid would have fled in terror! Glide, as it is affectionately called, is in the heart of San Francisco, and the traffic was terrible. In order to produce top quality video material, we traveled with state-of-the-art equipment – and a lot of it – along with a crew of five, including executive producer, director, sound man, grip and myself. Just the logistics of parking the vans and getting the equipment into the church was overwhelming. Crowds were lined up in front of the church waiting to get in for the service. The rear entrance, the one we were instructed to use, also is the entrance for one of the truly humanitarian ministries within the Glide complex; assistance for San Francisco's large population of homeless people. Security, understandably, was tight, and no one knew we were coming.

As a case study in disastrous location shoots, this one was beginning to acquire all the necessary characteristics, especially when we found out that the man I contacted was no longer employed by the church. Finally, we were led into a crowded outer-office space and told to wait. Reverend Williams might be able to give us a short interview, but only after a third service at 12 p.m. that had just been added that morning.

At this point, it was a judgment call. Should we wait for three hours for a maybe interview or cut our losses and run? With all the diverse religious activity in San Francisco, there would always be something else of interest we could videotape. In the end we decided to wait and were well-rewarded. Not only did we obtain some fantastic footage of the 10:30 a.m. service which captures the experiential dimension of this energized ministry, but Reverend Williams proved to be an articulate, provocative, wise and brutally honest interviewee.

The segment we have included in Class 2 represents just a short part of the overall interview. We will be returning to reflect on Reverend Williams' wisdom at other appropriate points during the semester, but this initial interview is packed with provocative ideas. As you listen to his comments, reflect on our key class theme that religion, fundamentally, is about *identity-formation* and *relationship-guidance* in the face of the exigencies of life. Reverend Williams opens with an astounding statement, considering it comes from the mouth of a religious leader; "Be careful about religion because religion can be toxic." From the perspective of our key class themes, he seems to be saying that you cannot genuinely identify with a religion or call yourself a religious/spiritual person unless you *relate* to other human beings or form *relationships* that work to ease human suffering. In the timeless debate about whether true religiosity is measured by a person's belief or a person's works, Reverend Williams does not equivocate about coming down hard on the side of works. As he so eloquently puts it, "you can't have a new heaven until you have a new earth." And everything about his ministry, from the schools, employment offices, and soup kitchens for the homeless to the diverse and inclusive nature of the congregation, testifies to his "new earth" orientation.

The students do a good job of pulling this essential theme out of the interview. Chris relates the Reverend's comments back to our earlier discussion of *power*. Rather than anesthetizing believers into believing that identity and relationship can only be complete in some next life in heaven, the church has the power to inspire social action. Larry adds that he experienced *toxicity* in a strict fundamentalist Christian upbringing that, for him, was life-denying rather than life-affirming. Janet underscores her earlier call for compassion as the key to a *non-toxic* religious experience, while Warren offers a funny line designed to affirm that right action is more important than right belief if toxicity is to be avoided; "Religion should not be about pie in the sky, but Sam, I am!" From your own perspective, how do Rev. Williams' comments about religion illustrate our *identity/relationship* theme?

Six Dimensions of Worldviews / Lecture / Graphics

In the first section of this chapter, we have gone into quite a bit of detail on the *six dimensions of worldviews*, and it's not necessary to repeat that information here. It is interesting, however, as you view this segment of the class, to notice the students' response to the various dimensions. Almost unanimously, students appear to embrace myth and ritual but are nervous about the doctrinal dimension. Do you feel the same way? Is there a tension between religious experience and religious belief?

Doctrines and the accompanying ethical systems that develop out of doctrinal interpretations of experience, myth and ritual are highly important in defining individual and group identity and guiding relationships as *proper patterns of action*. Can it go too far? What happens when, as Phyllis notes, religious interpretations become androcentric and patriarchal and, thus, undercut the self-esteem and empowerment of woman? Janet asks a telling question; "Do you profess a belief or really believe it?" In other words, when a person becomes *indoctrinated*, are they addicted to a certain set of beliefs in a way that makes their relationship towards *the other* toxic? Or as Larry observes, do doctrines sometimes build walls around a given religion so that the beauty, peace and joy present in experience, myth or ritual cannot shine through? These are important questions. Please add to the list. Then let's hold the answers until we arrive at our investigation of the doctrinal dimension.

Mt. Beatitudes Roll-in

Though I am personally thrilled to have an opportunity in life to study religion, and there is hardly an aspect of that study that I would approach without enthusiasm, I am most excited about the development of new religious movements. When we explore the social dimension, we'll go into great depth on how and why new religious movements develop. But our Mt. Beatitudes roll-in is inserted here to underscore the *identity/relationship* theme. There are many complex reasons why a new religious movement begins, but one clearly is that a charismatic leader such Jesus of Nazareth redefines human identity and human relationships in a profound and powerfully moving manner.

Jesus, of course, was a Jew and grew up in the unstable and volatile world of Roman occupation in Judea. Not only were there numerous Jewish sects that argued over *identity and relationship* within Judaism, but there were numerous other Roman mystery religions, pagan practices and philosophies vying for the spiritual attention of the residents of first century Palestine. We might say there was a *competition* amongst sets of answers to profound life questions. As we will see when we arrive at the social dimension, religious and spiritual instability provides a fertile field for the development of new religious movements. No respected biblical scholar would claim that Jesus intended to *create Christianity* in his life and teachings. However, he offered such a novel interpretive approach to the fundamental religious features of identity and relationship, that, indeed, in time, a new religious movement did form.

Particularly if you come from a Christian background, the Mt. Beatitudes roll-in will test your nascent worldview analysis skills. If you have grown up with Jesus' Sermon on the Mount, you instinctively will relate to his sayings from a faith community perspective. Try to bracket your past history with these passages for a moment, and listen to how every one of his statements cuts directly to the issue of identity and relationship. Also note how he is transforming an older paradigm into something completely new. In doing so, he unleashed the *power* of religion. The reason *identity and relationship* are such powerful forces is that they are so fundamental to human experience.

Acra Roll-in

Where do the sacred symbols that resonate within all the religions of the world come from? From the most common everyday elements of our shared human experience. That is the theme of our Acra roll-in. Having just promised not to bore you with more "tales of the video journey," I'm compelled to share a bit of the background on the Acra shoot and garner some gratuitous sympathy for our hard working crew!!

Those of you familiar with intercontinental airline travel know the toll it takes on body and mind, if not soul. Our Israel trip began in Chicago (add four hours on a train for me to get from Macomb, Illinois up to Chicago), eight hours to Frankfurt, Germany, three hour lay-over, then a four hour flight from Frankfurt to Tel Aviv. Upon arriving, we endured a three hour stop-start bus ride from Tel Aviv to Nazareth, and finally hit the sack at about 11:30 p.m. after 26 hours of travel. No time for jet lag on this trip! We headed out the next morning at 8 a.m. and put in a 12 hour day of shooting. The next day we put in a 15 hour day, including eight full equipment set-ups and breakdowns; four in a day is considered excessive!

So the Acra trip, out to the Mediterranean coast on a beautiful, warm February Saturday (the Sabbath in Israel), seemed like a good way to unwind. We took the camera along to collect some B-roll (background tape to add color to the video productions), but we weren't expecting to do any extensive shooting. Well, I guess it was all my fault. We were meandering down the road by the port, when I noticed the fishermen tending their nets, people wandering through the market buying fruits, bread and vegetables. Music was in the air, and suddenly the muezzin (the crier in Islam who calls the people to prayer) sounded forth from a local mosque. Everyday ordinary activities were interrupted by a sacred activity, and I was suddenly struck by how we, indeed, do draw our most sacred symbols from the most mundane ordinary activities. Voila! The Acra piece was born!

The Sacred and the Holy

In our Lecture/Graphics material on the Sacred and Holy, we are drawing on the work of one of the greats in the field of religious studies, Professor Mircea Eliade (1907-1986), in later life a distinguished service professor in the Divinity School at the University of Chicago. In works such as "The Myth of the Eternal Return" (1949) and "The Sacred and the Profane" (1957), Professor Eliade sought to shed new light on the nature and substance of religious activity, not from the more popular *reductionistic* approach that attempted to explain away religion, but in a truly humanistic manner that revealed religion to be an essential part of all human cultural activity.

In our quest to understand the sacred and the holy, important subjects to explore before we officially enter the experiential dimension, we are indebted to Professor Eliade for making simple, at least in explanation, what is incredibly complex in the world of religion. Humans *create* their most sacred symbols out of the most ordinary (common) elements of human existence. Through a process he termed *hierophany*, meaning "something sacred shows itself to us," a tree, a mountain, a rock, or wine, bread, and fruit, can disclose a sacred or holy presence. We will explore symbols and symbol-making in more detail when we enter the ritual dimension, but for now, we might raise an interesting study question – can any human being live in a world completely devoid of anything sacred? For our study, the door by which we enter the experiential dimension and begin to answer the "Why?" question regarding religion swings back and forth between sacred and profane realms. In the next class on the *religious process*, we will try to come to a clearer understanding of why people are religious. But the religious process could not even begin were human beings devoid of this capacity to experience the sacred, the transcendent, and the holy and even more important in terms of human religious and cultural motivations, to respond to it by creating sacred symbols out of their ordinary experiences!

Videotape Graphics

 At this stage we suggest you watch the videotape. The graphics you will see on the screen are reproduced below to save you the trouble of copying them down. You might like to add your own comments as you watch the tape.

Six Dimensions of Worldviews

– Experiential (experience)
– Mythic (myth)
– Ritual
– Doctrinal (doctrine = belief)
– Ethical (ethics = behavior)
– Social (impact of religious beliefs on society)

Key Class Theme

   Beliefs
+ Believers
――――――――
= Behavior

The Sacred and the Holy

Sacred Space and Sacred Time:
Sacred and Profane modes of Being
(Mircea Eliade)

The Sacred and the Holy

Sacred = nonordinary, transcendent, wholly distinct
Profane = common, ordinary, utilitarian

The Sacred and the Holy

Hierophany = hieros means "sacred"
               phanein means "to appear"
Something sacred shows itself to us

The Sacred and the Holy

Key Point

The most common, profane object – a tree, a mountain, a rock – can disclose the sacred presence

Key Question

Can any human being really live in a completely desacralized world?

The Sacred and the Holy

The Holy = a breakthrough to the sacred, an opening to the divine; implies a hierophany

---

The Sacred and the Holy

Axis Mundi = the center of the world

– the space and time where communication with the divine is possible
– the original *time* when the cosmos was created
– cosmogony = the creation of the world
– imago mundi = reproduction of the creation myth

The Sacred and the Holy

Examples of Sacred Space and Time

– Mt. Zion, Jerusalem
– Mt. Tabor
– The Dome of the Rock
– Mt. Fuji in Japan
– The Ganges River
– The Jordan River
– Eyre's Rock in Australia

The Sacred and the Holy
Humans create sacred space and time out of the most ordinary, shared human experiences.

Class 2

Review Questions

Answering the following questions will help you review key class themes and prepare for the examinations.

1. What did Reverend Cecil Williams mean by the statement, "Religion can be toxic?" In your opinion, should religions and religious people put social action over "correct" belief?

2. List the six dimensions of religion, and offer a short definition of each one.

3. How do the key interrelated features of religion, *identity and relationship*, influence the development of a new religious movement? Please use the example from the Mt. Beatitudes roll-in in your answer.

4. What is the sacred and the holy? Where do human beings acquire the symbols to express the sacred? What did Mircea Eliade mean by the term, *hierophany?*

Sources and Further Readings

Eliade, Mircea. *The Sacred and Profane*, tr. Willard R. Trask. NY: Harcourt, Brace, & World, 1957.

Eliade, Mircea. *Cosmos and History: The Myth of the Eternal Return*. NY: Pantheon, 1954.

Smart, Ninian. *Worldviews: Crosscultural Explorations of Human Beliefs*, 2nd Edition. Englewood Cliffs, NJ: Prentice Hall, 1995.

BELIEFS AND BELIEVERS
Class 3 – Boundary Questions: Rites of Passage

Introduction

Reflection: *In the first two classes, we've tried to make the case that religion is worth exploring, intellectually or otherwise, because we are "homines religiosi." In order to understand human life in its fullness, we need to study humans as religious beings, just as we would study human activity from a biological, political, artistic or economic perspective. Before viewing our third class, please reflect on why humans are compelled to create religious expressions. What is it about human existence that has made and continues to make religious activity such a pervasive part of human cultural experience?*

In our first two introductory classes, we explored religion as a fundamental cultural phenomenon deeply rooted in the human condition. Put one way, our individuality causes us to be *apart*. Yet the religious impulse motivates us to seek a sense of *a partness* – to be whole within ourselves, within a community or with the cosmos. As human beings, we find ourselves faced with these seemingly conflicting impulses when pondering *boundary questions*, enduring a rite of passage, or struggling to see our religious ideals made manifest in political realities. Perhaps it is the tension between the sense of separateness and the drive for unity that makes it so difficult to accurately define our first dimension – the EXPERIENTIAL DIMENSION.

Before formally entering into a discussion of the experiential dimension, we still are in need of clarity on why we are religious humans, *homines religiosi*. Religious experience itself is part of the answer, but in Class 3 we want to dig deeper into the reasons, motivations and instincts that inspire the magnificent cultural expressions we now call *religion*. The map on this particular journey is the *Religion Process*.

Key Class Themes

This lesson focuses on the following themes:

1. The *Religion Process*
2. Pervasiveness of religion/spirituality in human experience
3. The spiritual/religious impulse in human kind
4. Rites of passage as a catalyst to human religious activity
5. The *seeker style* as a window into the *Religion Process*

Videotape Synopsis

- Class discussion
- Graphics, "The Religion Process"
- Video presentation on Pyramids/Egyptian museum in Cairo
- Video interview with Kate Cogan, self-proclaimed witch
- Video interview with Professor Paul Mundschenk

Class 3

Videotape Commentary

I suggest you read this section before you watch the videotape. You will find that it will help you organize your thoughts so that when you watch the tape it will be more meaningful. When you have finished viewing the tape, you may want to read this section again.

The Religion Process

By now, I'm sure you are aware that this teleclass, "Beliefs and Believers," is the second edition of this unique journey into the world of religion and religious studies. The original teleclass was recorded in 1990, only about a year after I created the course to meet the needs of my undergraduate students at Western Illinois University. While the teleclass has enjoyed national distribution and many thousands of students have had the opportunity to take the course, for the past eight years, I have been busy teaching the course virtually every semester in a traditional classroom setting at WIU. Like one of my own children, this course has grown and matured over the years, and in taking the second edition you will benefit from the maturation of the "Beliefs and Believers" teleclass.

As I mention in our opening class discussion, my primary motivation in teaching is to learn. I constantly learn from my students, and in that productive interaction over the years, I naturally have gained new insights into the nature and meaning of religious phenomena. In other words, there is nothing static about my approach to my classes or my approach to teaching. Over the years, in the creative environment of my WIU classroom, "Beliefs and Believers" has improved in the sense that I've found better ways to explain difficult class themes, acquired video material that better illustrates the point of view of a particular *believer*, or in the case of our six dimensions of worldviews, conceptualized a more dynamic explanation of how these dimensions interrelate and energize a given worldview. As a teacher who cares deeply about his subject matter and strives for a clear and entertaining classroom presentation, I'm thrilled to have another opportunity to teach "Beliefs and Believers" as a teleclass. Throughout this semester with the help of these top notch students in our television classroom studio, we will be working to bring you, the teleclass student, a more refined and hopefully more intellectually stimulating version of this course. The first example of new material drawn from my in-the-trenches classroom experience is the *Religion Process*. It will be worthwhile to review each of the five stages of the process here in the study guide.

The Religion Process

Over the years, I found that the *experiential dimension* is the most difficult dimension for students to grasp. There are probably many complex reasons why students struggle with religious experience, but it is vital to have at least some understanding of this dimension because without the extraordinary and unique phenomenon of religious experience, there would be no religion or religious activity. All the other dimensions are *driven* or *energized* by the first dimension, religious experience. Of course when we speak of *religious experience* in this class, we are using an expansive definition of the term.

In our quest to approach the *why question*, meaning *why do we have religion and religious activity*, we should be looking for an answer that is applicable to nearly every human being, in all times, in all places, and in all cultures; a gargantuan task, to say the least, but the *Religion Process* may come close to accomplishing two important steps in answering the *Why religion?* question: a) establishing the *pervasiveness* of religion/spirituality in human experience; and b) accounting for the spiritual/religious impulse in human kind. Let's review the five stages of the process:

The Religion Process

Five Stages

1. Self-consciousness
2. *Boundary Questions*
3. *Rites of Passage*
4. Spiritual dimension
5. Development of World Religions

By *self-consciousness*, we mean that extraordinary human capacity to *step outside of ourselves* and make judgments about the world we perceive, including nature, other human beings, the universe, even ourselves. Another way of putting it is that humans experience *self-transcendence*. While animals are conscious of being *a part* of their immediate environs, humans are also conscious of being *apart;* a gap exists between perceiver and perceived. This state of separateness, or self-consciousness, forces humans to ponder *existential questions,* and these questions inevitably lead to issues involving *identity and relationship*. Is it any wonder that *identity and relationship* are foundational in human religious activity? The pieces of the puzzle are starting to fit together.

Existential questions are *boundary questions*. Self-consciousness, the sense of being apart, compels human beings in all cultures to ask, "Who am I?" "Why am I here?" "What is the meaning and purpose of life?" "What is good and enduring?" "Why do we suffer?" "Where do we go when we die?" The impulse to ask these existential questions comes from a sense of separateness from that which we perceive. But self-consciousness alone is not enough to spark the *religious impulse*. Life itself demands that we come to agreed upon answers to boundary questions, and it does it through the identity-shaking and relationship-disrupting changes we call *rites of passage*.

Rites of passage, the third stage in our *Religion Process*, supports our *pervasiveness of religion* theme. Though the answers to the boundary questions that arise during rites of passage may be as different as the cultures in which they emerge, nevertheless, all human beings are faced with birth and death. In between are a series of events, also culture-based, that necessitate change in identity formation and accompanying changes in relationships. Rites of passage can include coming to adulthood, grouping (family, marriage, mating), love and tragedy, suffering and change or sacred vows.

Notice how religion traditionally steps in at these critical times to offer direction and supply answers to boundary questions that arise. In particular, the *ritual dimension* plays a key role during rites of passage. Consider, for a moment, how ceremonies and services touch all our major life events whether they might be religious or not; graduation, funerals, political holidays such as the 4th of July, the opening of the Superbowl or the All-Star Baseball game, heroic activity or natural disasters. Given an identity-shaking and relationship-disrupting event, you can bet humans will step in with some kind of ritual activity.

The fourth stage, the *spiritual dimension*, recognizes that *answers to profound life questions* must satisfy a set of complex, interrelated human needs. What we are referring to as the *spiritual dimension* includes emotional, psychological, intellectual and physical requirements that when met, help bridge the gap between *apart* and *a part*. In order for a self-conscious human being to cross a boundary generated by a rite of passage and successfully continue on life's journey, these needs have to be met. The spiritual dimension, then, is that aspect of human inner-experience that brings assurance and harmony in the face of identity and relationship changes. When we ask the *"Why?"* question of the world's great religious traditions, the *Religion Process* at least provides a sensible, working answer. As always, in a course like this, it is not the final answer; rather, it is a catalyst for a continuing conversation.

Stage five, the development of world religions such as Hinduism, Judaism, Buddhism, Christianity, Islam, Taoism/Confucianism, primal religions or alternative religions, is the inevitable process of human beings creating coherent answers to profound life questions that emerge during rites of passage. These religious systems have been proven successful in meeting the variegated human needs that make up the spiritual dimension and in doing so, help humans, individually and in community, make identity and relationship adjustments in the face of life's changes and challenges. As we move through the semester and meet believers from all of the above religious traditions, keep our *Religion Process* in mind. See if the stages we have listed make sense in the very real life experiences of true believers or, more importantly, in your own life.

Class Discussion

During our class discussion, Suzanne shares a moving experience that underscores our pervasiveness of religion theme. Of all the rites of passage that are an inevitable part of human experience, death understandably is the most challenging and, thus, demands resolution to identity/relationship questions. In one week, Suzanne witnessed the death of a good friend and consoled another friend whose child had committed suicide. Obviously, Suzanne is still processing this encounter with death, and her sensitivity brings out some powerful insights into human spirituality as a defining force at tragic moments.

She asks an important question in her own attempt to *find meaningful answers* to her encounter with human mortality: "Are we talking about religion or spirituality?" What she is grappling with is the fact that institutionalized religion, that is, religion with an identifiable set of answers to profound life questions, may not always help a person deal with an identity-shaking, relationship-shattering event like the death of a friend or family member. To find some resolution, some reconciliation, a person needs to *cross a boundary* out of a limited, selfish, materialistic view on life and into a more expansive realm where the ego is no longer the sole focal point for perceiving reality.

So often, the ups and downs of human existence are but the perceptual interpretation of the ego-eye looking out on the wonder and beauty of life through the encrusted aperture of self-centeredness. On a daily basis, most human beings think of themselves as the hub of the wheel around which all the other spokes revolve. A rite of passage such as death delivers a stern life lesson; not only are we not the hub of the wheel, but something far more powerful, call it the divine or simply call it life itself, is pulling the cart, and the direction or destination of the cart is something we will never know, at least not from the perspective of ego-consciousness. The painful emotions that accompany an encounter with death can never be resolved while a person huddles in a self-made bunker of pity, loss, and despair.

Suzanne intimates that *letting go* of a loved one who has crossed the boundary between life and death, a journey we all will take, can only be accomplished by experiencing a transformation on this side of death. From her perspective, spirituality is that aspect of human experience that works to initiate this change in identity and accompanying change in relationships. Religion is only effective during rites of passage if a person is spiritually attuned. If not, it offers only empty rituals and impotent symbols. Of course, this is Suzanne's opinion, and at this point in the course, it is best to leave it *out there*, so to speak, and put the spirituality/religion dichotomy to the test as we meet believers from a wide variety of religious perspectives. But it is an important question, one that will come up time and again as we explore the experiential dimension.

Egyptian Museum/Pyramids Roll-in

The pyramids are considered one of the *seven wonders of the world*, and I admit to being reduced to childlike wonderment standing before them. If you ever have a chance to visit them, take it! However, for all the majesty surrounding these ancient constructs, there is something, in the context of modern Egyptian culture quite disturbing about their presence on the borders of Cairo, a massive city of some 15 million people, many of whom live in poverty.

The tension is clearly between the glory of an old civilization and the struggle of a modern one. Of course religion plays a key role in both instances. The pharaohs who built the pyramids at Giza were captivated by the rite of passage we have just discussed, death. In their quest for immortality, they created one of the world's most magnificent, most colorful civilizations. However, as Barbara points out in class discussion, the pharaohs *bought* personal immortality with the blood of hundreds of thousands of workers who literally were worked to death building these launching pads to eternity.

In a similar way, Islam, the dominant religion of Egypt today, aspires to the highest of ideals, but in the day-to-day life of the average Egyptian, can bring as much misery as joy. This has nothing to do with Islam as one of the world's most sublime statements about identity and relationship. Later in the course, we will have an opportunity to study Islam and hear from the mouths of Muslim believers just how fulfilling a worldview it is. However, even the most idealistic religious system can be dragged down into the muck of human hatred and violence when it is mixed with an unstable social situation. That, unfortunately, is the Egypt of today.

President Mubarak, in his attempts to bring modernity and democracy to Egyptian society, has offended fundamentalist Muslims who fear the inevitable secularization that comes with these predominately Western ways of organizing society. The more extreme Muslims tend, also, to be from the poorest socioeconomic strata in Egyptian society. Literally, they have nothing to lose, and in the name of Allah, they have attacked Mubarak, modernity and secularization by attacking Egypt's primary industry – tourism. Tourists have been indiscriminately murdered in several gory incidents, and it was obvious that these terrorist activities are having a damaging effect on the tourist industry in Egypt.

I wanted to share these perceptions with you because it was out of this experience that the inspiration for our Egypt Museum/Pyramids roll-in emerged. In touring the Egyptian museum, I was struck, as anyone would be, by the grandeur of archaic Egypt and the complexity of a religious system that seems to have a single existential source; a pervasive desire on the part of those with power and wealth to *take it with you!*

From the perspective of "Beliefs and Believers," the rite of passage – death – sparked this veritable explosion of culture and civilization-making but also created hell on earth for the less fortunate who toiled to build these *wonders of the world*. At the same time, a trip to the Pyramids encapsulated all the current religiopolitical challenges the Egyptians endure today. Poverty and struggle, soldiers and hustlers writhe in the shadows of these grand monuments to the timeless human fear of our own mortality. In the strong desert winds blowing off the Sahara, the dust from the pyramids literally mingles with the dusty lives of soldiers, peasants, and police who cling to religious fundamentalism while the spiritual grains of Islam seem to be scattered beyond their reach.

Religious Styles

Before discussing our two remaining Class 3 interviews with Kate Cogan and Paul Mundschenk, I want to go through our last graphic, Religious Styles, in more detail.

Class 3

Belief Style

This style is clearly aligned with organized religion. The group is defined by what the members believe. All religious organizations must participate in this style to some extent. In fact, is that not what the leader of the group does for the most part during a given *sermon*? He or she outlines what is proper belief. Put another way, people believe in a set of answers of boundary questions and come together in religious services to reaffirm the authority of those answers be it through reading a sacred text like the Bible or participating in a familiar ritual. When you are in the middle of the dishes and someone knocks on the door to give you *the truth* about reality, you are being forced, unless you slam the door, to experience the belief style. Unfortunately, sometimes people lose their lives when two intensely held belief-oriented groups clash. Political worldviews are just as guilty of this as religious worldviews.

Communal Style

You would be surprised to find out how many people spend their entire lives in a religious organization and know very little about what it is they so fervently espouse. Here, we come back to our apart/a part considerations. Human beings need to belong. The combination of the belief style – the security of agreed upon answers to boundary questions – and the communal style – the comfort of group identity – is the glue that holds organized religion together. Theological purity is really not as important as seeing familiar faces in the pews and chatting about the local softball team or the weather after church.

Seeker Style

While the belief and communal styles of being religious are legitimate and time-honored ways for human beings to express their religiosity, it is the *seeker style* that serves best as a springboard into the often murky waters of religious experience. Why? Simply because seekers possess a *thinner spiritual skin*. Since they are seeking, they are more likely to be grappling with boundary questions. Perhaps the seeker just went through a jarring rite of passage, and found the *answers* offered within his or her chosen religion to be wanting. Or sometimes a person simply matures spiritually, and in that natural process, begins to ask new, more complex existential questions. There can be profoundly religious people who adopt the belief or the communal style of a particular organized religion. But we also have to take into account the fact that some people simply cannot find fulfillment in the stock answers offered by religious institutions. These religious questors need to break out of the ordinary and embrace the extraordinary with the totality of their being. Kate Cogan, in our next roll-in interview, is just such a seeker.

Kate Cogan Interview

Kate belongs to a group called CUUPs – Coven of Unitarian-Universalist Pagans. We will meet the Unitarian-Universalists later in the course, but in essence, the Unitarian-Universalists of America represent a very inclusive, open-minded, liberal form of Protestant Christianity. We are speaking historically, of course. There are probably many Unitarians who would be troubled with the label, "Protestant Christian," just as there may be some who don't agree with allowing a coven to organize under their institutional umbrella.

In any event, Kate provides us with an excellent example of a person who seeks *and finds!* As you view this short piece, notice how her seeking involves sorting out questions about identity and relationship. As a woman, she was frustrated with ordinary religious expressions that seemed to hold womanhood or the feminine element in disregard. Her *finding* was intimately involved in her own quest for self-esteem and empowerment. Once discovered, the world of *wicca* and neo-pagan ritual magic set her on a new and exciting spiritual journey towards self-actualization.

Interview with Professor Paul Mundschenk

Professor Paul Mundschenk is my office mate and colleague in the Department of Philosophy & Religious Studies at Western Illinois University. Paul's perspective is especially helpful at this juncture in the course, when we are about to formally explore the *experiential dimension*, because he has spent a lifetime studying spiritual transformation. For Paul, the seeker style and the religious quest are the most natural expressions of our shared human spiritual experience. We are, of course, engaged in the academic study of religion. Words are the tools we use to study and express our perceptions of religion and religious activity.

However, as Paul so succinctly puts it, if we really want to *experience* religion, we have to go beyond language, beyond speaking to another level of communication – one that in all the great religious traditions of the world calls for silence. And this is an extremely important insight as we move into our next class on the *experiential dimension*. Right from the beginning of our search to understand religious experience, we need to be aware that religious experience, by its very nature, *transcends* all our ordinary methods for communicating knowledge about a particular phenomenon. Thus, the *experiential dimension* is, indeed, the most difficult dimension for students to grasp. However, if we openly acknowledge the difficulties in expressing the nature of religious experience, we will be closer to understanding the *meaning* of this extraordinary experience as the fundamental catalyst to religious expression. That is the goal of Class 4.

Videotape Graphics

 At this stage we suggest you watch the videotape. The graphics you will see on the screen are reproduced below to save you the trouble of copying them down. You might like to add your own comments as you watch the tape.

What Is Religion?

The Religion Process

Key Themes
– pervasiveness of religion/spirituality in human experience
– the spiritual/religious impulse in human kind

What Is Religion?

Five Stages
1. Self-consciousness
2. Boundary Questions
3. Rites of Passage
4. Spiritual dimension
5. Development of World Religions

The Religion Process

1. Self-consciousness
   – a part (unity, belonging)
   – apart (individuality)
2. Boundary Questions
   – identity = who am I?
   – relationship = who are you?
   – meaning = why?
   – purpose = how?
   – orientation in space and time = when? where?
   – death, suffering, change = why me? why us?
3. Rites of Passage
   – birth
   – adulthood
   – grouping (family, marriage, mating, etc.)
   – love/tragedy
   – suffering/change
   – death
4. Spiritual dimension
   – emotional needs
   – psychological needs
   – intellectual needs
   – physical needs

   lead to

5. The Development of World Religions
   Religions develop to answer boundary questions
   and meet spiritual needs
   – Hinduism
   – Judaism
   – Buddhism
   – Christianity
   – Islam
   – Taoism/Confucianism
   – primal religions
   – alternative religions

   Ordinary religion =
   spiritual search practiced inside an identifiable
   religious organization

   Extraordinary religion =
   spiritual search practiced outside an established
   religion (seeker style, personal search)

Religious Styles

– Belief
– Communal
– Seeker

Review Questions

Answering the following question will help you review key class themes and prepare for examinations.

1. What is the *Religion Process*? Outline the five stages and try to provide one or two examples from your own experience.

2. Why is death such a powerful motivator for human religious activity?

3. Define the three styles of religion. Do you think they are mutually-exclusive, or could a believer embody all three styles at the same time?

4. In your informed opinion, is there a difference between spirituality and religion?

Sources and Further Readings

Schmidt, Roger. *Exploring Religion*. Belmont, CA: Wadsworth, 1988.

BELIEFS AND BELIEVERS
Class 4 – The Religious Experience

Introduction

Reflection: *A recent Gallup poll found that about 40 percent of Americans have had some kind of religious or para-normal experience. However, religious experience is a topic people rarely discuss. In terms of discussion of identity and relationship, why do you think people are hesitant to be open about these profound, life-changing experiences?*

Unless you are an extraordinary student, or a person who has pondered the nature of religion before taking this class, about this time in the course you should be experiencing some confusion. In a course like "Beliefs and Believers" this is not only natural, it is probably a necessary step in the learning process. One of the standard obstructions to learning in a religious studies class is that the familiar gets in the way of the unfamiliar. We are so used to thinking about *religion* as something expressed in a particular building, on a particular day of the week, in accordance with authoritarian doctrines, then labeled and categorized as Methodist, Catholic, Buddhist, Hindu, etc., that it is difficult to make the leap into understanding religion as inwardly powerful, personal and ever-present in our common human quest to make sense of our shared reality.

In the previous class, we discussed different styles of being religious, and in interviews with Kate Cogan and Paul Mundschenk, pinpointed the *seeker style* as the most appropriate for our exploration of *religious experience*. In the seeker style of religion, we are more likely to gather evidence that supports our key class themes, particularly *boundary questions* and *rites of passage*. Before entering into our formal notes on the religious experience, it will be helpful to review these themes in the context of the seeker style.

One way of thinking about religious experience is to consider boundaries. We have already noted that defining and dealing with boundaries is fundamental to human religious activity. Crossing boundaries necessitates a confrontation with *otherness*, both dangerous and intriguing at the same time. The formation of our identity as a human being is at the heart of inevitable confrontations with that which is *other*. Simply put, *other* is that which is *not me*; not myself, not my family, not my town, not my tribe, not my body, not my mind, not my space, not my possession, not my identity. Nature is other; human beings may be other; God or the source of the cosmos is other.

Life is safe when we don't cross boundaries, when we don't confront the "other." But if we don't go, then we don't grow. One of the most powerful and irrepressible human drives is to cross boundaries, confront the "other," absorb it, and make it one's own. It is all part of developing and expanding our identity. As we come to be aware of ourselves, as we grow through life, we often define our identity in relation to that which is other. Are we not confronting that which is other, new and different when we go through life's most challenging changes? And doesn't it make sense that religious experiences, if we are to have them at all, would happen during rites of passage?

The experience of *otherness* permeates these major life events. At birth we leave the security of the womb as we are literally pushed over the boundary into the *other* of separate existence. Similarly, we cross the boundary from childhood into the *other* of adulthood; from being single to marriage; from life into death.

Class 4

From our previous class discussion about death, it is clear that moving across these boundaries is not always easy. Any time you are legitimately confronting the other in a rite of passage your identity is challenged as it undergoes change. Thus, *boundary questions* are raised: who am I, where did I come from, where am I going, what is the meaning of life? And in this state of questioning, religious experience becomes vital and real to believers and non-believers alike.

Consider for a moment how many religious ceremonies are designed for rites of passage; christening, circumcision, baptism, Bar Mitzvah, confirmation, marriage ceremonies, funeral rites, etc. Is it any wonder that these fundamental life changes awaken the religious impulse, which then becomes translated via the medium of culture into any number of religious rites and rituals?

Even in the most secular (not sacred) cases, crossing boundaries generates ritualized human activity. Boundaries define territory, be it inner-psychological territory or outer-geographical territory. When you cross the border from one state to another in the United States, you inevitably encounter signs welcoming you, informing you of state laws, identifying the governor and directing you to an information/rest stop. All of us who have made a long cross-country trip know that special feeling when you have finally reached the last mile of a particularly long state and crossed the border into new territory.

People who don't consider themselves to be religious still cross psychological boundaries, confront rites of passage and, consequently, seek assistance from members of the secular priesthood in their life process of identity transformation. Think of the enormous growth in modern times of psychoanalysts, psychiatrists, psychologists, counselors, and persons offering any number of New Age remedies to assuage the perplexities of ancient boundary questions. If you haven't already considered it, reflect on how your transition from high school to college resulted in myriad changes in identity and relationship. How did you cope with this major *rite of passage*?

Sometimes, no matter how secular you may think you are, the power of boundary crossing can not be escaped. In the late 1980s, I attended what, for lack of a better cultural designation, had to be considered a *Yuppie* wedding. The 1980s are doomed to be characterized as a time of self- centered materialism, and *Yuppie* was an acronym for young, urban professionals. The happy couple stressed that there was no *religious* reason for the ceremony; getting married was just a casual move based on practical necessities. Yet at the moment when the judge performing the ceremony pronounced the couple man and wife both of them were overcome with emotion. And the otherwise *cool* participants shed a few tears on the leather upholstery of their BMWs. The power and emotional energy present in boundary crossing have little concern for cultural posturing or current social fads.

Religious experience *IS!* It may have happened to you, and assuredly it happens to people such as your colleagues at work, friends in the neighborhood or the total stranger sitting next to you on an airplane. According to the Gallup pole, almost half the people in the United States have had an experience that, like a minor rumble of *terra-firma* in California, shakes up ordinary life while pointing to something well beyond the *everyday* way of perceiving reality. In this class, we want to explore this most special aspect of human consciousness – religious experience.

Key Class Themes

This lesson focuses on the following themes:

1. The Religious Experience
2. Difficulties in determining religious experience
3. Seeker style and religious experience
4. Language, interpretation, and religious experience

Videotape Synopsis

- Class discussion
- Seeker/Finders testimonials
- Class discussion
- Interview with Professor Stanley Krippner
- Graphics/lecture, Religious Experience
- Class discussion

Videotape Commentary

I suggest you read this section before you watch the videotape. You will find that it will help you organize your thoughts so that when you watch the tape it will be more meaningful. When you have finished viewing the tape, you may want to read this section again.

Class Discussion

Class 4 opens with a lively discussion spawned by our identification of three styles of religion: belief, communal, and seeker. Chris notes that the tension between the communal and seeker style reflects the *apart* and *a part* dichotomy in human self-consciousness. This observation raises some interesting issues regarding the experiential dimension and the tendency for humans to institutionalize religion. Over and over again, we will hear words such as *unity, oneness,* and *belonging* being used to describe the religious impulse. Indeed, humans seem to have a deeply seated need to belong, to be *a part* of something. At the same time, we are individuals. No person experiences life exactly the same way. We all endure a slightly different set of challenges and changes, and those rites of passage call for a slightly different set of *answers* to the questions generated by these life-shaking events. Institutionalized religion offers a clearly defined set of answers expressed through myth, symbol and ritual. Is it reasonable to assume that a given religious teaching is applicable to every human being who claims adherence, who is a believer? This is another question *to live with* as we move through the experiential dimension.

Barbara remarks that "each person has their own religion," and Helen adds that some reconciliation is necessary with the religion of one's ancestors in order for genuine spiritual progress to occur. We have touched on a raw nerve in the study of religion – the tension between inner religious experience and outer religious expression. And believe me, the nerve will twitch and twang throughout the semester!

Another way to approach this tension between experience and expression is to contemplate an analogy between religion and education. Education, ideally, is about the creation, the expression, and the acquisition of knowledge. Like religion, when education becomes institutionalized in colleges and universities, it manifests something of a split personality; it is at once a force for change and transformation and a force for control and stability. Knowledge, like religious experience, exudes power, and humans understandably create educational institutions to control this power.

But what happens when a society undergoes change and transformation? Usually, the institutions of higher learning play a key role in revolutionary activity. Consider the 1960s and early 70s in the United States. Colleges became both the intellectual centers and, in come cases, the battle ground for the difficult cultural changes occurring at that time. Throughout history, institutionalized religion has played a similar role in culture-transforming revolutions.

To continue the analogy, imagine that you are about to graduate from college. In her closing remarks, the president of your university reminds you that you can never learn, never explore new fields of knowledge unless you come back and do it at your alma mater or branch schools thereof. That would seem absurd, but in a way, that is how religious organizations, particularly in manifesting the belief style, control the power of religious expression. Is it unreasonable to consider that as people grow they might *graduate* from a particular religious perspective and become seekers? Religious experience, because it can initiate profound changes in identity and relationship is, at the same time, an indispensable element in the creation of our great world religions and the force that can just as easily destroy the institutional expression of a given worldview.

Seeker / Finder Interviews

Before entering into our formal notes on religious experience, we thought it would be helpful to *gather* a group of what, for lack of a better term, I would refer to as *seeker/ finders*. In each case, the believers we interviewed were clearly seeking but had just recently found a religious path that satisfied the set of psychological, emotional, intellectual and physical needs we have termed *the spiritual dimension* (see the Religious Process, Stage 4). I simply asked them, "What does your religious path mean to you?" As you view this segment of the class, notice how their answers invariably come back to observations about their identity and their relationships. Can you identify other stages in our Religious Process in their comments?

Interview with Professor Stanley Krippner

Dr. Stanley Krippner is Professor of Psychology at Saybrook Institute and Distinguished Professor of Psychology at the California Institute of Integral Studies. He is the past president of the American Parapsychological Association. We wanted to interview him because any exploration of the experiential dimension of religion, particularly in an academic setting, requires an empathetic, yet realistic approach. Humans are naturally fascinated with paranormal phenomena, from near death experiences to channeling and clairvoyance, but we need to separate fakery from fact. Dr. Krippner points out that spiritual experiences can be studied using the scientific method. In fact, he has built a career doing just that.

He makes an important point in noting that a person can believe he or she is inspired by God then work tirelessly to help the sick and poor like Mother Teresa or pick up a gun and assassinate the president of Israel. This underscores one of the most important "Beliefs and Believers" themes. As people believe, so they behave. One might argue that religious/ spiritual experience is delusional, but from Krippner's perspective, these kinds of extraordinary experiences need to be studied because they engender human behavior that can impact on society at large.

He also helps us with his discussion of science and religion. Science also asks boundary questions, but the questions call for answers based on measurable, quantifiable aspects of material existence. Religion, on the other hand, seeks answers to more transcendent, more existential queries about the nature of reality. In our quest to understand what it means to be, science and religion need not be mutually exclusive.

Graphics / Lecture on Religious Experience

One of my professors in graduate school, Dr. Robert Michaelsen, used to tell a joke about a Baptist preacher who confronted a Methodist about the efficacy of infant Baptism. I love to use this story because absolutely nobody gets it! No laughs are forthcoming!

The story is set on the frontier prairie around the middle of the last century. An old, wizened Methodist preacher, dead tired from days on the road, rides into town and is tying his horse to a hitching post in front of the local store. A fiery young Baptist preacher eyes him, and being in feisty mood, strides over and accosts the tired Methodist. He says, "Sir, do you mean to tell me you believe in infant baptism?" The Methodist replies, "Sonny, believe in it? I've seen it!"

Of course you need to know that Baptists took issue with the standard Christian ritual of baptizing infants, holding that a person needed to be old enough to consciously accept Christ as his or her savior before the baptism ritual should be performed. But from the perspective of the experiential dimension, the story hits home. You can argue about the truth or falsehood of a given religious experience, but like our Methodist preacher, "I've seen it!" Without religious experience, human beings would never have gone to all the trouble of creating religious expressions. True, it is difficult to determine what people mean by *religious experience*. The lecture/graphics section of Class 4 are designed to help us sort out these difficulties and develop a more informed understanding of this seminal religious dimension.

Like the term "religion," the *experiential dimension* is not easily defined, categorized and placed neatly in some mental cubbyhole. We will be grappling with some of the difficulties involved in analyzing different types of religious experience. As we move through the graphics and enter into class discussion, five major *problems* arise: a) definitional problems, b) typological problems, c) contextual problems, d) problems of description vs. experience, and e) the accompanying problem of a person's role as an insider or outsider in relation to a given religion, a problem of interpretive orientation.

Definitional Problems

Whether a "religious experience" is a once-in-a-lifetime, identity-transforming experience or a repeated sense of serenity and resonance with something greater or transcendent to oneself, it seems to be spawned by some of the most human of experiences. Thus, the difficulty rests in the familiarity of events that people sometimes call *religious experiences*. Take love, for instance. Love is a *boundary crossing experience*. Most of us have experienced the *bliss* of infatuation. Falling in love is rising out of a limited, self-centered perspective on life. During those joyful days or weeks when the flame burns hot, everything looks more beautiful. Life is good! The familiar love experience may suggest what the great mystics and spiritual leaders intimate about a fuller, more complete love. Several traditions, including Christianity, identify God with love.

The challenge for the student seeking to understand religious experience is to sort out common, human experiences from something truly life changing. Whether a person experiences love or a sense of oneness with nature, the key to determining an authentic religious experience is the behavior of the person who had the experience. Does the experience change the person's behavior for the better? Is it an identity-transforming, relationship-improving event? If not, the experience should be seen for what it is; another good day at the beach!

Typological Problems

Religious experience comes in many flavors, and often the taste is dependent on the cultural environment of the believer. Numinous experience posits an encounter with an awe-inspiring, sometimes terrifying, but fascinating *other*. When someone says, "I saw God," they have had a numinous experience. The believer retains his or her sense of self and enters into a relationship with the divine being. Mystical experience, on the other hand, seems to *erase* the separate, ego-driven, sense of self that characterizes everyday human perceptual experience. Oneness with the divine is the message, whether it be oneness with nature, oneness with the Mind of God or the universal essence or oneness with a divine figure perceived, at first, in a numinous encounter.

Cultural Context Problems

The great mystics in all traditions are united in the claim that, ultimately, religious experience is ineffable. In other words, religious experience, by its very nature, transcends our ordinary methods of communication. But, as Helen points out in our class discussion, we are language-using creatures. If something wonderful happens, we want to communicate the experience to our friends or family. And the only tools we have to do the communicating are those we receive from our cultural background.

I like to use the prism analogy in explaining cultural context problems. Concepts, practical experience, language, and institutional structures including religious traditions are like the angles of a prism. Religion colors or shades the *pure white light* of spiritual experience. Consequently, when listening to the experiential statements of someone from a particular religious tradition, we have to have some background on their cultural experience in order to make sense of what it is they are trying to communicate.

Perhaps you have heard someone say something like, "All religions lead to the same Truth; people just describe that truth differently." The arguments for and against such a statement comprise some of the most heated debates in the field of religious studies. In terms of religious experience, opposing camps might rally around two perspectives: a) religious experience is everywhere the same; b) every religious experience is unique to the cultural context in which it arises. Of course, others try to find common ground in the middle. This perspective is presented in our graphic on cultural context problems. It does seem logical that in any given culture, conceptual, practical, discursive and institutional elements will have some impact on how religious experience is described.

Description Problems

General problems of describing and interpreting religious experience exist. Even if all of the above difficulties could be worked out, how can we be sure when a person is describing a religious experience, that his/her description is completely accurate? Language, by its very nature, is an interpretive adventure. As Suzanne notes in class discussion, we have only one word for love, but so many for hate. Or as Janet points out, the three stars of the heavenly body known in our culture as Orion, can be three stars, or they can be three men going fishing from the perspective of aboriginal culture of Australia. To add to these good observations, we might return to Paul Mundschenk's advice; if you want to understand human spirituality, shut up!

Prism Effect

Obviously, persons from within a particular religious tradition are likely to describe religious experience using language that contains numerous presuppositions about the nature of reality. Without meaning to, these presuppositions may *color* their description of the experience. For example, if I say that I experienced the *eternal unity with the Trinity, God, the Son, and Holy Ghost*, my description contains many presuppositions which would be securely placed in the consciousness of a practicing Christian. I presuppose that there is a God; He manifests as a Trinitarian Being; He has a Son, Jesus Christ, all of which may or may not be true but certainly cannot be proved experientially. An investigator of religious experience would have to turn to philosophical or historical analysis to prove such a description.

On the other hand, if you knew that I had no background in a religious tradition, and I told you that I experienced an *undifferentiated merging with pure light and bliss consciousness*, there is considerably less use of presuppositions. You might, at least, be willing to let my description stand as an experience of some altered state of consciousness.

All of this leaves us with another of those delightful *unanswerable questions* which we will continuously discover during this course. Is there a fundamental religious experience, available to all human beings, which has been described and interpreted throughout human history according to presuppositions about reality present in respective cultures? Again we are back to the same overarching question. Can we identify a pristine religious experience apart from the cultural trappings of the tradition in which it is clothed? Keep this in mind as you meet believers who want to explain the joy that energizes their belief system. It's a natural occurrence!

Videotape Graphics

 At this stage we suggest you watch the videotape. The graphics you will see on the screen are reproduced below to save you the trouble of copying them down. You might like to add your own comments as you watch the tape.

Religious Experience
Difficulties determining what it is

Religious Experience

Definitional problems:
– Joe falls in love with Mary
– Oscar climbs Mt. Shasta
– Sally has a "near death" experience

Religious Experience

Different types:

Numinous experience =
an encounter with the Divine/God; awe-inspiring; terrifying yet attractive; separation between Divine and human identities

Example= Moses encounters God in a "burning bush"
Rudolf Otto, *The Idea of The Holy*
"Mysterium, Tremendum, and Fascinans"

Religious Experience

Different types:

Mystical experience =
loss of personal identity; merging with the totality of Being (God, the Divine, Mind, Consciousness, etc.)

Three types:

– nature mysticism
– Monist mysticism
– Theist mysticism

Class 4

> **Religious Experience**
>
> Cultural context problems:
>
> Different context = different *description* of
>   the experience
>
> – Conceptual = ideas in culture
> – Practical = day-to-day living
> – Discursive = language
> – Institutional = social structures "color"
>   religious belief and experience

> **Religious Experience**
>
> Description problems:
>
> – Discrepancy between actual experience
>   and interpretation of that experience
> – Is the description of the religious experience
>   "colored" by interpretations drawn from a
>   particular religious training, i.e., Christianity,
>   Buddhism, or Islam?

> **Religious Experience**
>
> *Prism Effect*
>
> Religion colors or shades the "pure white light"
> of spiritual experience

Review Questions

Answering the following questions will help you review key class themes and prepare for the examinations.

1. Why is it difficult to define religious experience?

2. In your informed opinion, is there a difference between religion and spirituality?

3. Identify the types of religious experience we have explored in class. Can you provide an example for each one?

4. Can a person have an authentic religious experience outside of a religious organization?

Sources and Further Readings

Smart, Ninian, *The World's Religions*. Englewood Cliffs, NJ: Prentice Hall, 1989.

BELIEFS AND BELIEVERS
Class 5 – Religious Experience: Mystics and Meditation

Introduction

Reflection: *Religion is a powerful force for change in the world. However, in nearly all religious traditions some believers have chosen to turn from the world and devote their entire lives to worship, prayer or meditation. Do you think the monastic or mystical impulse is a world-denying, selfish mode of spirituality? After viewing this class session, has your opinion changed?*

When I was an undergraduate student at the University of California, Santa Barbara, I had the opportunity to study with the late Professor Walter Capps. Walter Capps would later become my mentor and advisor in graduate school, but in many ways, the seed for all my future ventures as a student and teacher in the field of religious studies was planted in that first class, *Monastic Impulse*, Religious Studies 187. From his own experience as a gifted teacher, Professor Capps knew that, while theory and intellectual rigor were important in the classroom, students also learned from *experiencing* religion in the field. Thus, every class he offered included a field trip to a religious site or spiritual center where students could meet real believers and join in productive dialogue.

Monastic Impulse offered students the opportunity to visit the Our Lady of Guadalupe Monastery in Lafayette, Oregon. Our Lady is a Trappist Monastery, one of the most austere in the Roman Catholic faith, where silence is enjoined at all times, and the monks obey the classic monastic vows of poverty, chastity and simplicity in life style. Each student was given his or her own cell, and we were invited to meditate and pray with the monks, eat with them, and join in their daily work activities. Though silence was the rule, twice a day a monk would join us for a teaching/dialogue session. It was during one of these sessions that I begin to grasp the *monastic impulse*.

Father Paschal led the session, and opened with a classic story about why he chose to join a monastery. Paschal was a high pressure lawyer in Los Angeles, fresh out of law school, and working 18 hour days trying to prove himself in one of the most competitive L.A. law firms. One morning he found himself in bumper-to-bumper rush hour traffic on Wilshire Blvd. He was driving a knock-about Chevrolet. The car right in front of him was a shiny new Mercedes, and he noticed that the driver was one of the partners in his firm. At that moment, Paschal was struck by the fact that in 20 or 25 years, the driver of the luxury car would be him! All the struggle and effort he would put in to rise in a law career would simply get him a fancier car to be stuck in during rush hour traffic. The glories of material success vanished for Paschal, and the next day he resigned from the law firm and joined a monastery.

What causes human beings to turn from ups and downs of everyday life in the material, secular world and devote their lives to prayer, meditation, and the life of the spirit? From the perspective of "Beliefs and Believers," it is *religious experience*. Not everyone has a knack for experiencing profound, life-changing religious insights. But the mystics in all faiths certainly do. In this class, we want to explore the mystical experience, meditation and the monastic impulse in order to further our understanding of the power of religious experience and its effect on the life of believers.

One other important point is that during this class session, we will meet two extraordinary human beings, Swami Prabuddhananda and Bishop Thomas. The Swami is a Hindu and resides in a quiet religious center in San Francisco, California. Bishop Thomas is an Eastern Orthodox Christian from central Egypt. By tradition and geography, these believers are literally half a world apart. Yet notice that they express the same sentiment when it comes to mysticism, meditation, and the monastic life. Far from being world-denying or saving yourself while all the rest of the world can go to hell-in-a-hand-basket, they teach us that the deeper you go inwardly through prayer and meditation, the more caring and compassion you have for all creation, including other human beings, nature, and believers from other faiths. Notice how Bishop Thomas and Swami Prabuddhananda make an extraordinary statement about the transformation of our ordinary sense of identity and relationship.

Key Class Themes

This class focuses on the following themes:

1. Styles of Religion (review)
2. Nature mysticism
3. Monist mysticism
4. Theist mysticism
5. Monasticism
6. Meditation

Videotape Synopsis

- Class discussion
- Graphics/lecture on Types of Mystical Experience
- Interview at the Vedanta Society of Northern California
- Class Discussion
- Interview with Brother Mark and Bishop Thomas, St. Makarios Monastery
- Interview with Professor Wendy Wright

Videotape Commentary

I suggest you read this section before you watch the videotape. You will find that it will help you organize your thoughts so that when you watch the tape it will be more meaningful. When you have finished viewing the tape, you may want to read this section again.

Class Discussion

We've made the case several times already that the best way to get the most out of "Beliefs and Believers" is to begin to see the world around you with "BNB" eyes. Class 5 opens with a discussion of any events students might have experienced that illustrate key class themes. Rites of passage, boundary questions, identity and relationship examples abound! Barbara asked me if she might read a short passage from the book, "Two Against the Sahara," by Michael Asher.

After our previous discussion of religious experience in Class 4, Barbara felt it would make a moving addition to our exploration of religious experience. Indeed, it does! In fact, the author captures the essence of the *nature mystical experience*. Note that these desert travels experience a kind of *axis mundi* in which they are attached to the earth by a nurturing umbilicus. The key element in all mystical experience, *unity*, is expressed oneness with the earth, connection with all beings past, present and future and the realization that our variegated planet is, indeed, the mother of all life. In our class on primal religion, our Native American spokesperson, Thomas Drift, an Ojibwe Indian, will elaborate on this experience as it arises during the popular *sweat lodge* ritual (see Class 12).

"BNB sightings" continued to be mentioned well after the class was over and the studio cameras were still. Mary recognized key "Beliefs and Believers" themes while attending the graduation of her daughter. Notice how we use the term "commencement" when speaking of the graduation ritual; the graduate *commences* on a life characterized by a new identity and new relationships. Lynne attended an outdoor baptism ceremony. In the Christian context, baptism is a major step in the process of being *born again* in Christ. Here, a rite of passage, baptism, redefines the participants' sense of self and relational patterns in life. Chris observes the same transformative activity in a wedding ceremony and following ritual. The point is, folks, that we are not just making this up! Though they may be colored and shaped by cultural differences, the fundamental features of religious activity are part and parcel of basic human existential experience in all times and in all places. Have you begun to see evidence of our key class themes in your own day-to-day experiences?

Since the course ended, my 11-year-old daughter, Lily, came face-to-face with mortality; her beloved first pet, a parakeet named Mikey, died. Mikey lived a long life for a little bird, about six years, but Lily was devastated by the loss. Instinctively, she knew that a rite of passage of this magnitude demanded some kind of ritual activity. We decided we would give Mikey a funeral and bury him in the backyard under a huge spreading elm tree. Lily found one of the boxes that checks come in which was the perfect size for a parakeet coffin. Along with Mikey, she put flower petals, a few special trinkets and cotton to make a soft bed for him. Then she did something truly amazing. She cut off a small piece of her hair and placed it on his stilled feathers, as if to say, a part of me is going with you on your journey. Wow! We dug a hole, put the coffin in, covered him up, then wished him well on his transformative journey, wherever it might take him. The ritual was finalized by setting up a stone ringed by smaller stones around the grave site. I was obviously feeling pain for Lily's loss and emotionally involved in this impromptu ritual, but I couldn't help reflecting on how, from the dawn of human consciousness, human beings must have been moved to perform ritual activity in the face of death – pervasiveness of religion at its most obvious!

Lecture / Graphics on Types of Mystical Experience

Because mystical experience is the most common kind of religious experience, it will be useful to explore the following three types: nature mysticism, monist mysticism and theist mysticism. Notice, however, that though there are differences, there is a central theme in each experience, expressed over and over again in words such as oneness, unity, and interconnectedness.

Nature Mysticism

We will hold off on having a *believer-spokesperson* describe nature mysticism until we come to our future classes on *primal religion*. In terms of religious expressions of nature mysticism, primal religions provide the clearest examples. When we speak of primal religion, we are talking about an extraordinary variety of beliefs and believers. One estimate is that more than 200 million people in Central Africa, the Amazonian Basin in South America, the Arctic regions and on reservations in North America, practice primal religion. However, it is important to recognize that when we use the term "primal religion," we are not talking about worldviews that are primitive, backward or unsophisticated. They are in fact enormously complex and coherent. In addition, primal religion is being recovered in the so-called *advanced* countries such as the United States by followers of the neo-pagan movement, by practitioners of ritual magic and other manifestations that crop up under the general heading of New Age religions.

For our purposes, at this juncture in the course we might call nature mysticism *natural mysticism*. Surely, in its religious expressions primarily found in primal religions, nature mysticism emphasizes an earth-centered spirituality and a pervasive sense of the interconnectedness of all phenomena in creation. As *natural mysticism*, the variety of spiritual experience seems to touch more human beings, inside and outside of any identifiable religious organization. Whether on a lonely mountain top beneath a crescent moon or on a solitary walk beside the pounding ocean waves, you've been touched by natural/nature mysticism if you are overwhelmed by feelings of interconnectedness or unity with the cosmos. Usually the experience brings a sense of complete inner-peace, assurance that all will be well, cosmic confidence or a total reduction of stress. Bliss and joy are words people use to describe the experience. Of course, as is the case with all types of religious experience, does the experience lead to positive life changes or is it just a passing movement in some kind of altered state of consciousness? Naturally, there is some debate about what constitutes a genuine mystical experience. Many mystics in all traditions point to a positive and complete transformation of identity which leads to a more compassionate, caring set of relationships.

Monist Mysticism

Swami Prabuddhananda is our spokesperson on monist mysticism. He is the director of the Vedanta Society of Northern California, a sect of Hinduism dating back to the 19th century teachings of Ramakrishna (1834-86) and Swami Vivekananda (1863-1902). The Vedanta Society posits the essential truth of all religions and the divinity present in all human beings which makes a religious leader such as our Swami a perfect *believer* to explain the oneness, or monist mystical interconnection, that envisions the divine in everything.

He also makes the important connection between mystical experience and meditation. Actually, our usage of the word *meditation* does not adequately express the meaning that a devout Hindu or Buddhist ascribes to the word. For the meditator seeking a monist mystical experience, meditation means a rigorous discipline of mental, spiritual and physical development that proceeds through a set of practices leading to a higher level of concentration, compassion, wisdom, mindfulness and, ultimately, enlightenment. As we will see in the next class on Hinduism when we revisit our Swami, the ultimate monist mystical experience for the Hindu is *moksha* or release from the karmic cycle of births and deaths and attainment of oneness with the Divine. The importance of meditation is evident in this quote taken from one of the great leaders in the Vedanta tradition,

> *Meditation is the very center and heart of spiritual life. It matters not whether you are a follower of the path of karma, or of devotion or knowledge, whether you are Christian or Buddhist or a Hindu, sooner or later you have to practice meditation, you have to become absorbed in divine contemplation; there is no other way.*

Notice in the Swami's tone, his demeanor, as well as in his words, how he seems to manifest this sense of monist mystical unity that he has developed perceptually from a life time of meditation.

Theist Mysticism

Theist mysticism begins as a *numinous* experience. While not common, it is the type of mystical experience found in Judaism, Christianity and Islam. In each case, the believer becomes so in love with the manifestation of the Divine, that the boundaries between perceiver and perceived blur until the all-important experience of unity, oneness or interconnectedness is attained.

Like meditation in the Hindu tradition, the monasticism provides a fertile field for theist mystical experience in Christianity. We were very fortunate to be able to talk to two

Christian mystics, Brother Mark at St. Makarios monastery, a Coptic (Egyptian) Orthodox Christian monastery in the deserts of Egypt and Bishop Thomas. Our stop in the desert was particularly appropriate since it was in this same setting that Christian monasticism began about 17 centuries ago. Brother Mark, in our interview, notes that the root of the word *monastery* is <u>one</u>. And in the simplicity of the monk's life style, the devotion to prayer and meditation, and the roots of the monastic tradition itself, everything in the monastery guides the monk towards the theist mystical unity with God, Christ and the Holy Spirit.

In response to the question of monasticism as being world-denying or selfish, Bishop Thomas weaves a beautiful analogy. When you go deeper into yourself, spiritually, it is like a tree extending its roots deep into the earth. Strong roots allow the branches to reach out and intertwine with the branches of other trees. And beneath the surface, the roots also embrace. It is only through deep spiritual practice, regardless of one's chosen faith, that human hatred and violence will be overcome, and all peoples will be united in peace and harmony. Bishop Thomas calls this *Christian globalization*, a not-so-subtle jab at the secular notion that the techno-economic-information revolution we are experiencing will be the globalizing force. For him, the most practical path to the assuaging of all human ills is for human beings to wake up from their hypnotic fixation on the material aspect of life and to begin cultivating their innate spiritual sensitivities.

During class discussion, I relate my experience of the night before, at the local *Chuck E. Cheese* pizza parlor. Kids love the place, and once my daughters, Lily and Sophie, spotted the colorful marquee at a shopping center near the university, we were destined to visit. My comments are certainly not meant to denigrate this popular national chain, merely to reflect on what the attraction might be in light of our discussion of monastic simplicity and silence. In fairness to the chain's marketing technique, they do provide a safe, entertaining atmosphere for children. If you've not had an opportunity to visit a *Chuck E. Cheese*, I would describe the atmosphere as cacophony laced with chaos! Arcade noise mixes with amusement park frenzy, music videos blare from a seemingly endless number of TV screens and mobs of kids dash from one amusement to the next, gobbling down pizza and soda all the way, while their frazzled parents huddle in booths and try to bear up under the wash of sensory overload. Could it be that all the noise and frenzy humans tend to generate and call entertainment is an ultimately doomed attempt to fill some deep spiritual emptiness? I am sure that that would be the perspective of a mystic such as Bishop Thomas. What do you think?

In our final video interview in this class, Professor Wendy Wright, from Creighton University, speaks eloquently of a long tradition of theist mysticism in Christianity. While making the important observation that the great mystics of the world include as many women as men, she describes how common church rituals such as prayer, the singing of hymns, chanting, or the observance of silence are rooted in the desire of Christian believers to enter into a kind of inner sanctuary where the mysteries of God, Christ, and the Holy Spirit are revealed through theist mystical experience. Today, many Christians are turning to contemplative prayer to develop a deeper, living relationship with God and experience growth and personal transformation in their lives.

Though we've divided our study of mysticism into three types, it is not uncommon for the accomplished mystic to embrace all three at once. The class ends on a quote I read from "The Monastic Journey" by Thomas Merton (1915-1968), a Trappist Monk who, through his many, many books, did so much to bring the theist mystical experience that he cultivated in the monastery to spiritual seekers around the world. Notice how elements of nature mysticism, monist mysticism and theist mysticism are all evident in his poetic expression of a Christian mystical experience.

If therefore we seek Jesus, the word, we must be able to see Him in the created things around us - in the hills, the fields, the flowers, the birds and animals that He created, in the sky and the trees. We must be able to see Him in nature. Nature is no obstacle to our contact with Him, if we know how to use it.

Whether in Hindu meditation or Christian monasticism or any other inward practice present in the religious paths of the world, "knowing how to use it" is the key to developing genuine religious experience and applying the benefits of those experiences in our daily lives. So say the mystics of the world!

Videotape Graphics

At this stage we suggest you watch the videotape. The graphics you will see on the screen are reproduced below to save you the trouble of copying them down. You might like to add your own comments as you watch the tape.

> **Religious Styles**
> Belief
> Communal
> Seeker

> **Types of Mystical Experience**
> – Nature mysticism
> – Monist mysticism
> – Theist mysticism

Review Questions

Answering the following questions will help you review key class themes and prepare for the examinations.

1. Having viewed this segment of the teleclass, do you feel that mystical experience is world-denying or, on the contrary, in touch with the most practical aspects of human existence?

2. Describe nature mysticism, monist mysticism, and theist mysticism. Please provide an example of each type of religious experience.

3. Though we haven't gone into great depth in discussing meditation, why do you think the practice lends itself to monist mystical experience?

4. Are monks who join a monastery selfish?

Sources and Further Readings

Isherwood, Christopher. *Vedanta for the Western World*. San Francisco: Vedanta Press, 1977.

Merton, Thomas. *The Monastic Journey*. NY: Image, 1978.

Smart, Ninian. *The World's Religions*. Englewood Cliffs, NJ: Prentice Hall, 1989.

Keating, Thomas. *Open Mind, Open Heart*. Amity, NY: Amity House, 1986.

BELIEFS AND BELIEVERS
Class 6 – Religious Experience: Hinduism

Introduction

Reflection: *For the first time, you will be encountering believers representing a religion with which you may not be familiar, in this case, Hinduism. Do you have any preconceived notions about Hinduism or perhaps about members of the International Society for Krishna Consciousness (commonly known as the Hare Krishnas)? If so, jot them down. Before viewing Class 6, think about what it means to approach the interviews with Swami Prabuddhananda and Shankara Pandit with structured empathy. Remember; you don't have to become a Hindu in order to understand and appreciate the Hindu world view.*

Class 6 offers us an excellent opportunity to put our nascent *worldview analysis* skills to the test. Elements of the Hindu religion have intrigued the intellectual and spiritual sensitivities of Westerners for centuries. Take *karma*, for example, the inexorable cosmic moral law that determines rewards and punishments in a person's life; add the Hindu answer to what we have seen to be the most troubling of boundary questions, death. Driven by karmic law, the belief in *reincarnation* holds that humans do not have but one life to live but will experience literally thousands of lives. Through *yoga, meditation* or *devotion*, under the guidance of a *guru*, the Hindu seeks *moksha* or eventual liberation from the cycle of births and deaths. At that time, *atman*, the soul, will return to its essential oneness with *Brahman*, the one reality.

How fascinatingly different these answers are from those drawn from Western religious traditions! "Beliefs and Believers" is a tool to assist students in developing *worldview analysis skills*. It would be presumptuous of us (and also virtually impossible) to attempt to grasp the basics of the world's great religions in a single semester. When we dedicate a class to a particular world religion as we are in Class 6, we are asking believers, as guests or via video interviews, to help us understand the dimension we are studying, in this case the *experiential dimension*.

In previous classes, we have explored several difficulties in determining what religious experience might be. We have noted several types of religious experience, and we have had a lively discussion regarding the impact cultural context has on the explanation and interpretation of these profound, life-changing experiences. In addition, we've made the case that at the heart of religion and religious experience is the quest to clarify *identity* and *relationship* by answering profound life questions.

As you *hear* Hinduism described by two believers representing two dynamic Hindu sects, keep focused on our study of the experiential dimension. If you find Hinduism intriguing, at the end of the semester with newly-honed worldview analysis skills in hand, you will be able to go back to this religion and continue your investigation on your own. The primary objective of "Beliefs and Believers" is to provide you with the curiosity and confidence to make your exploration of religion and spirituality a life-long learning experience.

Class 6

Key Class Themes

This lesson focuses on the following themes:

1. Hindu *answers to some profound life questions*
2. The Vedanta sect of Hinduism
3. The Hari Krishna sect of Hinduism
4. *Karma/Reincarnation*
5. *Moksha/Dharma/Yoga*

Videotape Synopsis

- Graphics/lecture on key elements of Hinduism
- Interview with Swami Prabuddhananda
- Interview with Shankara Pandit
- Class discussion

Videotape Commentary

I suggest you read this section before you watch the videotape. You will find that it will help you organize your thoughts so that when you watch the tape it will be more meaningful. When you have finished viewing the tape, you may want to read this section again.

Graphics / Lecture / Class Discussion

Any class on Hinduism and the *experiential dimension* should open with an invocation, and Janet Cowser, class student, biology teacher and Hindu believer, is kind enough to provide us with a beautiful and genuine rendition of the Hindu chant used to invoke Lord Patanjali, the provider of great knowledge. From a comparative perspective, as Janet chants, reflect on how human beings use chanting, drumming, singing or dance to move from ordinary, secular consciousness to a higher level of spiritual understanding; from the mundane to the magical, mysterious and mystical. In our section on the *ritual dimension*, we will explore how and why this transformative practice touches all worldviews.

We met Swami Prabuddhananda during our exploration of monist mysticism in the previous class. When we asked the Swami to place Hinduism in world history, he replied that Hinduism can be divided into three historical periods: ancient, medieval and modern. He added, however, that in reality Hinduism was *not* a historical religion. Rather, Hinduism, the religion, expresses a single eternal spiritual truth, that God, or *Brahma*, resides in us as the eternal indwelling spirit, the same consciousness or Mind that energizes all creation. Experiencing that one truth is the supreme goal of human existence.

From the perspective of "Beliefs and Believers," Hinduism lends itself to the exploration of the *experiential dimension* for that very reason. While the outward manifestations of Hindu belief are incredibly diverse, all the myths, rituals, doctrines, ethical systems and social constructs are mere props on the stage of life. Life's dramas are all for naught if they don't eventually lead the believer to a *fully-realized* spiritual experience of oneness with the Divine. Why humans do not instinctively realize that *atman* and *Brahman* are one, or as Larry asks in our discussion, how did we ever lose our sense of oneness with the Divine, are *boundary questions* in Hinduism that are answered in myriad colorful myths and acted out in equally magnificent rituals.

The point is that all roads eventually lead to the Divine, and Hinduism, with an openness almost unparalleled in any other major world tradition, says, "Choose a path, any path, but get on the trail and start walking!" Thus, it's important to recognize that our interviews with

Shankara Pandit and Swami Prabuddhananda are representative views of two walkers on two of hundreds of possible paths on the road to *moksha*, or liberation. However, both travelers would feel at home with some basic *answers* to boundary questions that, like road signs on the highway, guide the pilgrim towards the ultimate destination. These *answers* are explored in our class graphics.

Before seeing how these key teachings in Hinduism combine to create a coherent worldview, it's useful to note that a *religion* survives and grows into a major world tradition only if it satisfies three basic functions. The sociologist of religion Professor Robert S. Ellwood from the University of Southern California, describes these needs as *fundamental features of religions:* the theoretical, the practical, and the sociological. By theoretical, Professor Ellwood means what we are describing as *boundary questions*; the religion must provide a believable, applicable set of answers regarding identity, relationship, means, purpose and destiny. The practical feature tells the believer what he or she must <u>do</u> in order to achieve the end goal of the religion (salvation, liberation, oneness, etc.), and is understandably expressed in such activities as worship, rituals and variegated ethical re-quirements. In terms of *establishing* the path as a *bona fide* world religion, the first two important features would go nowhere without the third, the sociological. We'll talk more about this important dimension in the last part of the course, but as Professor Ellwood notes, the sociological feature concerns the preservation and implementation of the religion's teachings and practices, and the relationship of the religious institution to other institutions in the larger society and hierarchical structure of the institution, including the all-important sub-feature of leadership.

 I bring up these three features at this early point in the course as yet another helpful set of analytic tools you can apply as we explore the major world traditions. In the case of Hindu-ism, and as we look at some key Hindu answers, it is obvious that a religious expression that has had such a long institutional life must be successfully satisfying the theoretical, practi-cal, and sociological features, and in doing so, meeting the spiritual needs of a broad and diverse religious community. Translating Professor Ellwoods's features into "Beliefs and Believers" terminology, we can equate the theoretical feature with *identity* and the practical and sociological features with *relationship*. And that is exactly how we have divided up our key Hindu *answers* on the graphics.

As we've already mentioned, the heart and soul of Hinduism is *experiential*. Thus, the answer to the all-important *identity question* is simple; *atman* and *Brahman* are one. To experience this *eternal truth*, as Swami Prabuddhananda described it, is to BE the eternal truth. Of course, as are all things involving religious experience, the goal may be easily defined but the processes leading to that goal are often so complex and diverse that, for the student, any attempt to fully-grasp the nuances of a given religion seems hopeless. Please don't be frustrated if, after a single class on a religion like Hinduism, you feel that "I just don't get it." Our goal is not to *"get it"* in this class. Our goal is to explore with an open mind, develop worldview analysis skills and use them in the future to continue the learning process. As we encounter Hindu answers to *relational questions* - karma, reincarnation, moksha, yoga, dharma – you will be doing fine if you can simply see how these *answers* combine to create a coherent worldview that provides millions of believers with a sustaining and inspiring vision of reality.

Interview with Swami Prabuddhananda

In Hinduism, there is great variation on the relationship between *Brahman* and the world and the human soul, *atman*. Depending on the school of Hindu philosophy, Brahman is both different and not different from creation. In our quest to understand *monist mysticism*, we were naturally drawn to the Vedanta Society because Advaita, or Nondualistic Vedanta, dating back to the teachings of Sankara (eighth century c.e.), makes the strongest case for the oneness of the soul and Brahman, and the illusoriness of the world as multiplicity.

Advaita Vedanta has been one of the most influential Hindu philosophies in modern time, particularly in the West. Swami Vivekananda (1863-1902), disciple of the Hindu saint Sri Ramakrishna, ignited American interest in Hinduism when he taught at the 1893 Parliament of World Religions in Chicago. Due to the warm reception of Eastern *answers to profound life questions*, the Swami remained in America where he founded numerous Vedanta Societies. Swami Prabuddhananda is the current leader in one of those societies, the Vedanta Society of Northern California. As you listen to the Swami explain his understanding of Hinduism from the Vedanta perspective, notice how he stresses *religious experience,* the experience of the eternal indwelling spirit, as the primary goal of his chosen path but also the ultimate goal of all religions. Do you agree?

Interview with Shankara Pandit

Of the many varieties of Hinduism that arrived in the United States in the mid-1960s and early 1970s, perhaps none has been more visible than the International Society for Krishna Consciousness, popularly known as the Hare Krishnas. The sight of colorfully dressed young devotees chanting and dancing on the street corners of American cities was a common one; and particularly in the early 1970s, it was practically impossible to pass through an airport without being accosted by book-selling, saffron-robed believers.

Because of their exotic appearance, strange customs, and unfamiliar beliefs, these devotees of Krishna have often been portrayed as a *new age cult* with little or no significant relation to the historic heritage of Hinduism in India. The story we get from Shankara Pandit, an American adherent of Krishna Consciousness, is, however, quite a different one. He stresses that his religion is very old indeed with deep roots in the Vedic religion of ancient India. The International Society for Krishna Consciousness (ISKCON) is a form of devotional Vaishnava Hinduism that originated with the 16th century Bengali ascetic and saint, Chaitanya Mahaprabhu (1486-1534).

Chaitanya was himself a convert to Vaishnavism. As a *bhakta* (devotee) of Vishnu, Chaitanya believed it possible to experience the divine mysteries. By single-minded devotion to Vishnu through his incarnations as Krishna and Rama, he thought it possible to establish the divine presence in consciousness and so attain pure consciousness free from the illusion of the phenomenal world around us. Chaitanya's devotion was often intensely emotional, frequently accompanied by ecstatic dancing, singing and chanting. And today, members of ISKCON continue this devotion through the use of the mantra made famous by the chanting in airports, parks and street corners:

> *Hare Krishna, Hare Krishna*
> *Krishna Krishna, Hare Hare*
> *Hare Rama, Hare Rama*
> *Rama Rama, Hare Hare*

Worship and devotional practices of the Hare Krishnas also include service to temple statues of the God, the public chanting of the names of God, study of Vedic culture and the history of *bhakti yoga*, the marking of the body with clay pigment in 12 places with each place signifying a name of God, and the eating and distribution of prasadam, the vegetarian food offered to Krishna.

Krishna Consciousness was brought to the Unites States by A.C. Bhaktivedanta Swami Prabhupada (1896-1977) in 1965, and the following year ISKCON was founded in New York City. Prabhupada, known to his followers as "His Divine Grace," also established the Bhaktivedanta Book Trust which has become an important instrument for propagating the movement's beliefs and its founder's studies of Krishna worship and the Bhagavad Gita. Shankara Pandit, after exploring many different religions in the *seeker style*, met Swami Prabhupada in the early 1970s and soon after decided to become a full-time Krishna devotee. Since his conversion to ISKCON, he has risen within the community to become president of the Chicago temple. During our interview with Shankara, notice how chanting, for the Hare Krishna devotee, initiates the same *experiential* sense of the *indwelling eternal spirit* as meditation does for the member of the Vedanta society.

Video Interview with the Western Convert to Hinduism, Loleta

This interview was a spontaneous event with an amusing story behind it. Our remote video excursions had to be well-planned events since a great deal of time, effort and expense goes into such a journey. We traveled with the director, the producer, audio and video technicians and one or two assistants. The equipment itself requires a van to haul it around.

We had contacted the Lemont Hindu Temple in Lemont, Illinois three times to confirm the time of arrival. Each time we were assured that all was well, just show up and start filming. When we arrived, whomever we had spoken to was not there, and no one seemed to know anything about us. We started to roll the camera equipment into the temple per our phone instructions, and were told frantically that no photography was ever allowed in the temple!

Having come all that way, we wanted some footage to take with us. In the middle of our frustration with the protectors of the temple, Loleta arrived and agreed to be interviewed. Loleta might be considered to be an independent Hindu convert. And in her interview she does an excellent job of explaining just what it was about the Hindu worldview that caused her to convert from Christianity. Notice her explanation of the *experiential dimension* in relationship to the Hindu perspective. Can you pick out key class themes such as *identity and relationship*, *boundary questions,* and *the seeker style* in her comments?

Videotape Graphics

 At this stage we suggest you watch the videotape. The graphics you will see on the screen are reproduced below to save you the trouble of copying them down. You might like to add your own comments as you watch the tape.

Some Key "Answers" in Hinduism

Identity

Brahman: the ultimate ground of Being; existence, consciousness, bliss, the One Mind, all-in-all

Atman: the human soul or the eternal aspect of all living things; ultimately, Atman (the essence of the self) and Brahman (the essence of the cosmos) are ONE

Class 6

Some Key "Answers" in Hinduism

Relationship

Karma: the cosmic law of cause and effect; deeds in this life affect human events, for good or evil, in this life and future lives

Reincarnation: rebirth of an individual soul in subsequent life form; governed by the law of Karma

Moksha: liberation from the karmic cycle of death and rebirth through Yoga

Yoga: a spiritual practice designed to unite Atman and Brahman

Dharma: the external order of the cosmos or the obligations and duties of this life

Some Sacred Texts

– Vedas
– Upanishads
– Bhagavad-Gita (a section of the)
– Mahabharata

Review Questions

Answering the following questions will help you review key class themes and prepare for the examinations.

1. How do Hindus answer *boundary questions* concerning identity?

2. What are some of the Hindu answers to *boundary questions* concerning relationship? Be sure to include some discussion of *karma, reincarnation, moksha, yoga,* and *dharma* in your answer.

3. What are Professor Robert Ellwood's three fundamental features of religions, and in what ways are they evident in Hinduism?

4. What is the ultimate goal in Hinduism? After viewing Class 6, would you agree or disagree that the Hindu goal is, in reality, the goal of all religions?

Sources and Further Readings

Ellwood, Robert S. *Many Peoples, Many Faiths*, 5th edition. Upper Saddle River, NJ: Prentice Hall, 1996.

Gelberg, Steven, ed. *Hare Krishna, Hare Krishna*. NY: Grove Press, 1983.

Melton, J. Gordon. *The Encyclopedia of American Religions,* 5th edition, Detroit: Gale Research, 1996.

Smart, Ninian. *The World's Religions*. Englewood Cliffs, NJ: Prentice Hall, 1989.

BELIEFS AND BELIEVERS

Class 7 – Religious Experience: Buddhism

Introduction

Reflection: *What does Buddhism, and the Buddhists we will meet in this class, have to tell us about the relationship between the religious impulse, boundary questions and the experiential dimension?*

If we think of the religious impulse, unclothed or unadorned by cultural trappings, as the raw essence of the *experiential dimension*, then there is no better way to examine the *clothing process* than by turning to Buddhism. Siddhartha Gautama, the *Buddha* or "man who woke up," was born around 560 b.c.e. in the part of the Indian sub-continent now known as Nepal. It is a bit difficult to separate fact from legend, but the story of his life leading up to his enlightenment in 519 b.c.e. provides us with a classic example of a human being's encounter with *boundary questions*. And the Buddha's extraordinary answers to those questions developed, over time, into the constellation of worldviews we call Buddhism today.

Siddhartha grew up in a Hindu family at a time of intense religious turmoil. After approximately a thousand years of development, the Hindu worldview, as is so often the case in the history of world religions, had hardened into a set of cold doctrines and systematic rituals. People were beginning to rebel against the priestly Brahmin class who controlled temple life. Legend has it that the Buddha's father, Suddhodana, who was a king in that region, had a vision that his son would be a world ruler if he remained in the palace. If the child left the palace, he would become a spiritual savior. Naturally, the politically-oriented king wanted Siddhartha to be a world ruler.

In order to keep him in the palace, the king surrounded young Siddhartha with every imaginable luxury and pleasurable distraction. He was tutored in the arts and sciences and was groomed to be a successful political leader. But as the young lad grew to manhood, he became increasingly dissatisfied with life. From our perspective, he begins in earnest to confront *boundary questions*.

The cause of his discontent lies in the legend of "The Four Passing Sights." In order to keep young Siddhartha's mind attached to the world, his father gave strict orders that no ugliness intrude upon his son's life experience, specifically sickness, decrepitude and death. He was also forbidden to witness Hindu ascetics who had turned from the world and were following a spiritual path. In order to shield Siddhartha from these *boundary question generating* experiences, his father sent runners ahead to clear the roads of these sights whenever the young prince left the palace. Alas, whether by divine intervention or negligence on the part of the king's servants, Siddhartha, on three separate occasions, witnessed the suffering of the world in all three forms: a decrepit old man, a sick person racked with pain, and a funeral where mourners wept and wailed for their departed friend. He had encountered the impermanence of human existence in the ever-threatening forms of old age, sickness and death.

On a fourth journey, he met a Hindu monk who seemed quite content to travel about the country with his begging bowl. Siddhartha realized that in a world of change all joys and pleasures are fleeting. Determined to find the true knowledge about reality, he resolved to leave home and enter into the harsh life of a Hindu ascetic.

After six years of extreme self-denial, all he had accomplished was to ruin his physical health. Hindu practices had not revealed the answers to life's questions, so in desperation, he decided to leave Hinduism behind, sit under the shade of a large bodhi tree, and meditate until he attained true knowledge. On the third night of meditation, the *Four Noble Truths* were revealed to him. Siddhartha Gautama woke up and became the Buddha.

The story of the Buddha's enlightenment is fascinating in its own right, but also reveals a number of key class themes. First, it tells us something about how new religious movements emerge. When we explore the social dimension later in the course, we will discuss the dynamics of religious organization at length. For now, we can simply note that the Buddha was a devout Hindu who, nevertheless, could not find complete satisfaction with Hindu answers to life's most profound questions.

If we stay with our *clothing* analogy, we might say that he, Buddha, in his driven quest to find the truth, stripped the religious impulse of its Hindu garb, and in a state of pristine religious experience, discovered a new set of answers to these troubling questions. He somewhat reluctantly set the wheel of the *dharma*, or teaching, in motion by gathering a group of disciples and wandering the country, spreading the word until his death at age 80.

The point is that he didn't sit down and say, "Hey, I think I'll start a new religion." In fact, during his lifetime, Buddhism was seen as a sect of Hinduism. Over time, his unique religious experience became clothed in a veritable wardrobe of cultural expressions as his unique perspective on life moved out of India, through China and other Eastern cultures and on to the West. Today, like any major world tradition, there are innumerable varieties to be found: Theravada, Mayayana, Zen Buddhism, Tibetan Buddism, Japanese sects, Korean Buddhism and even a uniquely American Buddhist *dharma*. And each form of Buddhism is colored by the cultural customs present in the country in which it arises. Slightly different twists on a doctrinal point may set a group off on a new organizational journey; another sect is born. Here in the United States, Buddhism is growing to such an extent that in Chicago there are enough different Buddhist groups to necessitate a city-wide Buddhist council.

Another key class theme is that religions are living, dynamic entities, always expanding, always undergoing change like all institutions in society. A comparative example: a charismatic leader named Jesus with new spiritual insight into the Jewish law begins a Jewish sect that becomes a major world religion. Today, in the United States, there are more than 900 different varieties of Christianity. As long as human beings share the exigencies of the human condition, as long as they continue to ponder boundary questions, which will be with us until humanity goes the way of the dinosaur, new worldviews will emerge.

In this class, we examine the Buddha's answers to life's *boundary questions*. In addition, in our video interviews we will have a chance to see how two different groups of Buddhist believers structure their behavior around these ancient revelations.

Key Class Themes

This lesson focuses on the following themes:

1. The experiential dimension clothed in Buddhism
2. The Four Noble Truths
3. The Eight Fold Path
4. No-self/dependent origination
5. Zen Buddhism
6. Tibetan Buddhism

Videotape Synopsis

- Introduction
- Graphics/lecture
- Class discussion
- Interview with Dr. Nancy McCagney, University of Delaware
- Interview with Paul Haller, San Francisco Zen Buddhist Center
- Interview with Greg Conlee, Dharmadatu/Shambala Meditation Center, Chicago

Videotape Commentary

I suggest you read this section before you watch the videotape. You will find that it will help you organize your thoughts so that when you watch the tape it will be more meaningful. When you have finished viewing the tape, you may want to read this section again.

Class Discussion / The Four Noble Truths and the Eight Fold Path

Our class discussion along with the graphics on the Four Noble Truths and the Eight Fold Path raise some fascinating issues regarding the Buddha's answers to *boundary questions*. More than one analyst of religion has questioned whether the Buddha was *in the religion business* at all. Certainly, his original teachings carry none of the *clothing* normally associated with religion. In fact, the Buddha eschews the dimensional structure of religion, including the mythic dimension, ritual dimension, and doctrinal dimension. The ethical and social dimensions are evident in the Eight Fold Path, but they only function as outer manifestations of the all-important experiential dimension.

Theravada Buddhism, the religious expression closest to the Buddha's original insight, has often been referred to as a *psychology* rather than a religion. Indeed, the Buddha's assessment of human suffering and the therapy he prescribes, represented respectively by the Four Noble Truths and the Eight Fold path, could well be the prognosis of a modern psychoanalyst. The first *truth* is that humans suffer. Why do they suffer? According to the Buddha, it is *tanha*, the desire for private fulfillment generated by the ego-centered drive for separate existence. How can humans *wake up* from this delusional dream of separate, ego-oriented existence that causes so much suffering? The fourth *truth* contains the prescription. Follow the Eight Fold Path.

As Suzanne notes in our class discussion, the Eight Fold Path is as much good, solid, practical advice as it is a *religious* program for self-actualization. And as Chris points out, the Buddha's teachings are demonstrably similar to those of the popular psychoanalyst and author F. Scott Peck, author of the popular book "The Road Less Traveled." And how could it be otherwise? Good psychological advice is applicable whether it was perceived and expressed 2,500 years ago or five years ago. Let's review the steps in the Eight Fold Path and reflect on how even a non-religious person might benefit from applying these insights in his or her life.

1. Right Belief

The Buddha taught his devotees to avoid religious systems and seek their own path to enlightenment. However, even a pathless path needs some road map. The first step on the Eight Fold Path calls upon the believer to recognize the validity of the first three *Noble Truths* not just intellectually, but as a fundamental observation about the human condition. Life is suffering. We suffer because we seek permanence in a constantly changing world, but we can wake up from this dream and experience *Nirvana*, the cessation of desire and liberation from the cycle of rebirth, the goal of Buddhist spiritual practice.

2. Right Purpose

Once the believer's mind is settled that the goal of life is to end suffering by transcending separateness, a successful journey along the Eight Fold Path is dependent, as are all worthy goals, on the determination and intense aspiration of the traveler to reach the desired destination. Seeking liberation from *tanha* requires total commitment. It is not something that will work with a few exercises, meditative practices, or rituals that are ventured into halfheartedly at a certain day at a time of the week. Once assured that enlightenment is really the goal of life, the believer traveling the Eight Fold Path focuses all his or her energies with single-minded intensity on realizing that goal. This means using every event, every relationship throughout the day, as a test to determine if separate ego is defining reality or the eternally perfect oneness of being.

3. Right Livelihood

Unless we're born wealthy or win the lottery, the struggle for the legal tender will occupy most of our waking hours. Thus, it becomes highly important for the spiritual traveler to pick an occupation that is conducive to advancement along the spiritual path. The Buddha did point out a few professions he considered incompatible with spiritual growth, including poison peddler, slave dealer, prostitute, and caravan peddler (in his day, probably the equivalent of our traveling salesman!). It is interesting to reflect on which occupations in our own time would be detrimental to achieving enlightenment. Any occupation that becomes more than a means to the end of providing food, shelter, and clothing could be dangerous to your spiritual health. If the occupation feeds the ego or demands manipulation of others, *tanha* will flourish. Of course an occupation that forces one to lie, steal or cheat is frowned upon. Whatever one chooses to do for a living, it should be done selflessly, with less attention on remuneration, and more on serving others. That is the Buddhist way.

4. Right Speech

In Class Four while we were exploring the difficulties in determining the nature of religious experience, we entered into a lively discussion on the power of language. Our daily use of language reveals who we are and, from the Buddhist perspective, where we are on the Path to Enlightenment. For instance, language can be used to protect and nurture the ego. Skillful use of language to perpetrate some deceit, to hurt or slander others or in any way to deviate from the truth indicates that the speaker is using language to protect the walls of the ego. Fear is the primary motivator in these cases. What the Buddha meant by *right speech* is a reminder to the traveler on the Path to pay attention to the motives that prompt the words that arise in any life situation where verbal communication becomes necessary. Compassion and selflessness should be the motivating force, not fear and deceit. If at first it is not always possible to *speak the truth*, at least be aware of how language use can be a liberating force or just another brick in the wall of separate existence.

5. Right Conduct

Sometimes referred to as the "Ten Commandments of Buddhism," this stage on the Path lays out some familiar ethical territory: Do not kill, do not steal, do not lie, do not be unchaste, do not drink intoxicants. But this is more than just a list of admonitions. Like the Ten Commandments in the Hebrew Bible, these ethical requirements help formulate identity and definitely guide relationships. Again, the *motivation* behind acts that harm is all-important. Acts that hurt are inevitably based on self-seeking motivations while acts of kindness and caring are inspired by a genuine sense of interconnectedness to the *other*, be it other people, places or things. Right conduct requires that the traveler be attentive to his or her behavior. Even the thought that, say, stealing is possible indicates that the potential thief is still perceiving reality through the encrusted aperture of ego-consciousness. From the other side, or the enlightened perspective, there is nothing to steal and nothing could ever be stolen. All is One!

6. Right Effort

The second *fold* on the Path calls for right purpose. As we have noted, right purpose gets the traveler going. But the act of will necessary to continue on this arduous journey towards enlightenment must constantly be fueled by right effort. Beginner's enthusiasm will inevitably wane. It is only through steady, day-by-day, effort that the traveler can make progress. In a nutshell, right effort means attending to the other seven stages on the path, and though the traveler may stumble from time to time, the will to get back up and continue the journey may spell the difference between success and failure on the Path.

7. Right Mindfulness

Right mindfulness is both a stage on the path and the end result. To be absolutely attentive to the *here and now* is a primary goal of Buddhist practice. Thoughts and feelings come and go as do the myriad experiences of life, but the traveler stays focused on the goal of selflessness. The ego-oriented mind-set consists of endless chatter usually in the form of "why me?" "what if?" "if only" generated by a fruitless quest for permanence in a constantly changing world. Mindfulness simply asks that everything from the most mundane task to the most glorious achievements are treated with the same level of detachment or equanimity. The ego by its very nature instantly categorizes life events as *good* or *bad* according to the mind's current desire programming. The way out of this trap is to be attentive, to observe how and why this mental chatter arises, and then *let go* of the desires that feed the ego and distract the traveler from what is happening *right now!*

8. Right Meditation

As we noted in the introductory section of the class, the heart of Buddhism is the *experiential dimension.* The Buddha didn't so much outline a new religion or philosophy as he did a *new experience.* A well-meaning person could read every book ever published on Buddhism and Buddhist practice but without meditation it would only be, one hopes, a rewarding intellectual experience. What the Buddha perceived is nothing less than a completely new way of perceiving reality. Meditation facilitates absorption into this new reality. Like the would-be vacationer who longs to experience the wonders of some exotic island, it is only an unfulfilled dream until the boat pulls away from the dock. Meditation is the vessel on which the traveler sets out towards *nirvana.*

Interviews with Nancy McCagney and Paul Haller at the San Francisco Zen Center

While the Four Noble Truths and the Eight Fold Path provide the central core on which all Buddhists agree, Buddhism is taught differently depending on the cultural context in which it is found. In class, I use the analogy of a ball covered with *velcro.* As this Buddhist ball rolls down through history and across the boundaries of varied lands and peoples, it quite naturally has picked up the cultural trappings characteristic of those regions. This has made for a great deal of regional variation resulting in new movements within Buddhism. For all the diversity in Buddism, however, we can divide Buddhism worldwide into three major schools.

Theravada Buddhism, which comes closest to preserving the austerity of the Buddha's original teachings, has virtually disappeared from India, but today can be found in Sri Lanka and Southeast Asia. *Mahayana Buddhism*, the Greater Vehicle, spread throughout East Asia, including China, Korea and Japan. It includes the Nichiren and Zen Buddhist schools. Paul Haller, our interviewee at the San Francisco Zen Center, learned Zen practices in Japan, and now lives and practices Zen in America. The third major movement is *Vajrayana*, the Diamond Vehicle, also known as Tantric Buddhism. Tibetan Buddhism is a form of *Vajayana Buddhism*, and in the next roll-in Greg Conlee introduces us to Tibetan Buddhism at the Chicago Dharmadatu Meditation Center.

Our first interview with Professor Nancy McCagney illustrates, once again, how important it is to *go directly to the believer* when attempting to make sense of an unfamiliar worldview. Nancy's discussion of hiking in the wilderness as a new form of Buddhist meditation shows how this ancient self-actualization psychology is applicable in the most modern trends. Notice how she speaks about being "absolutely" attuned to the natural setting as one hikes through the woods; the sound of the wind in the trees, the smell of the earth, the sunlight, birds and other animals. Being in the *here and now* of a wilderness experience stills the chatter of the mind, and brings the hiker into that special experience of interconnectedness with nature. As a scholar of both religious studies and environmental studies, Nancy uses Buddhist precepts found in the Eight Fold Path to underscore the need for ecological harmony between humans and nature. Perhaps the Buddha was the first ecologist!

Next we have an opportunity to chat with Paul Haller, a teacher and resident at the San Francisco Zen Center. Zen is a school of Mahayana Buddhism, colored and shaped by Japanese culture. The San Francisco Zen Center grew out of a small group of meditators which formed under the leadership of Suzuki-roshi in the late 1950s. Zen has been described as the mystical school of Buddhism. Sitting *zazen*, a typical Zen method of meditation, the practitioner follows the Buddha's path towards the experience of *satori*, described variously as total joy, bliss, full and perfect equilibrium with the cosmos, or enlightenment. Zen teaches that through meditation, one can cut through the illusion of the ego to the truth that underlies all things. In meditation, the mind becomes clear, the illusion of separate existence falls away, and life is experienced purely in the *now*. According to Zen practitioners such as Paul Haller, this is the *right meditation, right absorption* mentioned in the eighth stage of the Eight Fold Path. The experience of *satori*, sudden Enlightenment, will lead to *nirvana*, or the cessation of desire, an end to human suffering and liberation from the cycle of rebirth that is the goal of Buddhist spiritual practice.

As you listen to Paul Haller describe his daily meditation practices, his teaching, and the key Buddhist concepts of no-self and dependent origination, see if you can pinpoint several examples of the Eight Fold Path at work in this believer's life.

Interview with Reverend Greg Conlee of the Dharmadatu/Shambala Meditation Center in Chicago

Reverend Greg Conlee is a representative of the Tibetan Buddhist school of the *Vajrayana movement*, or Diamond Vehicle. This variety of Buddhism is representative of the Kagyupa sect founded by Lama Marpa of Lhagyupa in the country of Tibet during the 11th century. Rinpoche Chogyam Trungpa Rinpoche, who died in 1987, brought the tradition to the United States in 1970. Since that time, from the group's base in Boulder, Col., numerous meditation centers, or *dharmadatus*, have been established throughout the United States.

One additional skill you will pick up as you become more adept at worldview analysis is the ability to *see* what is going on around you. For instance, on our journeys to the various religious centers where we interviewed spokespersons, we came to *see* that the location of the centers, the actual buildings themselves had much to tell us about the worldview. Observing phenomena, as mundane as the type of furnishings in the reception room, decorations in the restrooms, or the clothes of the spokesperson can tell us much about the B + B = B equation even before the interview begins.

The Dharmadatu Meditation Center is the perfect exterior expression of the religious activity going on inside. It blends into the world around it in such a way that, unless you have a good set of directions, you would never find it much less see it. The center is located on the second floor over a row of small businesses, nestled beneath the elevated train tracks in a bustling commercial section of north Chicago. The reception area looks like the office of a travel agent (Air Meditation!). A short step down the hallway reveals an entrance to a simple, but beautiful meditation room. It is immediately clear that this is a room where people do something. It is functional; it has a purpose. Greg Conlee, despite the sense of peace that emanates from him, looks like and dresses like an executive of a major business firm. As a matter of fact, he is an executive for a telecommunications company.

The overall impression you receive is that the center is a place for being here, now. Contrast that with an ornate Gothic Catholic church. That structure points to the beyond; inside, worshipers focus their attention on God, the transcendent, Heaven and salvation in some other realm. For the meditators at the Dharmadatu center, heaven, or *nirvana* as the Buddha referred to it, is to be found right where you stand.

How do we account for this religious *behavior*? Let's look at some of the key beliefs in this form of Buddhism. The *dharma*, or teaching, pivots on a single frustration descriptive of the human condition, the desire for permanence in a constantly changing world. This single frustration has sparked everything in human culture from major world religions to Country & Western ballads about lost love, bad luck and broken dreams. A Christian looks for permanence in Heaven. A Hindu finds permanence in the escape from the karmic wheel of birth and death in mystical unity with Brahman. Though there are numerous explanations found in different varieties of Buddhism, the classical Buddhist finds permanence, paradoxically, in the rejection of the notion that such a thing could ever exist. All that is required to be *enlightened* is to let go, open your arms, and totally embrace change.

The two key beliefs, or doctrines, that address this process in Buddhism are *no-self* and *dependent origination*. As is stated many times during this class, in order to completely grasp these beliefs, you must adopt a particular kind of behavior. Like the Buddha, if you want to *experience* this spiritual insight, you have to *meditate*! To make a gross generalization, the entire human problem of lack of peace can be traced to the desire to cling to something mistakenly thought to be permanent in what is, in fact, a world of endless change. The idea that you have a solid, identifiable ego, or self, is the root cause of all suffering. Even the primary *boundary question*, "Who am I?" is misguided. While it may seem that you are an independent unit, this is only an illusion.

Here is where the second doctrine comes in. *Dependent origination* simply means that what you mistakenly see as solid is in reality a flowing stream of an interconnected, interrelated, constantly changing, dynamic collection of elements including the senses, the emotions and consciousness: of physical elements including the body, sexuality, hunger and sleep, and of cultural elements such as custom, beliefs and even religion itself. All these constituents of being are governed by *dharma*, meaning not only the teaching of the Buddha but the actual physical laws that govern the universe. We suffer because we fight against the dharma, cutting ourselves off from the natural flow of being.

Pretty heady stuff, to be sure! But try this exercise. Who were you seven years ago? Certainly you may have the same name, live in the same house, even have the same occupation. But are you really the same person? Do the same concerns preoccupy your mind? Do you have the same interests? Did you know that practically every cell in your body has reproduced itself over the past seven years? Do you have the same relationships? Did you pass through an extremely painful experience? Why was it painful? Could *tanha* have played a role in generating this pain, over and above the negativity of the experience itself?

Rites of passage come into consideration at this point. What really is painful about rites of passage? It is not that we struggle against the change? Part of ritual practice in initiation rites is to break the bonds that cause us to cling to that which is old so that we can enter into the new.

The Dharmadatu Center in Chicago reflects this perspective on life. You really can't tell where the center begins and the bustling world around it ends. The people who meditate at the center really aren't going anywhere in the sense that *nirvana* and *samsara*, the term for the physical world, are one and the same. Heaven is here, now. As we listen to Greg Conlee explain Buddhist teachings and practices at the Dharmadatu Center, a provocative thought arises. Perhaps one way of looking at the Buddha's answers to *boundary questions* is to say that the Four Noble Truths and the Eight Fold Path *erase the boundaries!*

Videotape Graphics

At this stage we suggest you watch the videotape. The graphics you will see on the screen are reproduced below to save you the trouble of copying them down. You might like to add your own comments as you watch the tape.

Buddhism

The Four Noble Truths

1. Life is suffering – "Dukkha"

   – trauma of birth
   – pathology of sickness
   – morbidity of decrepitude
   – phobia of death
   – tied to what one abhors
   – separated from what one loves

2. Cause of suffering – "Tanha"

   Desire – pulling apart from life
   Clinging – to ego-consciousness
   Craving

3. Tanha must be extinguished.

4. The way to extinguish Tanha and end Dukkha is to follow the Noble Eight-Fold Path.

Buddhism

The Noble Eight-Fold Path

1. *Right Belief*
2. *Right Purpose*

These involve the acceptance of the first three truths and the determination to effect a change

Basic Ethical Requirements

3. *Right Livelihood* – living according to Buddhist principles
4. *Right Speech* – avoidance of anger, gossiping, boasting
5. *Right Conduct* – "10 Commandments" of Buddhism

Meditation "Dhyana"

6. *Right Effort*
7. *Right Mindfulness*
8. *Right Meditation*

> **Buddhism**
>
> *Key Buddhist Insights*
> - Life is suffering. Humans suffer because they cling to, desire, struggle for permanence in a constantly changing world.
> - No Self = egolessness
> - Dependent origination
> - The self only exists in relationship with everything around it

Review Questions

Answering the following questions will help you review key class themes and prepare for examinations.

1. According to the Buddha, why do we suffer and what can be done about it? How does this insight relate to *boundary questions* and *rites of passage*?

2. What are the Four Noble Truths and Eight Fold Path? In your informed opinion, are these key Buddhist insights religious or psychological in nature?

3. Identify several examples of the Eight Fold Path in the comments of Nancy McCagney, Paul Haller and Greg Conlee.

4. Why do you think Buddhism is becoming so popular with Western believers in our secular culture?

Sources and Further Readings

Corless, Roger, *The Vision of Buddhism*. NY: Paragon House, 1989.

De Bary, Wm. Theodore, ed. *Sources of Indian Tradition*. NY: Columbia University, 1958.

Melton, Gordon J. *The Encyclopedia of American Religions*, 3rd edition. Detroit: Gale Research, 1989. See the chapters on Buddhism.

Smart, Ninian. *The World's Religions*. Englewood Cliffs, NJ: Prentice Hall, 1989.

Smith, Huston. *The Religions of Man*. NY: Harper & Row, 1965. See the chapter on Buddhism.

BELIEFS AND BELIEVERS
Class 8 – The Religious Quest:
The Ramtha School of Enlightenment

Introduction

Reflection: *Class 8 will be our last class in this opening segment of the course on the experiential dimension. In this class, we devote the entire hour to an exploration of the Ramtha School of Enlightenment. Here is an excellent opportunity for you to apply what you have learned so far in "Beliefs and Believers," particularly the useful skill of developing informed answers to the "Why?" question when it comes to unusual religious activity. Using our key class themes such as the religious process, pervasiveness of religion, seeker style, boundary questions, rites of passage and types of religious experience, see if you can determine what is it that motivates the students at the Ramtha School of Enlightenment. And remember to put on some Ramtha moccasins before you do any serious walking through this extraordinary worldview.*

Students often ask me how I find the believers we interview in our "Beliefs and Believers" class sessions. I'd like to be able to reveal some well-thought out master plan, but the fact is that serendipitous occurrences play as much of a role as hard-nosed research or organized networking. Such is the case with the Ramtha School of Enlightenment, one of the most innovative spiritual centers I have ever visited. About three years ago while vacationing in Santa Barbara, I arranged to have dinner with J. Gordon Melton, Director of the Institute for the Study of American Religion. During our post-dinner conversation, Gordon mentioned that he was co-organizer of a conference that would draw scholars from all over the world to investigate a woman, JZ Knight, who purportedly channels a 35,000 year old ascended master, named Ramtha. Physicists, psychoanalysts, sociologists, humanists, parapsychological experts and medical doctors had all been invited. Gordon needed one more paper on the ethical dimension of Ramtha's teachings, and asked me if I'd be interested. Always looking for a new challenge, I consented.

Participants in the conference were required to visit the school during a teaching session at least one time before the conference. This was a good idea in that scholars, so often left to their own devices in their respective theoretical worlds, really did need to see the school's operation, observe the students at work and meet JZ Knight. I flew to Seattle in November of 1996, rented a car, and headed down to Yelm, Washington, a modest little town nestled beneath the majesty of Mt. Rainier. As you can imagine, my anthropological/fieldwork approach to religious studies has taken me to some unusual settings. Nothing, however, had prepared me for my introduction to the school. I reached JZ Knight's opulent ranch just as it was getting dark, drove through the massive gates and was greeted by two genial employees of the school. They told me that the students were doing "field work" and asked if I'd like to observe. We walked past a huge horse arena and down towards a horse corral about the size of two football fields. As we approached the corral, a hissing sound, rather like steam escaping a pipe, became louder and louder.

I was doing my best to keep an open mind and do a little moccasin walking, but when we reached the corral, my immediate reaction was to run for the gates! Imagine 1,200 blindfolded people in the dark, wandering about a huge fenced-in field, with hands held out in front of them in a peculiar fashion and making a loud hissing sound with their breath. Had I suddenly been transported into a scene from "The Night of the Living Dead?"

The following morning we all had a good laugh about my brush with worldview paranoia. My guides apologized for not preparing me a bit for my first encounter with Ramtha's rigorous and most unusual training activities. As you will see on the videotape roll-ins, the next day I received a crash course in fieldwork, then actually tested the process myself. No doubt, it proved to be a consciousness-transforming experience, even on the first try by a novice practitioner.

The conference, which was held in February of 1997, proved to be a resounding success for JZ Knight and the Ramtha School of Enlightenment. During the 20 years JZ had been channeling Ramtha, she quite understandably had been the target for negative skepticism from religious leaders in the greater Seattle area – verbal attacks on her family and herself, ridicule by the media, lawsuits and even threats on her life. With major media in the region covering the event, the scientists involved in the conference concluded unanimously that whatever was happening during the Ramtha channeling sessions, JZ could not be perpetrating a fraud upon her students. What exactly was happening when JZ channeled Ramtha was still unclear from a scientific point of view. However, as the headline of a major regional paper proclaimed, "JZ Knight is not a fake!"

I make mention of this public validation of the school, JZ, Ramtha, and the students, because it led to one of the most extraordinary experiences I have ever had in exploring alternative religions. Spirits were high after the conference ended, and the scholars, a handful of devoted students, and JZ adjourned to a local restaurant for a post-conference celebration. Wine, good food and great conversation quickly transformed the gathering into a magical event. One could sense the relief on the part of JZ and the students in finally being legitimized by some of their most vociferous former critics.

Towards the end of the dinner, JZ and a handful of Ramtha's long-term, devoted students gravitated to an end table to share a special moment apart from the scholars and other guests present at the dinner. JZ sat in the middle with students at either side. At the risk of seeming sacrilegious, what I saw was a real-life representation of the Last Supper. The bond between leader and student was tangible, as was the sense of transformation. For these religious questors, some invisible boundary had been crossed, some new convenant made. It suddenly occurred to me that I was experiencing first hand, what it must have been like to be with Jesus, the Buddha, Moses or Mohammed, when their spiritual sparks ignited the religious sensibilities of their followers. True, the Ramtha School of Enlightenment may not last a generation. Or then again, it could be the start of a new spiritual movement that lasts for millennia. Either way, on that special night, I saw a charismatic leader surrounded by committed, devoted followers who were prepared to continue their religious quest into uncharted spiritual territory. Make no mistake, the great world religions have earned their place in human history. Time is an effective validator. But all had a start, and the spontaneity of their primal moments may well have been quite similar to those I experienced that night in Yelm, Washington.

Key Class Themes

This lesson focuses on the following themes:

1. The Religious Quest
2. Ramtha School of Enlightenment
3. The birth of a new spiritual movement
4. Personal transformation as a religious quest

Videotape Synopsis

- Guest - Pavel Mikoloski, from the Ramtha School of Enlightenment
- Ramtha School of Enlightenment roll-in; "student activities"
- Ramtha School of Enlightenment roll-in; "JZ and Ramtha"
- Ramtha School of Enlightenment roll-in; "the Ramtha experience"

Videotape Commentary

I suggest you read this section before you watch the videotape. You will find that it will help you organize your thoughts so that when you watch the tape it will be more meaningful. When you have finished viewing the tape, you may want to read this section again.

Keeping our "Beliefs and Believers" methodology intact, we wanted to have a representative from the school come to our class session to handle student questions from the believer's point of view. We were thrilled when Pavel Mikoloski agreed to make the trip from Yelm, Washington to the Chicago area to spend some time with us. The structure for this class combines short roll-ins that illustrate key points about this worldview with an open and lively interaction between Pavel, the students and myself. Let's turn to our first video roll-in.

First Roll-in: Ramtha School of Enlightenment, "Fieldwork"

In the various pamphlets and brochures that describe the school and its teachings, the Ramtha School of Enlightenment, is referred to as *The American Gnostic School*. Gnosticism, the quest for knowledge that reveals the secrets of the universe and all existence, may go back as far as the second century of the Common Era. Some scholars see the Gnostic quest as a perennial tendency in all human religious activity. Nevertheless, the primary motivation in any form of gnosticism is *personal transformation*. The Gnostic questor does not just learn theories about the power of the mind, the macrocosmic/microcosmic relationship between the universe and the human body, or the secrets that reveal the magical link between consciousness and reality. The traveler on the Gnostic path learns and practices secret techniques that actually *transform* reality. It is not a spiritual path for the dabbler; come committed or don't come at all.

Following the Gnostic tradition, only serious students come to this school. The starting point for their training is the Beginning Consciousness & Energy (C&E) Workshop, a two-day workshop designed to initiate the student into the power of consciousness-transformation. The unique breathing exercise you will hear during the student activities is actually a *yogic method* (my term, not theirs) for becoming aware of the power of your own consciousness and refocusing your energy in a more mindful, creative manner. There are three levels of C&E classes. After completing this introductory level, students who wish to continue are required to attend two mandatory sessions per year, a seven-day retreat and a three day follow-up. Students don't actually live at the school for extended periods of time. You attend teaching sessions with Ramtha, then you go back into the world and integrate those teachings into your everyday reality.

It is estimated that a primary student attends two events and contributes a minimum of $1,350 per year. But don't come to the Ramtha School of Enlightenment expecting plush hotel meeting rooms and soft beds. The accommodations are Spartan, to say the least. Students ordinarily will be assigned a "space" on the floor of the arena, just about big enough for a sleeping bag. They must bring their own food and a means to prepare it. Port-a-potties and make-shift showers must serve the needs of as many as 1,800 people at a given event. No one comes to the ranch for a vacation. The simplicity of accommodations keeps the focus turned inward on personal transformation and away from the distractions of life in a world of comforts and convenience.

Though JZ Knight has been channeling Ramtha since about 1978, the school did not begin until May 1988. Ramtha introduced the basic C&E exercise, then added additional practices as students became more advanced. Though the full explanation is quite complex, the purpose behind the exercises we will see on videotape is to learn to use completely new parts of your brain, what the teaching refers to as *the analogical mind*. In learning to focus and *know* in a powerfully new manner, the student is on the path to consciously creating his or her reality in day-to-day life. Finding your card in *fieldwork*, hitting a bullseye while blindfolded in *archery* or reaching the *center* while traversing the labyrinth known as *the tank* are not ends in themselves. They only represent a developing skill, a special *gnosis* that then is to be applied in the world. Far from being some airy New Age philosophy, the teachings at the school are decidedly pragmatic; students come there because they experience positive, personal transformation in themselves and in their lives.

Our first roll-in will give you some visual experience of what students do at the school. Diane instructs me on how to do fieldwork, then we see a short segment on archery, and a look at *the tank*. One observation – the students at the school see consciousness and energy as being the basic elements behind personal transformation. From the perspective of "Beliefs and Believers," I couldn't help equating *consciousness* with *identity* and *energy* with *relationship*. If that is an accurate comparison, then we are on the right track in "Beliefs and Believers" when we identify *identity* and *relationship* as being fundamental elements in all religions. After all, the religious impulse is towards personal transformation. While the other dimensions of religion might work to provide stability and permanence, the *experiential* dimension is about change; that is why the Ramtha School of Enlightenment provides such an appropriate end to our study of this fascinating dimension.

Second Roll-in: Ramtha School of Enlightenment, JZ Knight and Ramtha

In this roll-in and the following, you will experience some of the most extraordinary "beliefs and believers" testimony in the entire teleclass. JZ Knight describes her first meeting with Ramtha, the god, in her kitchen in Tacoma, Washington, in 1978. From our look at types of religious experience, JZ's first encounter with Ramtha is a classic *numinous* experience. Later, she will describe what actually happens when Ramtha "takes over" her body and mind and uses it as a vehicle through which to offer his Gnostic teachings.

As you know by now, in this class we do not promote or belittle any worldview. We leave it up to you to decide for yourself whether the spiritual practice makes sense or is simply unbelievable. However, it might be helpful in your assessment of JZ's relationship to have a little historical background on *channeling*. Channeling seemed to spring out of nowhere in the 1980s, as so-called New Age practitioners flocked in great numbers to hear quite a variety of channelers, including JZ, offer wisdom, healing or spiritual insight. Among this group of '80s channelers, JZ quickly rose to the top.

Channeling has its roots in 19th century Spiritualism. Belief that the living can communicate with the dead has probably fascinated humans down through history. In the most general sense, Spiritualism is the belief in the survival of the self after death, and the ability of human beings, especially those with unique gifts (mediums), to establish contact with those who have "shuffled off this mortal coil." The uniquely American form of Spiritualism was influenced by events in New York, in 1848, and by the writings of Andrew Jackson Davis, whose book, "The Principles of Nature" (1847), became the "Bible" of modern Spiritualism.

You may have heard of a ritual practice known as a *seance*, during which a medium contacts the deceased and establishes an open line of communication. The first modern seance probably occurred on March 31, 1848, in Hydesville, New York, when 11-year-old Kate Fox and her sisters established communication through mysterious rapping sounds from an entity, Mr. Splitfoot, who had been murdered in their cottage some years earlier. The subsequent seances set off a national sensation, and though the established churches of the time condemned the sisters, their seances drew enormous crowds of people wishing to commune with the dearly departed. Interest in Spiritualism, in one form or another, has been part of the alternative religious scene in America ever since.

Channeling is simply a more modern, more current manifestation of the conduit between this realm and the next, established in the Spiritualist practices of the previous century. In general, the characteristics of channeling are as follows: a) rejection of traditional Christianity and its scripture; b) belief in reincarnation; c) contact with spiritually-evolved beings who have migrated to higher planes of existence (like Ramtha); d) the belief that the soul evolves through higher and higher levels of consciousness. Though JZ Knight's experience as a channeler is without a doubt unique, we can still observe some of these characteristics in her experience. Of course what makes the Ramtha School of Enlightenment unique in the world of channeling is the school itself; the organization and teaching clearly emerges from the ancient Gnostic teaching tradition.

Third Roll-in: Critics and Supporters

Our final roll-in from our visit to the Ramtha School of Enlightenment includes JZ Knight describing her experience when Ramtha enters her body and "uses it" to teach. J. Gordon Melton attests to the fact that this transformation has been scientifically verified, part of the study done in concordance with the 1997 "In Search of the Self" conference.

We also hear from a local fundamentalist Christian religious leader, Pastor Walt Stowe, who clearly considers Ramtha to be a demon and JZ to be possessed by the devil. Pastor Stowe has attacked JZ on local radio and in the news media and even organized a prayer march outside the gates of her ranch to protest devil worship.

During the section of the course on the *social dimension*, we will explore some of the psychological and emotional reasons behind the attacks by established religions on new and evolving spiritual perspectives. For now, we can see Pastors Stowe's unease with Ramtha as a clash of myths. In the next class, we will learn about the important functions of myth in any worldview. For Pastor Stowe, any spiritual entity that is not from God must be from God's mythic counterpart, the devil. I sat for several hours with Pastor Stowe and found him to be a man of integrity. His identity is that of a fundamentalist Christian. Thus, all his relationships are colored or shaded by that rigidly cut prism. It is a classic example of our B + B = B equation. We will visit Pastor Stowe again when we look at Conservative Christianity during our exploration of the *doctrinal dimension*. For now, whether you agree with him or not regarding Ramtha and the school, at least observe how his religious beliefs make it impossible for him to accept JZ's own personal experience. Do you see any possibility for a peaceful resolution between these two believers? Now that would make a good final exam question!

Videotape Graphics

 At this stage we suggest you watch the videotape.
There are no graphics in this class segment.

Class 8

Review Questions

Answering the following questions will help you review key class themes and prepare for examinations.

1. Illustrate key class themes such as *identity and relationship*, *seeker style*, *boundary questions* or *types of religious experience* using examples from our investigation of the Ramtha School of Enlightenment.

2. What do Ramtha's teachings teach us about the *experiential dimension?*

3. In what way is the Ramtha School of Enlightenment characteristic of an ancient *Gnostic* school?

4. What are the 19th century roots of "channeling?"

Sources and Further Readings

Melton, J. Gordon. *Finding Enlightenment: Ramtha's School of Ancient Wisdom.* Hillsboro, OR: Beyond Words Publishing, 1998.

Miller, Timothy, ed. *America's Alternative Religions.* NY: SUNY, 1995.
(See the chapter on "Spiritualism and Channeling")

Ramtha School of Enlightenment
P.O. Box 1210
Yelm, Washington 98597 (360) 458-5201

WWW - http://www.ramtha.com

BELIEFS AND BELIEVERS
Class 9 – Myth and Ritual: The Dimensional Triangle

Introduction

Reflection: *As we enter into our study of the Mythic and Ritual Dimensions, try to observe the relationship between the experiential, mythic, and ritual dimensions in any recent religious service you might have attended. Understanding the relationship between these three important dimensions of religion will go a long way towards answering the why and how questions regarding the religious activity of human beings in all cultures.*

In "Beliefs and Believers" we are using the *six dimensions of religions* as tools to help us learn to understand and appreciate the religions of the world. We've made the case that no *believer* naturally divides his or her religion up into six dimensions. But from the perspective of the outsider, these dimensions provide us with important clues about how religion works in the lives of everyday people. Knowing how these dimensions interrelate is a critical step in developing worldview analysis skills, and that is our objective as we move out of our introductory classes and our sessions on the *experiential dimension* and into our exploration of *myth and ritual.* In "Beliefs and Believers" we never *finish* with a dimension. Though our focus is now on myth and ritual, we must always be concerned about how *religious experience* guides or drives mythic and ritual activity in a given worldview.

The *Dimensional Triangle* provides a simple and direct visual image of the relationship between the *experiential, mythic* and *ritual dimensions.* As we move through our classes on myth and ritual and on to our latter three dimensions, the dimensional triangle should help you understand the motivation behind religious activity, past, present and future.

Religious Experience
Raises Boundary Questions

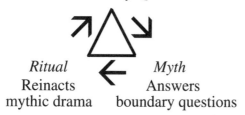

Ritual
Reinacts
mythic drama

Myth
Answers
boundary questions

Before viewing this class and observing examples of the dimensional triangle, let's summarize the relationship between religious experience, myth and ritual. Myth and ritual are both symbolic forms of communication; both dimensions are foundational in human cultural activity. Myths guide ritual practices which, in turn, validate human religious experience. The relationship works something like this: religious experience is the state in which human beings seek answers to *boundary questions*, questions as we have noted, that involve meaning, purpose, order, identity and relationship. These questions are answered in the *myths*, or paradigm-laden narratives, found in sacred texts or oral traditions in all religions. Myths contain stories of original *ritual* practices, usually initiated by the leader of the new religious movement or spiritual path. Jesus, for example, initiates the ritual of Communion at the Last Supper, part of the mythic drama in the New Testament. Myths guide ritual activity for future believers. Ideally, ritual activity answers *boundary questions*, and in doing so brings the believer back into a state of religious experience. A devout Muslim prays five

Class 9

times a day in the direction of the city of Mecca. Why? According to the mythic drama that undergirds Islam, the City of Mecca is where Allah revealed himself to the Prophet Mohammed, so the contact between heaven and earth had its most dynamic expression there. Buddha meditated; Buddhists meditate. The great myths in Hinduism speak of the Ganges river as the *mother of all life*; Hindus, by the millions, make holy pilgrimages to immerse themselves in the sacred waters.

Throughout this semester and beyond, see if you can recognize the *dimensional triangle* in the various religious expressions we encounter in class, or you run across in your own explorations. Here is an optimal opportunity to begin to use your newly-honed worldview analysis skills. I think you'll be surprised at how accurate an assessment of human religious activity the *dimensional triangle* is. Enjoy!

Key Class Themes

This lesson focuses on the following themes:

1. The Dimensional Triangle
2. The functions of Myth
3. Hindu myth and Hindu experience
4. Myth and ritual in Christianity
5. Myth, ritual and boundary questions

Videotape Synopsis

- Class discussion on Myth
- Dr. Davé explains the myth of the Ganges in Hinduism
- Graphics/lecture on the dimensional triangle and the function of myth
- Baptism ritual and interview with Pastor Walt Stowe
- Holy City graveyard roll-in
- Class discussion

Videotape Commentary

I suggest you read this section before you watch the videotape. You will find that it will help you organize your thoughts so that when you watch the tape it will be more meaningful. When you have finished viewing the tape, you may want to read this section again.

Class Discussion on Myth

Our lively and wide-ranging class discussion underscores a key point when considering myth; humans are story-creators. We love stories, and as Suzanne astutely points out, stories are so vital to human interaction that they might be considered a means of survival for humans in all cultures. Hit songs have intriguing story lines. Soap operas draw us into imaginary lives, and movies spin tales that keep us coming to the box office. Indeed, from cradle to grave, we surround ourselves with stories.

Of course *myths*, especially in the context of religious activity, are something special when it comes to the human love affair with narratives. The students' insights on myth are useful in clearing up some misconceptions that surround the study of myth. If you ask the average person-on-the-street to define *myth*, the likely answer will be a "false story." And, to be sure, that is how the word is used in our society by anyone from politicians to sportscasters to history teachers. But in the academic study of religion, the term *myth* has quite the opposite meaning. Myths in this sense are the most profoundly true stories that can be told.

Simply put, this is because myths cut right to the heart of those pesky *boundary questions*. These sometimes poetic, sometimes violent, but always fascinating sacred stories tell human beings who they are, where they come from, what is the purpose and meaning in life, why they must die, where they will go when they die and so on. And as we already have discussed, the answers to these questions provide a kind of *experiential glue* that binds communities together around our Beliefs + Believers = Behavior equation.

This brings up another point: when we say that myths are profoundly true, what do we mean by *true*? Ninian Smart points out that the word "mythos" came to mean false stories when the emerging Christian worldview clashed with ancient Greek and Roman *answers to boundary questions,* including all the colorful gods and goddesses present in their paradigmatic narratives. The Christians questioned the "truth" of the Hellenistic answers to life's perplexing questions.

Here is an everyday example for you: what happens at a family gathering? True, families are not as extended or as tight as they once were in this culture (the loss of agreed upon myths has much to do with this), but think back to a holiday celebration such as Thanksgiving when your family gathered together. Along with the ritual of munching down the turkey and mashed potatoes, the family experiences a sense of unity and belonging through story telling. Key family happenings are remembered; perhaps an enjoyable vacation, a tragic event or a humorous action that seems to represent a family member's quirky personality. At each gathering, the family looks forward to telling these stories, and though everyone has heard them a thousand times, they are never boring. They serve the purpose of establishing boundaries about who your family is, what they have done together and where they are headed as a unit. This, on a very small scale, gives you some sense of the power of story-telling as it defines community.

Now imagine how much more powerful these stories might be when they take on mythic proportions. For instance, in the next class we will examine the great mythic stories found in Judaism. This epic biblical narrative, stretching through the first five books of the Bible, has all the elements of myth. God creates the world, enters into human history through a covenant with Abraham, chooses a special people, liberates them from bondage in Egypt, then gives them the Law at Sinai after protecting them on a classic life journey in the wilderness. If these biblical accounts are familiar to you, consider them again from the point of view of *boundary questions*. Answers to questions regarding origin, alienation, the nature and identity of heroes, liberation, purpose, proper behavior, proper relationships veritably bubble up from the pages of these sacred texts. And as we shall see, when in the next class we listen to Rabbi Bronstein speak of the relationship between myth and ritual in Judaism, all Jewish religious holidays and ritual celebrations are *driven* by the great myths present in Hebrew scripture.

Consider, for a moment, the New Testament mythos and its effect on Christian experience and ritual practices. Jesus, as the central *hero*, accomplishes extraordinary deeds that absolutely defy all scientifically recognized laws regarding the physical world. He walks on water; raises the dead; dies and comes back to life, just to name a few of his *miracles*. Yet these stories form the basis for the predominant worldview of the most technologically advanced, scientifically-oriented nation in the history of civilization. When we speak of *truth* regarding myths, we need to understand truth as something different from scientifically verifiable information. Myths are true to believers at a level that is much more experiential, emotional, psychological, even mystical. A believer doesn't just know a myth; the believer lives, embodies the myth. And what does that myth do for the believer? Of course, it regulates behavior, particularly ritual behavior. This will be clearly evident in Dr. Davé's explanation of the power of myth in Hindu life.

One more example before turning to Dr. Davé and his recitation of the *myth of the Ganges*; one of the great made-in-America religions, Mormonism. The fight over whether Mormonism is *true* or not is over points of doctrine, to be sure, but it is also over the sacred story, the myth, of God's supposed revelation to Joseph Smith, founder of the religion. To the outsider, the story sounds fantastic. An angel, Moroni, led Joseph Smith to ancient gold plates that told the long, lost history of pre-Columbian America (America before Columbus visited the continent). Joseph was able to translate the Egyptian script on the plates into English with the use of two magical seer stones. Among other fascinating revelations, the plates explain that the Native American tribes were descendants of the lost tribes of Israel and migrated to this continent many years before the birth of Jesus. After Jesus' resurrection, he came to America to straighten out various doctrinal and ritual practices. Eventually, an evil branch of the tribe wiped out the noble branch, but the plates were preserved and buried in the hills of upstate New York until Joseph Smith discovered them in the 1820s. The most important demand the plates made upon Joseph and his followers was to build the true church of Jesus Christ on American soil in these, the Latter Days. Thus, the grand religious drama that ultimately found most of the Mormons settling in Utah was started.

Now critics of the Church of Jesus Christ of Latter Day Saints point out that the Book of Mormon, Joseph's translation of the plates, describes Native American tribes that bear no resemblance to any known group that occupied this continent. In addition, it is noted that every doctrinal dispute that raged in upstate New York during Joseph Smith's lifetime is resolved in his translation of the ancient plates. Also, critics have maintained that passages in the Book of Mormon are extremely close to passages from the Hebrew Bible or Old Testament.

But all of this is beside the point. The myth that Joseph Smith articulated struck a chord in the 19th century American psyche to such an extent that his people endured unspeakable hardship in their quest to build the kingdom of God on the North American continent. The zeal with which they went about their tasks was, no doubt, fueled by the power of myth in their lives. If you want a perfect example of how myth drives human history, look no further than the account of the Mormon effort to realize Joseph Smith's prophetic vision. In addition, the story provides us with a classic example of our B + B = B equation from the perspective of myth. In class discussion, Jamie asks why religious leaders confuse myth with history. It's not so much confusion or an attempt to deceive believers as it is the raw power of myth defining identity and guiding relationships. Truth exists in myth, but as we note in our class graphics on myth and history, it is not always "factual" truth. Nevertheless, as the Mormon example illustrates, it is a truth with enormous power!

Interview with Dr. Davé; the Myth of the Ganges

Dr. Davé's delightful rendition of the Myth of the Ganges provides an excellent example of how myth undergirds the belief system in a worldview. See if you can identify the functions of myth in his sacred story and recognize how key Hindu doctrines – karma, reincarnation, moksha – are informed by the *answers to boundary questions* present in the mythic drama.

Notice that Dr. Davé treats his recitation of the myth as a highly religious experience. The myths have moved him to ritual activity, in this case, a pilgrimage to the river Ganges. Also he is subtly demonstrating how the Ganges myth has helped form his identity and has provided a kind of *identity-essence* that his parents passed on to him and that binds his family together. Notice the relationship between the *experiential dimension* and the *mythic dimension* as Dr. Davé tells his story. Here we return to the question of the *truth* of myths. Obviously, Dr. Davé is very moved by this sacred story. It evokes genuine, powerful emotions in him, and he uses that power to make the story come alive for us.

Baptism and Interview with Pastor Walt Stowe

Like everything in life, creating a teleclass has its ups and downs, good days and bad. Happening upon a group of Christians participating in the ritual of baptism in the river Jordan in Israel was, well, one of those *good days!* I had been looking for some religious event to illustrate our *dimensional triangle*. What could be more appropriate and more familiar to the predominantly Christian audience of American students than the baptism ritual? And as Pastor Walt Stowe accurately notes in our interview, it is the biblical story of Jesus' baptism, the myth, that is the driving force behind the Christian ritual of baptism. In going through the ritual baptism, whether in the River Jordan itself or in a baptismal font half a world away in Roy, Washington, the Christian believer participates in Christ's essential transforming religious experience. In baptism, by immersion, a person goes down into the water and symbolically the believer dies with Christ, crosses a threshold and rises again to life with Christ through his resurrection, thus becoming part of the new community that is linked in substance with the Lord. Experience, myth and ritual combine to deliver the believer into a *born again* experience, complete with a new identity and new perspective on relationships, the dimensional triangle at work!

Holy City Roll-in

Our last roll-in illustrates how the *dimensional triangle*, in response to a troublesome boundary question like death, spawns religious activity. Jewish, Christian, and Muslim pilgrims, guided by the mythic drama in their respective sacred texts, travel to Jerusalem to ritually renew their faith. For instance, the Via Dolorosa, or way of the Cross, commemorates the path which Jesus walked bearing the cross from the Praetorium to Calvary. Every Friday, led by Franciscan monks, groups of Christian pilgrims from around the world, retrace these steps, starting at the Church of the Flagellation and ending at the Church of the Holy Sepulchre. Muslims pray at the Dome of the Rock or El-Aqsa mosque where, according to the Muslim mythos, Mohammed conferred with the great religious leaders of all time. Or Jews literally wail at the Western Wall, all that remains of the Second Temple. The Western Wall is never deserted. At any hour of the day or night, winter or summer, there are always Jews, many who have come from great distances, standing in front of the Wall in devout prayer or placing their messages to Yahweh in the cracks and crevices between the stones. In our next class on Judaism, we will meet Jews at the Wall who, with no prompting, provide evidence for our *dimensional triangle* theory; they are there seeking religious experience through ritual according to the mythic traditions of their chosen worldview.

Videotape Graphics

At this stage we suggest you watch the videotape. The graphics you will see on the screen are reproduced below to save you the trouble of copying them down. You might like to add your own comments as you watch the tape.

Dimensional Triangle
Myth and ritual are both symbolic forms of communication; both are foundational in human cultural activity and experience.

Dimensional Triangle

Religious Experience

Ritual   Myth

Dimensional Triangle

Religious Experience
Raises Boundary Questions

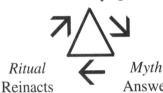

Ritual   *Myth*
Reinacts   Answers
mythic drama   boundary questions

Experience, Myth, Ritual
Their relationship:
– Religious experience is the state in which human
  beings seek answers to boundary questions:
  meaning, purpose, order, identity, relationship, etc.
– These questions are answered in the MYTHS, or
  paradigmatic narratives, found in sacred texts or
  in sacred oral traditions in all religions
– Myths contain stories of original RITUAL practices;
  Myths guide ritual activity for future believers. Ideally,
  ritual activity answers boundary questions; believers
  enter into a state of religious experience

Myth and History
Myth = paradigm-laden narratives

Myth and History
Key functions of myth
– answer profound life questions
– guide individual and collective behavior
– engender self-esteem and empowerment
– order existence
– provide reverence for the past;
  hope for the future

> **Myth and History**
> History = factual description of past peoples, places, events

> **Myth and History**
> *Key question:*
> Is history ever completely detached from myth?

Review Questions

1. What is a myth? How is the term used in religious studies?

2. Describe the relationship between the *experiential, mythic,* and *ritual dimensions.*

[handwritten: Identity keeps it alive   gives myths meaning]

3. In what way is a myth a profoundly true story? How does this relate to our B + B = B equation?

4. What are the key functions of myth in any given worldview? Using the Christian ritual of baptism, illustrate two or more of these functions.

Sources and Further Readings

Campbell, Joseph. *Hero With a Thousand Faces*. Princeton, NJ: Princeton University Press, 1968. Also try to watch the PBS series on the Power of Myth based on Campbell's lifelong work.

Eliade, Mircea. *Cosmos and History: The Myth of the Eternal Return*. NY: Harper Colophon, 1958.

Eliade, Mircea. *Myth and Reality*. NY: Harper Colophon, 1963.

Schmidt, Roger. *Exploring Religion*, 2nd ed. Belmont, CA: Wadsworth, 1988. Read his chapter on sacred stories.

BELIEFS AND BELIEVERS
Class 10 – Mythic Dimension: Judaism

Introduction

Reflection: *As we continue our discussion of myth, and especially as we ask Judaism to help us understand this dimension of worldviews, reflect on the power of myth. In the case of Judaism, a people have endured thousands of years of persecution because of their adherence to the meaning of their sacred stories. At the same time, it is those stories that sustain the believers during perilous times, an amazing saga of beliefs and believers!*

There is an old Jewish saying that anytime two Jews are together in a room, you will have *three opinions*. The point is that discussion, dialogue, argument, complexity and disagreement comprise the uniquely Jewish way of approaching reality, which from the "Beliefs and Believers" perspective, means sorting out questions regarding identity and relationship. At this juncture in our exploration of worldviews, Judaism is extremely helpful because the Jewish openness to many opinions means that *myth* is a *living experience* for these believers. If you still feel a bit uncertain about the mythic dimension and its power in answering profound life questions for believers, or if the *dimensional triangle* is more theory than actuality in your thinking, this class on Judaism should bring clarity to these key class themes.

In the case of Judaism, the great myths are encapsulated in the Hebrew Bible. Reflecting on why God created human beings, one ancient Rabbi said, "God created humans because he liked a good story!" And what a story it is in the Hebrew Bible. Comprised of three sections, the *Torah,* the *Prophets*, and the *Writings*, an unparalleled mythic drama unfolds. As we move through the types of myth and the characteristics of myth in this class, see if you can recognize a few examples drawn from biblical stories with which you might be familiar. Believe me, it is *all there* in the Hebrew Bible.

In discussing the various functions of myth, we observed that myths *order human existence*. The Jewish perspective on history, one shared by Christians and Muslims, provides a sense of order that tends to supercharge all the other functions of myth. Human history moves in a linear fashion from creation out of nothing, through historical vicissitudes and on to the end of history when God will bring the divine design to completion. God has provided revelations and prophets to offer guidance to humans on this wild ride towards judgment day, but humans exercise free will on the journey. Thus, in contrast to some other religions of the world where the ups-and-downs of life are deemed illusory and people have many lifetimes to complete the journey towards salvation, history is perceived as cyclical. In the *Abrahamic traditions*, you get one shot, and you better get on with it! The mythic dimension is ratcheted up to a higher level of intensity as human beings are *real players* in a drama that includes the most exalted aspirations and most debased actions as God brings creation towards fulfillment.

What makes myth a *living experience* for the Jew is the fact that these amazing stories are always open to *interpretation*. An analogy can be drawn from observing a group of talented musicians preparing to perform a Mozart concerto. The notes of the concerto do not vary. They are, from the musician's perspective, almost sacrosanct. No conductor would ever consider changing the notes in a Mozart concerto. However, it is the *interpretation* of the notes by skilled musicians that can lead to new insight into the power of the musical piece.

In the same way, Jews for millennia have *interpreted* their myths in a continuing quest to make sense of human experience in the present. As we listen to Rabbi Bronstein describe how the three great myths in Judaism guide all ritual activity, Dr. Lorberbaum explain the

Class 10

Talmud, and a Hasidic Jew speak reverently of the power of prayer at the Western Wall, notice how history and myth, the past and present, combine in Judaism to bring meaning and purpose to a people whose very survival is one of the miracles of human religious history.

Key Class Themes

This lesson focuses on the following themes:

1. Types of Myths
2. Characteristics of myth
3. The three great myths in Judaism
4. The Torah and the Talmud
5. The Dimensional Triangle in Judaism

Videotape Synopsis

- Class discussion: the Dimensional Triangle
- Graphics/lecture: Types and Characteristics of Myth
- Graphics/lecture: three great myths in Judaism
- Psalm 136 reading
- Rabbi Bronstein interview
- Dr. Lorberbaum interview
- Western Wall interview

Videtotape Commentary

I suggest you read this section before you watch the videotape. You will find that it will help you organize your thoughts so that when you watch the tape it will be more meaningful. When you have finished viewing the tape, you may want to read this section again.

Class Discussion

This open and lively discussion on the *dimensional triangle* could almost serve as a summary for the first half of the course. What makes it so helpful is that the students are describing real life events that happened within a week's time. Their experiences underscore one of the primary objectives in "Beliefs and Believers" – to learn to *see* human religious activity in the world around us. Then theory becomes reality, and you, the student, have gained skills that, if nothing else, will make your life much more interesting.

Chris' experience couldn't be better in illustrating how myth guides ritual activity which, in turn, brings the believer back into an extraordinary experience unique to the religion of the believer. Communion, the sharing of bread and wine, commemorates the Last Supper when Jesus initiated a *new covenant* with his disciples. For millennia, Christians have been ritually replicating this important part of the Christian mythos. For Chris, the symbolic embellishment of torches to light the path along with nature's gratuitous contribution of a beautiful full moon rising over Lake Michigan brought new meaning to an ancient ritual practice.

Janet and Suzanne have different experiences that support our observation that rituals are necessary to ease one through difficult rites of passage. Notice how the change inherent in Janet's experience at the kidney transplant survivor's meeting and Suzanne's singing of "The Heart Song" at a Separated and Divorced Catholics gathering evoke the need for ritual activity. Certainly in the world's major religions, ancient myths drive rituals that meet rite of passage needs. However, human beings will *create* rituals where none existed before in the poignant effort to withstand the suffering that life's more dramatic changes may bring. Two observations come to mind: a) once created, these *spontaneous rituals* generate their own mythic background in that believers will speak of the original ritual in the context of a distinct occurrence that evoked ritual activity on the part of the first participants; b) *spontaneous rituals* more often than not borrow symbolic elements from ancient rituals embodied in familiar religious activity. Thus, the passing of light from candle to candle, the singing of a meaningful and inspiring song or the sharing of food and drink in a solemn manner, all of which may be found in the ritual activity of the world's religions, may emerge *spontaneously* when human beings are moved to make sense of a wondrous or tragic event. Like Eliade's *hierophany*, ordinary human activities become empowered with sacred meaning when performed as a ritualized response to the exigencies of life.

As our discussion continues, one comment needs some clarification. Barbara makes a comparative leap between the ritual sacrifice of human beings in ancient Incan culture and Holy Communion in the Christian church. True, elements of death and rebirth are present in both examples of ritual activity, but we need to point out that the symbolic meaning *for the believers* in each context is quite different. The Incan ritual occurs in a mythic context, one that we will explore when we turn to *primal religion,* that bears little or no resemblance to the Christian context. Incan warriors or ritual specialists might eat the heart of an enemy or other *power person* to achieve strength, wisdom, agility, power or any other attribute that might help them attain a desired goal. Christians, once *erroneously* accused of cannibalistic practices because of the nature of the communion service, symbolically ingest *the body and blood of Christ* to either participate in or commemorate an extraordinary transformative act that is unique in all of human history. Quite a difference, indeed!

Psalm 136 and Video Interview with Rabbi Herbert Bronstein of the North Shore Congregation Israel, Glencoe, Illinois

We open our set of interviews with a reading of Psalm 136. In the beautiful simplicity of its verses, we find expressed the very heart of the Jewish mythos: creation, exodus from captivity in Egypt, the giving of the Law at Mt. Sinai and the fulfillment of the promise that the chosen people would receive a country in which to live and grow and prosper. The Psalms, part of the Hebrew Bible know as *the Writings*, are mythic stories that were originally sung, just as in medieval times, when an English troubadour might travel from village to village singing songs of heroes, bravery, tragedy and love. The Psalms are the songs that commemorate the realization of God's promise to Israel, and to this day, are ritually performed in Jewish rituals, the *dimensional triangle* at work.

Though they are at times hostile to each other, Judaism, Christianity and Islam share both a historical-cultural continuity and a religious relationship. Historically, roots are traced back to Abraham, a major mythic player in each religion, who lived in the Syro-Palestinian region (Syria-Palestine-Israel, today), around 2,000 years b.c.e. It might even be said that Judaism is a parent to both Christianity and Islam. Religiously, *monotheism* is the keystone, regardless of theological divergences. All three share the belief in a single, all-powerful, all-knowing God who is creator and ruler of the world. Though eternal and transcendent, God enters into creation through the historical process to initiate the grand mythic journey humans must make from alienation to reconciliation. In return for the maintenance of high standards of ethical behavior, in each case, God opens the door to paradise on judgment day.

As we mentioned in the introduction to this chapter of the study guide, we turn to Judaism at this point in our discussion of myth because all the other dimensions revolve around the *mythic dimension.* The story of a people, a land and the Law is lived by the devout Jew to the extent that every aspect of behavior is lovingly directed by this ancient collective experience. No other group of believers has withstood so much persecution for so long a time and survived.

Since myth is behind this tenacity to keep on striving, we wanted a spokesperson who would be able to describe what these sacred stories mean to a Jew. But we wanted it described in such a way that non-Jews could make sense of this great centering force in the Jewish experience. We chose to interview Rabbi Bronstein, a member of the reform tradition, which represents the most progressive, open-minded branch of modern Judaism. In this context some background explanation of the different types of Jewish tradition would be helpful. As is the case with all major world religious traditions, you will find sectarian groups that etch out territory on the liberal-conservative continuum of belief and practice. In the Jewish world, particularly in America, you will find three major traditions. *Reform* Jews reject following the Law legalistically but use the basic moral and ethical underlying principles drawn from the Torah to guide their lives. *Orthodox* Jews teach strict adherence to the Law and follow tradition in theology, Talmudic scholarship, worship, dress and forms of Jewish ritual practices. *Conservative* Judaism offers a middle path between Reform and Orthodox Judaism, taking the Law seriously but allowing for adjustments in behavior to meet the demands of modern life.

For the spiritual adventurer, there are other *paths* to follow in Judaism, particularly the mystical path of the *kabbala.* The *Zohar,* or Book of Spendor, composed within a developing tradition by Moses de Leon in Spain, about 1275, transforms the Torah into a metaphysical code book. God might be eternal and incomprehensible to the human intellect, but the Torah offers windows of insight into God's attributes. Meditating on these attributes can bring extraordinary spiritual experience to the *kabbalistic initiate*. Kabbalism has influenced everything from the development of Hasidic Judaism in the 18th century to the music videos of the rock star Madonna in current times. Despite the differing perspectives on the nature of belief and practice represented by Reformed, Conservative, Orthodox or Kabbalistic mystic Jew, all would share the power of the Jewish mythos. So we turn to Rabbi Bronstein to elaborate on the power of myth in Judaism.

In the interview, Rabbi Bronstein describes the three most powerful stories in Jewish mythos as Creation, Exodus, and the making of the *covenant* at Mt. Sinai. If you are a Bible reader, you know to find these accounts in the books of Genesis and Exodus. He refers to them as *archetypal stories*. We might think of an *archetype* as a paradigm, or model, deeply embedded in the subconscious mind that guides a human being on his or her life's journey. He describes these myths as being *genetically imprinted* in the Jewish people. The Rabbi also sees all other sacred stories in the Hebrew Bible as being substories of these three main myths.

Keeping in mind our *dimensional triangle*, the Rabbi makes a fascinating connection between the three myths and the life-cycle events in Jewish experience. In particular, he mentions circumcision, a birth ritual, and Bar/Bat Mitzvah, a rite of passage guiding Jewish boys and girls into adulthood and full membership in the community. Consider this observation in terms of our discussion earlier of rites of passage. Boundary questions are raised which are answered in myths that generate time-honored ritual practices. Looking at the Jewish experience from this perspective, can you begin to see how myths are more than just old stories? They have a profound impact on human life experiences and human behavior within the Jewish community. In fact, as Rabbi Bronstein observes, all the great Jewish holidays and festivals are ritualized acknowledgments of the grand stories in the Torah and provide continuity for Jews as they pass through the yearly cycle.

As Rabbi Bronstein attests, the concept of *covenant* is an extremely important part of the Jewish mythos. We have discussed the connection between *religion* and *relationship*. Both ideally bind people together. Covenant implies relationship. In fact, the covenant at Mt. Sinai, the Ten Commandments, is all about relationships, reconciliation, re-connection, religion in its broadest sense. On a vertical plane, the first four commandments tell human beings how to relate to God; the latter six tell human beings how to relate to each other.

The Rabbi describes this covenant as universal. The relational precepts in the Ten Commandments are for all peoples. Indeed, though all believers don't live up to these ethical commands, most traditional worldviews – Christianity, Buddhism, Islam, Hinduism and so on – have made very similar demands on their adherents. Though more conservative Jews might disagree, Rabbi Bronstein disarms the volatile notion of Jews as a *chosen people* by saying that Jews were chosen to receive the Torah, the Teaching. All peoples are chosen, are called to live up to the standards that will lead all humanity to peace and happiness, if obeyed. Once again, myths tell us how life should be lived. The obvious difficulty is that most human beings fail to fully live by the behavior models present in their sacred stories.

Interview on the Talmud with Dr. Lorberbaum of the Shalom Hartman Institute, Jerusalem

On the cover of the pamphlet describing the Shalom Hartman Institute, we find the following statement of purpose: "Israel must be a spiritual and moral light to world Jewry and participate with all humanity in the pursuit of justice and religious tolerance. The Shalom Hartman Institute is dedicated to keeping alive and nurturing this vision. Through its research and educational centers, the institute trains a new generation of scholars, educators and lay leaders capable of addressing the spiritual needs of modern Jews living in free and pluralistic societies."

Put simply, the institute exists to meet two major challenges that have changed Jewish self-understanding: a) modernity, and b) the rebirth of the state of Israel. Recognizing that religious pluralism is part of modern life and that Israel's survival may depend on its ability to get along with its neighbors, scholars at the Hartman Institute work to reduce religious fanaticism and intolerance by encouraging dialogue between different faiths, particularly, Christianity, Islam and Judaism. The *Talmud* provides the model for this dialogue. In an atmosphere of goodwill and intellectual respect, individuals of different faiths can explore questions regarding *identity* and *relationship* just as Jews for millennia have sought a clearer understanding of God's will through Talmudic dialogue. The Hartman Institute makes use of ancient myths, found in the Torah and Talmud, to make sense of life's complexities in the modern, pluralistic society of Israel today.

Interview at the Western Wall

The Western Wall in Jerusalem is one of the most holy sites in the world. For Jews, it serves as an *axis mundi,* a conduit where prayer flows freely from the *profane* world of human needs and desires to the sustaining realm of the divine. The Wall is all that remains of the Second Temple, a glorious structure built under the direction of Herod the Great. The Temple was destroyed by the Romans during the Jewish revolt of 66-70 c.e. Pilgrims come from all over the world to pray at this holy site. Sometimes called the *Wailing Wall* because of the somber tone of Jewish prayers, the Western Wall is never deserted. As I mentioned in the discussion on myth in Class 9, in any season, day or night, one can always find Jews there, standing before the Wall in prayer or placing their messages in the cracks and crevices between the stones. The Wall *experience* provides an excellent example of our *dimensional triangle.* Religious *experience, myth* and *ritual* intertwine in this most meaningful spiritual activity for the devout Jew.

Videotape Graphics

 At this stage we suggest you watch the videotape. The graphics you will see on the screen are reproduced below to save you the trouble of copying them down. You might like to add your own comments as you watch the tape.

Types of Myths

Origin/Creation Myths
– Genesis, Gaia

Alienation Myths
– Noah's Flood
– Adam and Eve

End-Time Myths
– Apocalypse now!

Myths of Salvation or Liberation (heros)

Characteristics of Myths

– Myths are symbolic; imaginative, like art
– Myths are revelatory; they reveal special truths
– Subject matter
  • primeval origins
  • ancestral models
  • heroic lives
  • ritual specialists
    - shamans
    - priests
  • future expectations

Myth in Judaism

Three great myths in the Hebrew Bible (Torah)
or Old Testament

– Creation (Genesis)
– Liberation (Exodus)
– Covenant (Exodus)
  the giving of the Law on Mt. Sinai – these myths
  guide all Jewish rituals

Review Questions

Answering the following questions will help you review key class themes and prepare for examinations.

1. What are the three great myths in Judaism?

2. According to Rabbi Bronstein, how is our *dimensional triangle* evident in Jewish religious life?

3. Illustrate two types of myth using examples from the Hebrew Bible.

4. According to Dr. Lorberbaum, in what way does the ancient Jewish text, The Talmud, provide a model for harmonious life in Israel today?

Sources and Further Readings

Anderson, Bernhard. *Understanding the Old Testament*, 4th ed. Englewood Cliffs, NY: Prentice Hall, 1987.

Smart, Ninian. *The World's Religions*. Englewood Cliffs, NJ: Prentice Hall, 1989.

BELIEFS AND BELIEVERS
Class 11 – Religious Symbols/Civil Religion

Introduction

Reflection: *If we live in a supposedly secular society in the United States, yet we know that human beings must live their myths in order to have a successful society, then myths must arise outside of established religious institutions. How does this happen in the United States? What is the American mythos? How do American myths define identity and relationship for American citizens? How is this experience expressed symbolically through the ritual dimension? If you are a citizen of a country other than the United States, can you see patterns of mythic and ritual activity that bring a sense of pride and self-understanding to your nation?*

If you are reading this Study Guide, congratulations! You have mastered a highly complex set of symbols, the English language. Like the proverbial fish in water, we are so used to living in a symbolic world, we never notice how we constantly use symbols to make sense of our world as we go about the most mundane or the most glorious tasks. Words are symbols. Have you ever been in a foreign country and not known the language? When that happens, hand and facial gestures become critical symbols. Likewise, television bombards us with symbols, as does advertising in general. Try to make a telephone call without using symbols.

Traffic signals are symbols. Can you imagine driving across town in symbolic ignorance? What does red have to do with stopping? What does a red metal octagon with the letters S-T-O-P have to do with your driving behavior? That siren blaring behind you says, "You better know!" Symbols are human-created, agreed upon signals that become associated with specific kinds of behavior. Our forebears in pre-history learned to read the signs of nature. Clouds meant it would probably rain, and the silence of birds meant a tiger was near. As human civilization became more complex, so did our symbolic activity.

Both myth and ritual are symbolic modes of communication. Symbolic activity, then, is at the very heart of human religious activity. One might say that symbols provide the fuel that ignites the mythic and ritual dimensions. As we move through the material in this class, reflect on the power of symbols in your own life. Like so many other phenomena we've explored in "Beliefs and Believers," our investigation of symbols and Civil Religion will again demonstrate that the most basic of human cultural insights are raised to new heights within the world of religion.

Key Class Themes

This lesson focuses on the following themes:

1. Myth and Ritual as symbolic modes of communicating
2. Types of Symbols
3. Key features of Ritual activity
4. Civil religion; its function in American society

Class 11

Videotape Synopsis

- Class discussion
- Graphics/lecture on symbols
- Graphics/lecture on ritual
- Graphics/lecture on Civil Religion
- Class discussion

Videotape Commentary

I suggest you read this section before you watch the videotape. You will find that it will help you organize your thoughts so that when you watch the tape it will be more meaningful. When you have finished viewing the tape, you may want to read this section again.

Class Discussion

Our opening class discussion underscores one of our most important overall class objectives, the development of worldview analysis skills that will enable "Beliefs and Believers" students to actually see the impact of the six dimensions of religion in the world around them. The students in our teleclass session do an excellent job of describing experiences that reveal our key class themes. Jo Ann comments on the observation that professional wrestling – the glitzy, colorful world of testosterone giants – is popular because we live in a culture that is mythically and ritually impoverished. How true! Human cultures cannot function for long without the mythic and ritual dimension; and, if they can't find an authenticity in traditional myths, they will create new ones, even ones that are predicated on phony athletic contests.

Annette adds to our store of knowledge on ritual by pointing out her feelings of alienation at a Catholic wedding when most of those in attendance weren't familiar with Catholic rituals. We've all had this experience. Whether in a religious service or a secular gathering such as a dance, if you don't know the steps, you just don't fit in. That is because one important feature of ritual is to bind people together in a collective experience. Over time, words and gestures become second nature, rather like driving after many years. Ritual activity of this sort allows the participant to move out of a separate sense of self and bond with the group. This seemingly simple occurrence releases the person, at least momentarily, from the pressures of individuality; we are back to our "apart" and "a part" theme. As you listen to other students describe their " 'Beliefs and Believers' sightings," reflect on your own experiences over the past week. Did any of our key class themes "jump out at you?"

Interpretation of Myth/Civil Religion

Our class session on Symbols and Ritual needs little expansion. However, it will be helpful in our exploration of myth to say a few words about *interpretation of myth.* As you might imagine, complex mythic dramas can be interpreted in a number of ways. The scholarly term for this kind of interpretive activity is "hermeneutics." The focus of the second part of this class is on one particular variety of interpretation, myth as a validation of the social order or what we will call *civil religion.* But there are other important systems of meaning which investigators have culled from myths.

For instance, in the sacred stories of the Torah, we encounter "ontophany," a disclosure of ultimate existence, or to put it bluntly, what really counts. In an ontophany, God or gods are revealed, the human relationship to the Divine is defined and proper patterns of behavior are delineated. Myths can also describe mediation of the conflicts and contradictions that beset human existence. One of the perplexities of the human condition is that we must constantly confront binary opposites: life and death, good and evil, male and female, reason and emotion, hope and despair, sickness and health and the list could go on and on. Depending on the myth, from these stories we might learn how to reconcile two opposites such as male and female; perhaps the myth might define male and female roles in a way that was complementary. Or, as we heard in Dr. Davé's myth of the Ganges, life and death are sorted out.

Another and more modern style of interpretation describes myths as archetypes or "public dreams." Here we find the work of the great psychoanalysts such as Sigmund Freud or Carl Jung. Joseph Campbell's series on myth also delves into this area. The basic concept here is fascinating. As Campbell has shown in his life-long study of myths in practically every culture known to human kind, there is a striking similarity in the myths that emerge. The suggestion, to borrow Rabbi Bronstein's phrase, is that all human beings carry a mythic genetic imprint in their collective unconscious. This concept is much too complex for further explanation here; you might want to read some Jung or Campbell. But for example, the mythological figures that peopled Mt. Olympus in Greek lore – Zeus, Athena, Apollo, Mercury, Pan, and so on – actually might be psychic beings who reside somewhere in our own unconscious. The myths may seem to come from some kind of Divine-revelation, but in fact they necessarily bubble-up from within whenever a given culture finds itself at a point of collective confusion regarding answers to profound life questions. Interesting theory!

Myth as Validation of the Social Order

Since one of the overall themes of "Beliefs and Believers" is the pervasiveness of religion, the interpretive variety we want to explore in this class is myth as validation of the social order, or *Civil Religion*, particularly as we find it in American culture. If myths disclose the ultimate reality to human beings, then civil religion in America might be described as an attempt on the part of American citizens to understand their nation's history in light of that ultimate reality. Remember the comparisons we drew between the Jewish and American mythos? Well one reason modern-day Israel and the United States are such good friends goes beyond politics; Israeli and United States citizens share similar mythic precepts about the founding and destiny of their respective nations – a chosen people with a special covenantal relationship with God who protects and guides the nation as long as His people maintain the high moral/ethical demands of the covenant.

As we've mentioned several times, human beings cannot live without myth. In the space created by the Constitutional separation of church and state in this nation, a grand mythic liturgical year has emerged through which we regularly move as the months pass. This cycle is what scholars have termed *civil religion*. If you want to really *see* the mythic drama unfold, just camp out at your local K-Mart and drink in the decorations. The purple and yellow of Easter; the red, white, and blue of Memorial Day; the yellow and black of Halloween; the red and green of Christmas. This explosion of changing hues isn't just designed to loosen up your wallet. It means something highly important in terms of social cohesion. The blend of religious and political holidays helps create a sense of common national identity and shared religious commitment to the ideals of the nation. President's birthdays merge into religious holidays such as Easter, then back into political holidays like Memorial Day or the Fourth of July. Consider our discussion of types of symbols and the features of ritual, then reflect on the meaning of holiday colors, the songs that are sung, the parades and other rituals that are performed during each of these special times. Do you see how this yearly cycle binds American citizens together and gives them a sense of belonging, identity, and purpose? All this activity is driven by myth as civil religion.

Notice the tendency for human beings to create festivals, holidays, holy days on given dates throughout the year then, year after year, pass through the cycle of occasions. Most religious organizations do this – the Catholic liturgical year, for instance – but nations also create celebratory cycles. This pattern of human behavior tells us something very interesting about the pervasiveness, the power of the mythic dimension. Myth functions as a means of transforming the mundane into the extraordinary, or to use Eliade's terminology, the profane into the sacred. We will discuss primal religions in the next session, but just consider that the earliest observations human beings made about their relationship with nature was that events happen in cycles.

Seasons change, hunting habits change as animals migrate, day turns into night into day, people are born, people die and so on. The raw weight of passage through the same cycle over and over again, the experience of the mundane, became so unbearable that humans, creative beings that we are, found ways, through myth, to re-define natural cycles in sacred terms. If planting or harvest has a "divine plan" or purpose behind it, or if it is a microcosmic activity modeled after some grand cosmic scheme, then the drudgery of the task is transformed into sacred drama. Even in the sports world, think of how many sports fans ease the monotony of their lives by vicariously living the glories of basketball players, hockey players, baseball players and football players. Then the cycle starts over again unless, of course, the neglected spouse tosses a brick through the TV set!

Besides providing social cohesion through a liturgical cycle of holidays and celebrations, civil religion infuses public policy and social ideals with mythic significance. Our discussion of the Lincoln monument and other types of granite symbols erected to honor war heroes and past presidents illustrates this function. Several key points emerge in class discussion. Janet mentions that her brother's experience in the Vietnam conflict changed his attitude, negatively, towards the American flag, a primary symbol of this nation. However, as Janet noted in an earlier class, visitors to the Vietnam Veterans Memorial, almost to a person, pass the dark granite structure in sad contemplation and reverence. Perhaps because the tragedy of the Vietnam conflict is still so real and so recent for Americans, the Vietnam Veterans Memorial evokes an almost overwhelming sense of civil religious presence. If you have some intellectual doubts about civil religion, a visit to this monument will provide you with the *experience* behind the theory.

Great presidents, such as Abraham Lincoln or Dwight Eisenhower, actually seemed to embody a kind of *civil religious mythos* to such an extent that they had no need to belong to a specific religious organization. It was almost as though their faith in America was faith enough. Lincoln certainly saw himself as a kind of Old Testament prophet charged with redeeming the nation from her sins. Extreme political behavior such as going to war has always been justified from an "Onward Christian Soldiers" mentality. Other examples of this blend of public policy and religious sentiment can be found on any piece of American currency, "In God We Trust." Or consider the Pledge of Allegiance to the Flag, "One nation under God, indivisible, with liberty and justice for all." Here again, is expressed a conviction that the policies, the causes, the wars, the very ethos of the nation is empowered with religious significance.

Of course, when considering civil religion, it is important to keep in mind that the mythos supports ideals over social reality and shapes history to suit religiopolitical convictions. Consider the fate of the indigenous peoples of the North American continent. In the next class, we will discuss in more detail the clash of cultures between Native Americans and the European invaders. Put simply, the Native Americans were run over by a high-powered civil religious steam roller! From early colonial times Americans have seen themselves as having a special destiny due to their unique relationship with God. Americans are to be a "light to all nations," protectors of freedom, a nation of the pure, just and free. Prosperity would be the reward for building the "kingdom of heaven" on American soil. However, continued success rested on the nation's ability to maintain high ethical standards, which balanced the covenantal bargain with God. In other words, the political principles of this nation can be expressed in terms that are decidedly biblical. Though the Constitution prohibits the *establishment* of any one religion as the religion of the land, mythically, the United States is unquestionably a Judeo-Christian nation.

For Native Americans, this Old Testament reading of reality by the Europeans had dire consequences. Myths can be re-enacted at later times if a particular culture finds profound meaning in a sacred story. Following the biblical example found in books such as Joshua, Judges, 1 & 2 Samuel, 1 & 2 Kings, early settlers on this continent replicated the behavior of the "chosen people" towards the inhabitants of the land they saw as promised to them by God. Few people acknowledge the incredibly bloody persecution on the part of the Hebrews towards the Canaanites which fills most of the historical section of the Hebrew Bible known as "The Writings." Just as the Hebrews found the peoples of Canaan to be sub-human, godless pagans who were completely expendable, the frontier inhabitants of America were easily swept aside in the rush to build God's kingdom. The behavior of Native Americans was seen to be immoral because it didn't measure up to the biblical standards upheld by their Christian conquerors. Since they were not included in the civil religious covenant, they could be used, abused, removed to reservations, and killed.

As Chris and other students accurately point out in our lively closing discussion, for the United States to remain united, we have to *remythologize* our civil religious sentiments in a way that finally is inclusive. Diversity, as a social reality, may well provide the catalyst that finally causes our collective national experience to live up to the sacred ideals present in our guiding documents; all human beings have certain inalienable rights including life, liberty and the pursuit of happiness.

Videotape Graphics

At this stage we suggest you watch the videotape. The graphics you will see on the screen are reproduced on the next page to save you the trouble of copying them down. You might like to add your own comments as you watch the tape.

Symbols

The Symbolic Process

Symbol = something that stands for or points to something else: a flag, a cross, a word, a flower

---

Symbols

The Symbolic Process

Types of Symbols
– signs
– representational symbols
– presentational symbols

Symbols

The Symbolic Process

Sign – something that is regularly or causally connected in experience with something else

– disease . . . symptoms
– dark clouds . . . rain

Representational symbols – ties things together that are distinct or different from each other: words, traffic light, flag, cross, stop sign

Symbols

The Symbolic Process

Presentational symbols – are similar to, but not identical with the thing symbolized: map, photograph, icon, certain road signs, sacramental service

Ritual

Ritual is a symbolic mode of communication

Ritual

– Ritual is a mode of religious expression that unites words and gestures to form a sacred drama
– Ritual transforms the ordinary into the extraordinary
– Ritual implies action or doing on the part of believers

Principal Features of Rituals

Sacramental
ordinary transformed into extraordinary

Performative
doing something

Repetitive
ritual activities are repeated

Social
rituals provide social cohesion; people do rituals together

Civil Religion

A form of myth that validates the social order

> **Key Functions of Civil Religion**
>
> – to provide social cohesion through a liturgical
>   cycle of holidays and celebrations
> – to infuse public policy and social ideals
>   with mythic significance
> – supports ideals over social reality
> – shapes "history" to suit religiopolitical convictions

Review Questions

Answering the following questions will help you review key class themes and prepare for the examinations.

1. Identify the three primary types of symbols and provide some examples for each one.

2. Define ritual. Describe the principal features of ritual using any ritual in which you recently participated.

3. What is *civil religion*, and how does it function in American society?

4. In your informed opinion, does civil religion have a positive or negative effect on life in this nation?

Class 11

Sources and Further Readings

Chidester, David. *Patterns of Power*. Englewood Cliffs, NJ: Prentice Hall, 1988.

McLoughlin, William. *Revivals, Awakening, Reform*. Chicago: University of Chicago Press, 1978.

Schmidt, Roger. *Exploring Religion*, 2nd edition. Belmont, CA: Wadsworth, 1988.

BELIEFS AND BELIEVERS
Class 12 – Ritual Dimension: Primal Religion, Part I

Introduction

Reflection: *Thomas Drift, our guest in this class who is a full-blooded Ojibwe Indian from Minnesota, is very much the diplomat when questioned about the relationship between Native American answers to profound life questions and those that were embodied in the religious expressions of Europeans who, in service of those powerful ideas, brought Native American cultures to the brink of extinction. Today, primal religious sentiments are finding renewal, not only in traditional cultures of Native Americans in America, but in modern movements such as the environmental movement or even feminist eco-spirituality. As we move through this class on primal religion, reflect on the difference in worldview between Native Americans and the predominantly Christian Europeans who came to this continent centuries ago. No matter which side you take in this violent encounter between religiopolitical perspectives, you can't deny the power of religious ideas in guiding the behavior of both groups in this tragic struggle. Once again, B + B = B!*

On January 9, 1855, Chief Seattle delivered a famous address to the governor of the Washington territory. The occasion was a response to a treaty proposal from the United States government that would relocate his tribe in the Washington territory. Government officials promised that his people would be given enough land to live comfortably and would be provided military protection from their traditional enemies.

Chief Seattle thanked the governor for his concern, but went on to point out the grave differences in *worldview* between the "white man" and the "red man." In a poignant and poetic manner, he provided a stinging critique of the fundamental religious ideas that motivated the European invaders. He questioned how the all-loving Christian God could possibly love the Indian. He accused the Christian God of prejudice. This God protected and fulfilled the white man, but rained death, destruction and loss down upon the Indian.

The God of the white man was an angry God who gave the white man laws written on tablets of stone, but the religion of the Indian was written on the hearts of the people. EuroAmericans accused the Indians of being purposeless wanderers who made no real use of the land. From Chief Seattle's perspective, however, it was the white man who had forsaken the graves of their ancestors to pursue an unsettled, wandering existence in foreign lands. The chief ended his speech with an eloquent testimony to the sacredness of the land and presence of the divine in the world:

> Every part of this earth is sacred to my people. Every hillside, every valley, every clearing and wood is holy in the memory and experience of my people... The ground beneath your feet responds more lovingly to our steps than yours because it is the ashes of our grandfathers. Our bare feet know the kindred touch. The earth is alive with the lives of our kin.

Less than 40 years after Chief Seattle's speech, the West was *won*, and Native Americans would either be subjugated or killed, a complex set of cultures effectively destroyed. From the perspective of "Beliefs and Believers," it is important not only to know that this happened but why. And the *why* is power of religious ideas, the energy of *identity/relationship* questing and the impact all of the above has on human behavior.

Class 12

Key Class Themes

This lesson focuses on the following themes:

1. Characteristics of primal religions
2. Features of the primal world
3. Ritual techniques in primal religion
4. Native American rituals and spirituality
5. Religiopolitical conflict between Native Americans and EuroAmericans

Videotape Synopsis

- Graphics/lecture on Primal Religion
- Pow-wow roll-in
- Interview and class discussion with Thomas Drift, Ojibwe Indian

Videotape Commentary

I suggest you read this section before you watch the videotape. You will find that it will help you organize your thoughts so that when you watch the tape it will be more meaningful. When you have finished viewing the tape, you may want to read this section again.

Graphics/Lecture on Primal Religion

Our encounter with primal religion will provide you with an excellent opportunity to "walk-a-mile" in a very different set of moccasins. Again, we have to be careful not to let the glare of the familiar blind us to the distinctive and important features of an unfamiliar worldview.

When we speak of primal religion, we are talking about an extraordinary variety of beliefs and believers. One estimate is that there are more than 200 million people in Central Africa, the Amazon basin in South America, and the Arctic region and North America practicing some form of primal religion. However, it is important to recognize that when we use the term "primal religion," we are not talking about worldviews that are primitive, backward or unsophisticated. They are, in fact, enormously complex and coherent. In addition, primal religion is being recovered in the so-called advanced countries such as the United States by followers of the neo-pagan movement, practitioners of ritual magic and other manifestations of earth-centered spirituality.

Consider once again our discussion of the relationships between humans and *the other* of nature. The need to establish patterns of interaction with nature may very well have been the earliest ritual practice of human beings. Think back to when you were a child and encountered your first thunderstorm. If your parents had not given you some watered down scientific explanation for the light and noise, you might still think the activity represented anger on the part of frightening spirits in the clouds. Wouldn't you want some kind of ritual practice to assuage the anger of the "cloud-spirits?"

We also have discussed the cycles of nature and the primal religious impulse to place these cycles in a kind of sacred, cosmic drama. Thus, in primal religion, the passing of the seasons demands rituals in honor of the divine beings who personify Sun, Moon, Winter, Summer, Spring and Fall. Earth, air, fire and water need to be ritually recognized, as do the four quadrants of space and time. You don't petition these powerful spirits; you enter into balance or harmony with them through the dimensions of myth and ritual. Animals may be sacrificed to assure that the group, tribe or clan is ritually pure. A portion of the harvest could be set aside in honor of the spirits of fertility. Statues of totem animals – coyote, bear, lion, eagle – could protect the home from marauding demons. In the world of primal religion, everything is alive; everything has power.

Cultures in Conflict

Though Thomas Drift graciously asks that Native Americans and EuroAmericans put aside past conflicts and search together for political justice and spiritual unity, the brutal historical fact remains that when these two cultures clashed, the Native American way of seeing the world put them at a disadvantage during the political and military struggles that ensued. Almost everyone has seen Kevin Costner's movie, "Dances with Wolves," which is a poignant testament to the tragic dismantling of Sioux culture in the upper-midwest. In "Beliefs and Believers," we always want to be cognizant of how religious ideas shape political realities, or to put it in our terms, how belief impacts individual and collective behavior. As sad a story as the culture clash between Native Americans and EuroAmericans is, it has much to teach us about this key class theme. Let's explore the difference between these two rich cultures, and see how religious ideas set the stage for success or failure in the political/military arena.

If religion presents an ideal vision of how the world (or reality) really is, then those who *believe* in that vision will wish to see it *realized* in the world around them. Belief is almost unconsciously linked to behavior in the mind of a true believer, not unlike an instinctive impulse traveling at light speed through the synapses of the brain. Religion and politics are dimensions of human experience engaged in the exercise of power. Religious and political ideas are cognitive tools human beings use to remake reality, in day-to-day experience, in the image of the ideal world expressed in those respective ideas. Religion and politics are both in the *identity and relationship* business.

It follows then, that a religion or spirituality that presents a view of the world that more closely reflects actual in-world experience will have less of a need to exercise broad strokes of power in order to insure political control over day-to-day experience. Other than to fulfill the needs required for physical survival, there is little need to manipulate or change the world to make it conform to some other, more perfect reality.

On the other hand, a religion that paints a picture of reality in which the source of being, the Divine or God, is *separate* from the world (ontological dualism) and views in-world experience as a threat or stumbling block to *real* experience – be it in Heaven or some other transcendent realm – will thrust believers into a pattern of using force to remake that world. Here lie some extreme differences between the religiopolitical perceptions of the varied Native American tribes who had been living on the North American continent for millennia and those of the European invaders who disrupted the Indian way of life.

We can begin to put the pieces of the puzzle together regarding our clash of cultures when we realize that Christianity, the religion of the European invaders, is a religion that in its traditional teachings presents a picture of reality that posits a huge distance between the Divine and in-world experience. Humans are inherently sinful, fallen from the source of all being, God. Their natural desires and instincts are not to be trusted. The world is merely a testing chamber where, according to behavior, a person is deemed fit or unfit for entrance into the realm of true reality, Heaven. If that didn't present enough of an ideational challenge, the world is also the domain of an evil being, Satan, who may use the pleasures and joys of this world to tempt humans and trick them into a bond with worldly delights that will ultimately result in eternal punishment.

There is no *either-or* in this picture. Jesus, God's only begotten son whom He allowed to die a torturous death by crucifixion as vicarious atonement for the sins of human kind, is God's life-line thrown down to save human beings from an evil, Satan-ruled world. As we will hear Pastor Walt Stowe testify during our class on Conservative Christianity, there is *no other way to salvation*! If a human being does not accept Jesus as his or her personal savior, then according to this worldview, he or she must be under the sway of Satan. Human beings under the sway of Satan have two choices: repent or die. As you can imagine, Native Americans who could not accept such a drastically different worldview, and who, thus, rejected Christianity, were slaughtered for their cosmic indiscretion.

The Europeans had a very clear understanding of the natural realm and what was to be done with it. God made *man* in His image, over and above other parts of the creation, and *man* was called upon to have dominion over nature, to control nature. To *use* the land meant to live by a utilitarian standard. Simple survival was not *using* the land. A human being was called upon to force nature to bring forth excess. Survival was for animals. Wealth, derived from a variety of manipulative processes culminating in the industrial revolution, was a subtle testimony to the fact that humankind was in the good graces of God.

Though not outwardly stated, a person's ability and skill in controlling and manipulating nature, and earning rewards for the effort, was considered a determining factor on whether or not one was chosen, that is, whether or not one was selected to be one of those human beings destined to go to heaven. This extraordinary religious idea which has come to be known as the Protestant work ethic or the spirit of capitalism was and is a powerful behavioral motivator of Christians, especially Protestant Christians.

If the Native Americans would not convert to Christianity, work the land and *join civilization*, then from the European perspective, they had to be displaced or killed. To not play the Christian game was to violate the very nature of reality. In the eyes of the Christian invaders, the reluctance of Native Americans to share their worldview made them less than human and transformed by divine *fiat* into animals and Christians had a divine mandate to control them or remove them from the playing field.

In contrast, the Native American perspective saw ultimate reality in day-to-day experiences. Sacred power was diffused throughout the natural world. As Thomas Drift explains during his remarks about the Sweat Lodge ritual, the earth is our mother, the very womb from which we come. Chief Seattle's speech certainly attests to this fact. Of course, in fairness, Native Americans were also capable of brutality and viciousness like all human beings. Wars, torture, rape and all the other crimes humans perpetrate upon one another were present in Native American cultures. However, the motivation behind the behavior, brutal or sublime, could not be traced to a power play to remake the world in the image of some distant, invisible, perfected reality. Nor was earthly existence seen as some waiting room or testing station preceding a more important leap into ultimate reality.

Herein is the power of religious ideas. In our discussion of the diversity of Native American cultures, it is clear that for millennia, Native Americans had enjoyed a rich, full and complex cultural experience. Their set of religiopolitical ideas allowed for a lifestyle that blended harmoniously with the natural ecosystem in which they lived, moved and had their being. One might expect that without the entrance of Europeans onto the scene, North America today might look very much like it did 600-700 years ago.

But enter they did. Pretend for a moment that you are an observer from another planet. You understand the worldview of the Native Americans; you understand the worldview of Europeans. Apart from the human tragedy involved, if these two cultures clashed, which one would you pick to survive given the motivating potential of their respective religiopolitical ideas? History provides us with a stark answer to that riddle.

Interview with Thomas Drift

Thomas Drift does an excellent job of introducing the students to Native American spirituality. From the beginning of the interview/discussion, he makes the important point that we are *seeing* Native American spirituality through his eyes, the eyes of an Ojibwe Indian. Accurately, he points out that Native American cultures are incredibly diverse. However, they do share common ground with our characteristics and ritual features of *primal religion*. As you view the tape and listen to his responses to student questions, see how many characteristics of primal religion you can identify in his explanation of Native American spirituality. Also, keep our key class themes in mind. How often do Thomas' comments reflect on questions or answers regarding *identity* and *relationship*? When do ritual practices play a role in *rites of passage*? How do myth and ritual intertwine in the daily lives of the Ojibwe Indian?

Notice that our guest is treating our time together as a spiritual exercise in itself. Obviously, he is taking it very seriously. He contacted his own spiritual teacher before the class to assure a successful venture. Following the ritual practices of his tribe, he opens our interaction with the giving of gifts, followed by a purification ritual. "Smudging," the burning of sage and sweetgrass and the wafting of the smoke with an eagle feather (totem animal) not only is designed to clear the mind and remove impure or negative thoughts, it in effect, transforms the classroom from ordinary space to extraordinary, ritual space. Thomas takes on his role as a spiritual teacher, in this case teaching outsiders the dimensions of his spiritual perspective. In our next class, we will meet two women, Cynthia Jones and Patricia Storm, who are recovering earth-centered spirituality and the ritual way of magic. They also use ritual to transform the class setting into a conducive environment for understanding the knowledge they wish to pass on to the students. Once again, the power of the ritual dimension in human spirituality is evident.

Since moving from Minnesota to the Chicago area, Thomas has taken on the role of ritual leader who conducts the Sweat Lodge ritual. As he mentions in our discussion, this particular ritual practice is common to almost every Native American tribe. Thomas passed out a hand-out to the students that describes the Sweat Lodge rituals, as it is performed by his tribe. I include it below. Once again, see if you can detect how myth guides ritual which, in turn, brings the practitioner back into a state of spiritual awareness; our *dimensional triangle*.

Sweat Lodge

1. *Offering/Gifts:*

This is respectful that we give tobacco or some gift to the leader who is holding the Sweat Lodge ceremony: The leader who is holding the ceremony needs much support as he/she is purifying all that we use for the ceremony, offering his/her prayers to bring in all our relatives to help hear our prayers.

2. *Acknowledgment/Preparation:*

Before we enter the Sweat Lodge we need to smudge ourselves with sage or sweetgrass to clear our minds and purify our thoughts. We give an offering of tobacco to the rock, fire, and tree spirits. The Grandfathers (the rocks) are our connection with the Great Spirit, who is represented by fire. With the tobacco we must also inform the four directions and our Mother Earth (all my relations) of what we are about to do.

FIRST DOOR
Giving Thanks:

To all that we use in the Sweat Lodge, to the four directions, to our Father the Creator, to our Mother the Earth, to our Grandfathers and Grandmothers the rocks, the water, the sacred pipes and medicines, your brothers and sisters in the lodge, the door man, the tree people, the winged, the crawlers, the swimmers, the four-legged and the two-legged. Always keep in mind the Creator or Great Spirit is in everything and of everything, also acknowledge that we are all related. We are their relatives, and they are ours. Humbly ask that our prayers will be heard. "All my friends and relatives."

SECOND DOOR
Purity and health for those in prisons, foster homes, nursing homes, treatment, etc.:

Always acknowledge the Creator or the Great Spirit before and after your prayer. Always end your prayer with, "All my relations."

THIRD DOOR
Family, loved ones, and our connection to your people:

That we may recognize and accept who we are and change the things that need changing in our lives, so that we can be more respectful to our families, loved ones, elders, leaders and our own spiritual life. Remember, we live in a world where it is easy to get attached to the senses and the things of the world. So pray hard for our children, families, etc., that they may have good health and be attentive to our way of life.

FOURTH DOOR
For yourself:

The prayers for the first, second and third doors should be acknowledged. Then you pray for yourself. We always give thanks for ourselves last (It is the Indian way) yet we are first through other's prayers.

The ceremony is now complete. Remember that through our sacred pipe and ceremonies, peace may come to those who can understand, an understanding which must be of the heart and not the head alone.

Videotape Graphics

At this stage we suggest you watch the videotape. The graphics you will see on the screen are reproduced below to save you the trouble of copying them down. You might like to add your own comments as you watch the tape.

Primal Religions
Myth / Ritual link

Characteristics of Primal Religions

– local and insular; closely linked with area and land
– embrace a worldview that is pre-scientific; cause and
  effect guided by myth and ritual
– "religion" deals with practical matters of survival
– emphasize ritual techniques

> **Features of Primal World**
>
> *Mana*
> unseen spiritual force present everywhere
>
> *Animism*
> natural world alive with spirits
>
> *Fetishism*
> protection by the power of special objects
>
> *Taboo*
> spiritual power in people, places, things
>
> *Totemism*
> special relationship with a "power" animal

> **Features of Primal World**
> Myth and ritual are an integral part of daily life

> **Ritual Techniques**
>
> *Magic*
> coercion of spiritual powers
>
> *Shamanism*
> ritual specialist; knows the ancient myths and rituals
>
> *Purification*
> the ritual removal of pollution; relates to Taboo
>
> *Sacrifice*
> gifts to spiritual power (Gods need to be informed, manipulated)
>
> *Funeral rites*

Review Questions

Answering the following questions will help you review key class themes and prepare for the examinations.

1. What do we mean by primal religion? Can you identify some of the characteristics and features of primal religion?

2. In the Sweat Lodge ritual, as described by Thomas Drift, how is our *dimensional triangle* evident?

Class 12

3. Provide some examples of instances where primal religious features infiltrate our supposedly logical, scientific world.

4. Identify the major religiopolitical ideas embraced by European Christians that clashed with Native American descriptions of reality.

Sources and Further Readings

Albanese, Catherine L. *America: Religions and Religion,* 2nd ed. Belmont, CA: Wadsworth, 1992.

Cavert, Edward, et.al., eds. *The Long Search: A Study of Religions*. Dubuque, IA: Kendall/Hunt Publishing, 1978. See the chapter on the "Way of the Ancestors."

Chidester, David. *Patterns of Power: Religion and Politics in American Culture*. Englewood Cliffs, NJ: Prentice Hall, 1988.

Drinnon, Richard. *Facing West: The Metaphysics of Indian-Hating and Empire Building*. Minneapolis: University of Minnesota Press, 1980.

Gill, Sam D. *Native American Religions: An Introduction*. The Religious Life of Man Series. Belmont, CA: Wadsworth, 1983.

Schwartz, Regina M. *The Curse of Cain: The Violent Legacy of Monotheism*. Chicago: University of Chicago Press, 1997.

BELIEFS AND BELIEVERS
Class 13 – Ritual Dimension: Primal Religion, Part II

Introduction

Reflection: *Obviously the human race has reached a crisis point. The last 45 years represent 1/100,000,000 of Mother Earth's life span. Yet in this minuscule period of time, human beings have harnessed the atom, cracked the genetic code, broken out into space, and changed the face of our planet. The negative side of such progress has been a meteoric increase in deforestation, desertification, population, human suffering, atmospheric pollution, extinction of non-human life forms, depletion of elemental resources, climatic dislocation due to depletion of the ozone layer, war and massive human atrocities toward one another and nature. In somewhat harsh terms, what this amounts to is the rape of our mother, Earth. And, like retribution in some mythological nightmare, the price to be exacted for this crime may be the extinction of our species. What can you detect in Cynthia Jones' religious perspective that might help us out of this mess?*

In this extraordinary class session, we will spend the entire hour with Cynthia Jones and Patricia Storm, co-founders of *Diana's Grove*. Myth, magic, ritual and *experience* are all part of this recovery of primal religion, a spirituality that is *earth-centered* as opposed to *heaven-centered*. For these women, the location of the divine is here, now. It is not in some transcendent realm or place otherwise separate from the physical life of our earthly biosphere. Since much of the discussion in this class has to do with the differences between Christianity and primal religion in its pagan or neo-pagan manifestation, it might be helpful to make some distinctions between two very different perspectives on the nature of reality, both of which have a long history in the world of human religious thinking. Both dramatically impact on our B + B = B equation.

The two perspectives are dualism and monism. Dualism posits a cosmos or universe in which the Creator, God, is separate and distinct from the creation. We have already discussed the implications of this viewpoint in the previous class. Monism has many varieties: a) some would say that God is everything; b) others might insist that God is the reality or principle behind nature; c) others might say that only God is reality; all else is illusion. The commonality between these different types of monism is the essential willingness to see all reality as ONE, whole, not divided into a sacred realm and a profane or human or natural realm, depending on how you might want to label it. God is the ground of being and is the enlivening, creative spark behind all that exists.

Obviously, dualism is about being two – two realms, two forces in the universe, two expressions of being. Here, once again, we see the fascinating relationship between the *experiential, mythic* and *ritual dimensions*. The great myths in dualistic traditions, such as Christianity or Judaism, emphasize human relationships with the Divine Creator who is apart from the creation. Humans are to fear God, pray to the Deity, rule over the Earth, but hope for final peace in some transcendent heaven. Thus, in terms of religious experience and ritual, we find rituals are mostly done in a numinous atmosphere designed to honor God or beg forgiveness for sin, the inability to live up to the moral standards of the divinity or petition God to ease the suffering of life *east of Eden*.

In addition, myths developed that expressed the dualism of being *(ontological dualism)* as a battle between two powerful forces, good and evil. Since the source of being, God, was not in and of nature, then the Earth, the realm of nature, became a kind of citadel for the evil forces ruled by Satan. The forces of good resided in Heaven. Humans lived a rather perilous existence, caught between the forces of good and evil. In the more literal interpretation of biblical dualism, the Devil rules the planet and is in competition with God for the souls of humans. This struggle will continue until, as foretold in the biblical book of Revelation, the forces of good once and for all vanquish the forces of evil.

It follows that if the planet Earth is reduced to just a convenient battleground or stage for this divine conflict, there is not much of an impulse to respect or preserve Mother Earth's treasures. However, a very different attitude emerges in the monistic view. Echoing our characteristics of primal religion, the divine enlivens and empowers all life. As Cynthia and Patricia poetically describe this worldview, the *magic* of life is knowing that the divine is *immanent* in the Earth which, indeed, is our mother. Thus, the only *divine charge* for human beings is to live in a harmonious relationship with the land, the plants, the animals and other human beings. Notice the *identity/relationship* theme throughout this class session.

As we go through this session, one that is extraordinary in that these spiritual leaders actually get the students to *experience* earth-centered spirituality, reflect on the power of religious ideas. Dualistic and monistic ways of mythically ordering reality have had a profound effect on the behavior of believers. Both perspectives historically have positive and negative behavioral patterns attached to them. Since we have been blunt about the negative aspect of the dualist perspective, in fairness we should mention that the drive to *build a divine kingdom worthy of the Creator on earth* has been a creative force behind the beautiful art and architecture that grace the great cities of Western civilization. The monistic quest for peace, harmony and balance has often relieved believers of that incessant need to create, to do, to accomplish. In any event, let's turn to these representatives of Diana's Grove and for this hour, look through their eyes on the power of myth and ritual in human spirituality.

Key Class Themes

This lesson focuses on the following themes:

1. The *dimensional triangle* in earth-centered spirituality
2. The recovery of primal religion by women
3. Witches, magic, neo-paganism
4. Differences between monist and dualistic perceptions of reality

Videotape Synopsis

- Interaction with Cynthia Jones and Patricia Storm from Diana's Grove

Videotape Commentary

I suggest you read this section before you watch the videotape. You will find that it will help you organize your thoughts so that when you watch the tape it will be more meaningful. When you have finished viewing the tape, you may want to read this section again.

Background on Diana's Grove: Reclaiming the Garden

There really is no need for commentary on this amazing class session because Cynthia and Patricia are such excellent teachers. They don't just describe their chosen path, they actually get the students to *experience* what it means to participate in an earth-centered spirituality.

As you prepare to watch Cynthia and Patricia in action, I thought it would be helpful to offer some background on the Diana's Grove movement. A few years ago, I presented a paper on the Diana's Grove movement at the American Academy of Religion national meeting. It was entitled, "Chronicling the Emergence of an Ecofeminist Spiritual Movement in the Conservative Midwest." As you will be able to tell from viewing this class session, Cynthia is a little uncomfortable with *labels* that might narrow the horizons of her spiritual path. However, she did agree with my term, *ecofeminist spiritual movement*. In a nutshell, Diana's Grove embodies a constellation of religious/spiritual/New Age/Old Age ideals and ideas in its manifestation as an egalitarian goddess-conscious, earth-based, moon-based, ritual-based, wiccan spirituality. Through magic, Diana's Grove calls forth, honors and embraces the divinity of all life, the seasons, the cycles, the elements and all the inner and outer processes of *being human*. It is a legitimate new religious movement, meeting the spiritual needs of an ever-growing constituency.

The short history of Diana's Grove can be divided into three eras: the Earth Magic store which opened in 1987 in Springfield, Illinois; the creation of Edge of Perception in 1990 and the unfolding of Diana's Grove in Missouri which was envisioned in 1993, and is in the process of physical and spiritual evolution today. Though we still live in a decidedly patriarchal culture where the contributions of women are too often ignored, any accurate reading of history tells us that it is often women spiritual leaders who reclaim authentic spirituality and guide the collective soul in times of cultural upheaval. Diana's Grove is another chapter in that grand story.

In preparing for that presentation, I asked Cynthia to send me an audio tape describing the history of her movement. She did, I transcribed it, and I offer it to you here.

> *"There truly is no way to recreate the history of women in religion without having it come close to incite to riot! It took five years to get past the anger into the position we presently hold."* — Cynthia Jones

> *"Feminism is not the opportunity to repeat all the unkindness done to women in the past. Diana's Grove is non-hierarchical and non-sexist. We are committed to women and men."* — Cynthia Jones

In 1987, I offered a 15-week Tarot class in Springfield, Illinois. Fifteen weeks demands quite a commitment, and I wondered if people would want an in-depth study. But I couldn't present the magic of the cards, the philosophy of becoming, numbers, symbols and doorways to the past and future in a less respectful format. The class was from 7 to 10 on Thursday nights. I began with an overview and proceeded through the numbers 1 to 10, then on with the four royalty cards.

Not only did people commit to 15 weeks, that class remained on-going for seven years. A second 15-week class began on its heels with interested students joining the on-going class. Patti (Patricia Storm) was in that first class. She later gave up her job in the mundane world and joined me in creating the Edge of Perception, adding her skills and training in psychology to my metaphysical classes. Since that first class, my life has been totally consumed by creating classes, teaching, gathering skills to empower seekers and writing books in the form of class material until my attention shifted to plumbing and recipes for 150 people; Diana's Grove was born!

If all the experiences of humanity are contained in the stories told by a Tarot deck, many of those cards were played in the seven years we served as the Edge of Perception –

stories better told in a book than a letter. Soon we were teaching four nights a week – astrology, wicca, magical arts and offering full moon and seasonal rituals on Fridays. Our commitment to excellence in teaching and ritual pushed us to our edge for creative learning. Finding no college of the transformative arts, we devised our own program. We attended every midwest *reclaiming* camp, Jean Houston's mystery school in New York, a one year's training in Hypnotherapy in California, and drumming workshops and pagan festivals to develop our skills as teachers and priestesses. But teaching gave us our greatest learning; standing five nights a week before wise and insightful individuals and offering our creation, the evening class, was our most profound discipline.

Our work kept us on the financial edge as well as the perceptual edge. In 1992, Tom Hammes began the long and tedious process of obtaining our not-for-profit status as a church. To classify our work as educational would have required less red tape, but it would also have denied the spiritual core of our work. We became the Sanctuary of Formative Spirituality ministering to 50 students weekly through classes and rituals. In the earthly realm, without the ability to receive contributions, we could not continue. Even though we charged for our classes, the expense of maintaining a center was greater than our income. Contributions gave us one more year.

Just after Candelmas 1993, we attended an intensive weekend with Starhawk in Chicago. We wandered down a path into our future. Neither Patti nor I found ourselves in Springfield, teaching in our brick center on a corner lot in our visions of the future. We were in the woods, in a magical ritual space with the fire dancing on our faces!

During the spring equinox ritual of 1993, we told our community that we had been *sponsored by a vision*! We would begin the search for land to dedicate to magical use, a place for reconnecting, reunion, regeneration and, yes, *reclaiming of the Garden!* Our local community formed a collective to continue offering seasonal rituals to the public in Springfield, and the search began.

What a trial by the fires of the secular world! After selling our home and center in Springfield, we were refused a bank loan because we were a "religious cult." However, we were saved by the kindness of one who was willing to contribute generously to our dream and co-sign for our loan. We arrived at Diana's Grove just before the spring equinox, 1994. Community was present at every step of our journey.

Patricia and I gave all our resources, and all the hours in our day to the gestation of Diana's Grove. In July of 1994, we gave up the notion that this place could be brought into being by camp attendance and our own labor. The dream was too large for the two of us to dream alone. Struggling under the weight of impossibility, we gave Diana's Grove to the Fates, the Goddess; we asked for a miracle, we asked for help! And you (all supporters of the group) came, each of you became a part of that miracle. Campers, workers, contributors, you came showing us that Diana's Grove was the child of community, and in community she was born.

Hand by hand we weave the thread. Here we are, an alternative spirituality that calls to people suspicious of the monetary demands of organized religion living in a world of mortgages, electric bills and postage stamps. As a Wiccan center in Missouri, we do not get a special rate. Here we are, a religion of mavericks, in a time of self that asks, "What's in it for me?" taking on the work of recreating a spirituality of community. We are rediscovering what community is, what a collective can do, and realizing that care of ourselves alone has made us lonely adults.

We discovered that only by being a part of community can we create community. Magic is made by weaving and spinning, mending and healing, taking a dream and working together to make it real! Diana's Grove is a collective dream built from collective labor and resources. Strangers wandered too close and found themselves captured by a vision that asked them to become weavers and spinners.

That is our history. What is our future? It is up to you. There are no classes without students, there is no camp without campers, there is no community without members, there is no dream without dreamers, and there is no fabric of reality without weavers and spinners. Blessed be!

Videotape Graphics

 At this stage we suggest you watch the videotape.
There are no graphics in this class segment.

Review Questions

Answering the following questions will help you review key class themes and prepare for the examinations.

1. Describe the differences between a monist and dualist perspective on reality. How do you account for the development of dualism?

2. How do religious experience, myth and ritual intertwine in the worldview presented by Diana's Grove?

3. Do you see any connection between monism, neo-paganism and Eastern religions such as Hinduism and Buddhism?

4. Compare the spiritual insights offered by our Native American representative, Tom Drift, and those of Cynthia Jones.

Sources and Further Readings

Adler, Margot. *Drawing Down the Moon: Witches, Druids, Goddess-Worshippers, and Other Pagans in America Today*. Boston: Beacon, 1979.

Ellwood, Robert and Harry Partine. *Religious and Spiritual Groups in Modern America*. Englewood Cliffs, NJ: Prentice Hall, 1988.

Starhawk, *The Spiral Dance*. San Francisco: Harper & Row, 1979.

Wilson, Colin. *The Occult*. NY: Vintage Books, 1973.

www.dianasgrove. com

BELIEFS AND BELIEVERS
Class 14 – Doctrinal Dimension: Christianity

Introduction

Reflection: *Believers must have doctrines. Doctrines not only tell believers what to believe but they act as boundaries, defining who is inside the group and who is excluded. As we begin our first session on the doctrinal dimension, think about the positive and negative functions of this very necessary dimension as it impacts on the behavior of true believers. Thus, the doctrinal dimension and the ethical dimension are at the heart of our B + B = B equation.*

Have you ever been involved in one of those late night bull sessions out at the local coffee shop or in a friend's dorm room when the subject of religion came up? After the "what religion are you?" question, immediately, the follow up is, "what do you believe?" People never seem to ask, "what are your most powerful myths?" or "tell me about your key rituals." The first substantial question is inevitably a query generated by the *doctrinal dimension*. In this lesson we will begin our exploration of this powerful, yet paradoxical dimension. Authoritarian doctrines are the life blood of our major world religious traditions. They provide believers with the official view of reality, define the theological, philosophical, and institutional boundaries of a given worldview, and by the very force of their presence, act to weed out heretical views that would besmirch the pure vision of reality presented by the worldview. We could even go so far as to say that the *doctrinal dimension* is the mortar that holds the other five dimensions in place.

Yet the earthquake of human religious creativity, time and time again, rumbles through world traditions cracking the doctrinal mortar. Then the negative side of the *doctrinal dimension* emerges as people fight and die over how the dimensional bricks are to be rearranged. We are speaking, in metaphorical terms, of the fact that doctrines manifest in established religions in two seemingly paradoxical ways: a) they bind believers together around an agreed upon set of beliefs; b) yet when doctrines turn to hardened dogma, they cause adherents to split apart as new living interpretations of traditional doctrines arise from within the group. In this class, we will be exploring this aspect of the *doctrinal dimension* and identifying other important functions of doctrine in any given worldview.

In addition, we will be asking Christianity to help us understand the *doctrinal dimension*. In terms of our understanding of different worldviews - which, of course, is what we are about in "Beliefs and Believers" - we have noticed that the familiar may get in the way of appreciating the unfamiliar. In the case of Christianity, within the cultural context of the United States, it is the *familiar* that obstructs understanding of the *familiar*! Since most people who belong to an identifiable religious organization in the United States belong to some variety of Christian organization (though this is changing as the country becomes more religiously diverse), there is a tendency to a) identify "religion" with Christianity to the exclusion of all other worldviews, and b) take for granted that one understands this complex, diverse, and mysterious faith simply because it is such a familiar fixture in the life-style of so many Americans.

For many Christians, faith is the better part of understanding. Thus, the quest for knowledge about the historical and cultural roots of Christianity or the examination of the diverse institutional expressions of this faith is deemed inappropriate if not dangerous to the maintenance of faith. Since we will be exploring many different varieties of Christianity and listening to spokespersons from varied Christian perspectives over the next several sessions, it will be helpful to establish some general guidelines regarding Christian beliefs and the historical, institutional manifestations of these beliefs.

As we mentioned in our chapter on Judaism, Christianity is directly descended from the Jewish faith and shares many of the basic assumptions about the nature of reality. Scholars of course differ on the who, what and why of the historical Jesus, but most would agree that Jesus was a Jew who was well-versed in Jewish scripture. Accordingly, a set of *Judeo-Christian beliefs*, found in the Hebrew scripture and the New Testament may be summarized as follows:

Judeo-Christian beliefs

1. *Monotheism*

This is the belief in one, all-powerful, all-knowing God who is Creator and Lord of the universe. God is transcendent, that is, He is apart from His creation, yet, at the same time, God is immanent in creation, guiding history and judging human activity.

2. *Sin or alienation from God*

God made human beings in His image but human kind disobeyed the Creator. This "sin" has resulted in human kind's banishment from paradise (life lived in the presence of God). Because of their sinful, alienated state, humans stand in danger of God's judgment.

3. *Reconciliation*

However angry God might be with the pinnacle of His Creation, He is a just and merciful Deity. Because he is a righteous judge, he revealed the Law to the Hebrews at Mt. Sinai and established a covenant with his "chosen people." God revealed Himself to His people so that they would have a model for the type of moral and ethical behavior which would, ultimately, reconcile them to God.

4. *Salvation*

Though the world is inherently sinful, one day the Lord would send his appointed agent, the Messiah, who would vanquish all the inner and outer enemies of the people and establish the kingdom of heaven in which righteous believers would live in peace, reconciled to God.

Of course, having agreed on the above basic beliefs, the fundamental difference between Jews and Christians is the person of Jesus. Jesus' lifetime was one of enormous cultural upheaval. The Jews strained under the yoke of Roman oppression; the area of Palestine where they lived was a hotbed of competing worldviews; people were seeking, hoping for truth. Jesus, a leader of a small but evidently powerful Jewish reformation movement, died on the cross, the Roman punishment for rebels, traitors, and criminals.

Within a generation of his death, many followers, both Jews and Gentiles (non-Jews), who would later adopt the name *Christian* after the Greek root for "Messiah," came to believe that Jesus was, in fact, God's chosen agent. For these people, the presence of Jesus on Earth signaled that God's plan for reconciliation, as foretold in Hebrew scripture (the Old Testament), had already begun to happen. Thus, the very purpose of life and every human activity, from the most trivial to the most profound, took on new meaning.

The story of the development of Christianity in the First century is the fascinating story of the birth of a new religious movement. To Jewish doctrine is added a set of striking new doctrinal elements all centered on the person of Jesus Christ. These are as follows:

Christian beliefs

1. Jesus died on the cross but overcame death and visibly appeared in physical form to his disciples. He then ascended into Heaven where He participates in God's divinity. He will return again at the end of history to carry out the final judgment and bring in God's eternal reign of peace and justice.

2. His resurrection had enormous implications in terms of the Christian mythos. The event confirmed that Jesus was divine, the only son of God whose death on the cross, vicariously, redeemed Christian believers from a world of sin.

3. The path to salvation no longer was through the Law, the *Old Testament* or covenant revealed at Sinai and written in the Torah. Only through faith in the person of Jesus could a human being be saved.

In addition, the person of Jesus radically changed concepts of God, church, and behavior as the Christian community developed. The Christian God became a trinity: the Father, creator; the Son, Jesus, savior; the Holy Spirit, comforter, guide, sanctifier. The Church became "the body of Christ," a community of all believers who followed Jesus. Christian behavior was to be at the highest level of morality, stressing perfection and holiness. The sense of being "reborn in Christ" necessitated an ontological change, that is, a change in the very being of a person. It required turning from sin and entering into a holy relationship with God through Jesus Christ.

For more than 1,000 years, the Christian church had the remarkable ability to maintain unity even though, in reality, there were two powerful centers in Christendom - a Latin center in Rome and a Greek center in Constantinople. After centuries of theological and political infighting, in the year 1054 c.e., the Eastern churches formally severed relations with their western counterparts. In the 16th century, Christendom divides again during the Protestant Reformation, a time of tempestuous doctrinal and institutional struggle within the Roman Catholic church that eventually leads to the schismatic birth of the variegated Christian sects we term "Protestant." Conservative Protestantism, so steeped in doctrine, will be the focus of our next class.

Key Class Themes

This lesson focuses on the following themes:
1. The relationship of the six dimensions
2. Doctrine and Ethics
3. Christian doctrines
4. The impact of religious behavior on the social dimension
5. Belief + Believers = Behavior

Videotape Synopsis

- Jonestown interview with Dr. Rebecca Moore
- Class discussion
- Video interview with Reverend Cecil Williams of Glide Memorial Methodist Church, San Francisco
- Sacred text and doctrine interview overlooking the Holy City in Jerusalem
- Myth and doctrine at the Church of the Holy Sepulcher

Class 14

Videotape Commentary

I suggest you read this section before you watch the videotape. You will find that it will help you organize your thoughts so that when you watch the tape it will be more meaningful. When you have finished viewing the tape, you may want to read this section again.

Jonestown: Interview with Dr. Rebecca Moore

On November 18, 1978, more than 900 people living on a religious commune in the South American country of Guyana, drank a potion of Fla-Vor Aid laced with poison. The Reverend Jim Jones, hounded by real and imaginary enemies, called upon the members of his People's Temple to drink the death-brew, and they followed his orders. To this day, questions remain on whether everyone willingly committed suicide, but the fact is that mothers, fathers and babies died that night in the name of religion.

When the news media broke the story, Americans were stunned by the tragic effects of the power of religious belief. Because most of the dead were United States citizens, the news media, as they are wont to do, tried to make sense of the event. Unfortunately, "making sense" came to mean casting Jones as a psychotic megalomaniac and his followers as brainwashed, cult-obsessed robots. In the grand media tradition of reducing something truly extraordinary to bite-sized, cereal sound-bites suitable for breakfast consumption, Americans were able to dismiss the event as something aberrant. To make matters worse, a racist tone entered the coverage as Jones was white and most of his followers were black. It is a sad commentary on American cultural mores that tragedy involving African American citizens can be pushed to the back pages of our social conscious.

In any event, Dr. Rebecca Moore, Professor of Religious Studies at the University of North Dakota, debunks most of the misinformation that has surrounded this unparalleled B + B = B event. And I can't thank Dr. Moore enough for her honesty, courage, and strength in sharing her own tragic Jonestown experience with our collective "Beliefs and Believers" audience.

Rebecca lost two sisters and a nephew on that night in November 1978. And there but for some protective intuitive rejection of Jim Jones' apocalyptic doctrinal twist on Christianity, she may well have perished in the Guyana jungle. What we hear in her account of the tragedy bears little resemblance to the media portrayal of brainwashed cultists. Her sisters joined the People's Temple because they believed that the movement offered a unique opportunity to *realize* Christian faith in a society, American society, that hypocritically claimed Christianity as its faith while violating every integral notion of justice, peace, hope, and love. These weren't daughters of marginalized citizenry, but daughters of middle class, white, Protestant Christian America. What went wrong?

On May 13, 1931, James Warren Jones was born to financially-strapped parents trying to make ends meet in central Indiana during the Great Depression. Perhaps that is why Jones would always be suspicious of the rich and powerful and would embrace communist ideology as part of his own social vision. Though materially poor, Jones experienced a wealth of Protestant faiths during his youth including everything from mainstream Methodism to the Pentecostal faith with its experiential revivalist style, faith healing, and speaking in tongues.

By the time he reached high school age, Jones was already a charismatic preacher. To his credit, he condemned segregation in the churches and by 1955 had established a lively integrated church in Indianapolis, the People's Temple. He created a doctrinal mixture that combined Pentecostal religious experience with the liberal, social gospel ethic of the liberal Protestant churches. His church grew, but not without controversy. Indianapolis was a conservative city, and his outspoken and progressive civil rights policies angered the establishment. Like so many oppressed pilgrims in the American mythos, Jones set out to find a sanctuary where his vision could be realized.

California offered just such a promised land, and Jones' church became very successful during its California heyday of the mid-1970s. Jones skillfully interpreted Christian doctrine in such a way that Christianity stood for economic justice, peace, inclusiveness, and social activism; a perfect fit in the liberal San Francisco Bay area. By 1975, Jim Jones was a major player in the left-wing political activity of San Francisco and was even appointed to the San Francisco Housing Authority by Mayor George Moscow.

Success, as it often does, brought greater scrutiny, and the United States Government began to investigate the Temple's tax status. Meanwhile defectors from the movement accused the Temple of psychological and physical abuse, faked healings, and unfair financial practices. A group of former members and relatives of temple followers, calling themselves "Concerned Relatives" convinced Leo Ryan, a California congressman, that what Jones had created was a dangerous, manipulative cult. The news media picked up on the story, adding fuel to the fire of Jones' already smoldering paranoia. During the summer of 1977, Jones ordered the collective migration of temple followers to the jungle compound they had been building in Guyana.

Unlike the pilgrims or later the Mormons, Jones was not able to escape the pressures of secular society by creating his own religious community in *the wilderness*. In November of 1978, Congressman Ryan, members of Concerned Relatives, and various news reporters descended upon Jonestown with demands that Jones submit to external scrutiny or face the consequences. What happened next is open to debate, but as the congressman, his crew, and several defectors were preparing to leave by plane from the jungle airstrip at Port Kaituma, temple followers opened fire with pistols and rifles. Congressman Ryan, NBC reporter Don Harris, two other newsmen, and defector Patricia Parks lay dead on the tarmac. Shortly thereafter, Jones called upon more than 900 of his followers to commit "revolutionary suicide." Four men managed to escape by running into the jungle, but everyone else in the compound died.

As you listen to Rebecca Moore describe her own insights into this extraordinary example of belief and behavior, please reflect on just how powerful the *religious impulse* can be. If we consider human religious activity from a much wider historical perspective, the events at Jonestown, while being terribly tragic, are not all that unusual. By its very nature, religion tends to move human beings to extremes. True, in American society, we have somehow learned to "keep a cap" on religious extremes, but the cap is always under pressure and always ready to pop! When we explore the relationship between the doctrinal and ethical dimensions, we come face to face with the *power* of religious ideas. Jim Jones knew how to wield that power, but, ultimately, the very same power destroyed him and his movement.

Class Discussion

In our class discussion following the roll-in at the mass grave in Oakland, California, Karen raises a question that underscores the power of the doctrinal dimension. Having noticed that the headstone refers to the dead as "victims," she asks, "Were they really victims?" Her point is that members of the People's Temple willingly followed Jim Jones to the Guyana jungle commune, allowed him to create what Helen later refers to as a "totalitarian state," and even practiced "revolutionary suicide" at his command. Chris adds to the conversation in his remarks about the biblical book, *Revelation*. Indeed, embedded in Christianity, the religion that is familiar and comfortable to most Americans, is a volcanic vision of a world that must come to a fiery, violent end. Whether people who wish to follow the teachings of Jesus become "victims," may well depend on their doctrinal interpretation of his life and teachings.

J. Dominic Crossan struggles with our "victim question" in his book, *The Historical Jesus: The Life of a Mediterranean Peasant*. Crossan paints a portrait of Jesus as a sage who preached a radical social egalitarianism. In other words, the "end of the world" that Jesus envisioned was not a violent end to the physical planet in some apocalyptic Armageddon, but the end of an ethical system characterized by economic and political injustice. To paraphrase Reverend Williams, Jesus demanded that "everyone be invited to the table." For that simple yet radical call for justice, he was crucified.

In his early years, Jim Jones interpreted Jesus' teaching in much the same light. He saw through the fundamental hypocrisy of American society, a society in which the vast majority of the citizens claimed to be Christians yet these Christians turned a blind eye to poverty, prejudice, hurting, and hatred. Jones founded the People's Temple with the intention of being true to Jesus' teachings. Following his doctrinal interpretation of Jesus' life and teachings, he set out to create a "church" in which all people were equal, regardless of cultural background or socioeconomic status.

Of course, like a character in a Shakespearean tragedy, Jones was possessed and tormented by inner-demons. In the end, those demons drove him to ignite his own violent, apocalyptic conflagration on that steamy jungle evening in 1978. But the "victim question" continues to haunt us all. If human beings continue to create social structures based on the exploitation and domination of an impoverished majority by a well-heeled minority, then we can surely expect to be visited again and again by messiahs who so clearly point out the folly of that doomed social endeavor. When they come, we kill them or drive them to insanity. In that collective act, we are all victims. Or we can interpret their teachings in ways that finally work towards a just and fair world.

Interview with the Reverend Cecil Williams, Glide Memorial Methodist Church, San Francisco, California

We have already had the chance to meet the delightful Reverend Williams in our earlier class on the experiential dimension. One of the key functions of religious doctrine is to make sense of or bring order to the wide-ranging, symbolic religious drama present in the mythic dimension. The Christian mythos, quite naturally, is the story of Jesus' life and teaching. But how is that story to be interpreted? Putting Reverend Williams' always colorful comments in "Beliefs and Believers" terms, what he is saying is that *doctrine* can never be separated from the *ethical dimension*. Christians are only *Christianing* when they work for justice, inclusiveness, compassion, caring, and community.

Of course, Reverend Williams embraces a liberal interpretation of what Jesus' ministry means and how a Christian is called upon to behave in this world. In our next class, we will meet a conservative Christian, Reverend Walt Stowe, who has a very different view on how the Christian mythos is to be applied in day-to-day living. In typical conservative fashion, the most important thing a Christian minister can do is get people *saved!* Whereas Reverend Williams' focus is on creating heaven on earth by helping those who have less, Pastor Stowe looks to heaven in the next life for his just reward. When you consider that, in the United States, we have somewhere between 900 and 1,000 different *flavors* of Christianity, it is clear that the *doctrinal dimension* plays a huge role in delineating how a Christian responds to the life and teaching of Jesus.

Reverend Williams hits the nail on the head with his "old dog" analogy. He says that the challenge to Christians, especially in the United States, is to "get off the porch" and "take a bite out of" the injustice that characterizes the cultural experience for which we are all responsible. If Beliefs + Believers = Behavior, then, according to Williams, it's time for Christians to stop being victims and "practice what you preach."

Roll-in Overlooking the Holy City in Jerusalem

While visiting a beautiful little chapel overlooking the Holy City in Jerusalem, the spot where, according to the *mythic dimension* present in the New Testament, Jesus cried for Jerusalem, I was struck by the important relationship between sacred scripture and the *doctrinal dimension*. Of course the authoritative scripture in Christianity is the New Testament. For most Christians, the New Testament has something of an eternal quality, but it took almost four centuries for the 27 writings that make up this body of sacred scripture to be agreed upon. Official lists of sacred scripture began circulating by the second century, as Christian leaders worked to build the doctrinal walls that would both describe the unique Christian worldview and weed out heresy. It wasn't until 367 c.e. when Bishop Anthanasius of Alexandria sent an Easter letter listing the 27 writings that alone were to comprise Christian scripture, that we find a listing of the Gospels, Paul's letters, pastoral epistles and the Book of Revelation that corresponds to today's *canon*, or authoritative scripture.

Imagine that you are a follower of Jesus, living in a time when most people are illiterate. You witness miracles, remember his teachings, recall other amazing events. As you grow older, you pass these stories on to your children. Eventually, this oral tradition is written down by scribes so that the tradition can be preserved. But wouldn't there be many stories, many different renditions of Jesus' ministry? Sacred scripture functions as a form of *doctrinal interpretation*. As a new religion develops, people need to have a clear definition of their beliefs. A sacred text, like the New Testament, brings authority to belief, guidance to ethical practices, and structure to religious institutions in society. Once again, in the New Testament, the relationship of the six dimensions becomes evident.

Roll-in at the Church of the Holy Sepulcher

The Church of the Holy Sepulcher is one of the holiest shrines in Christendom, and a place where myth, ritual, doctrine, and sacred architecture meet. The church is at the end of the way called the "Via Dolorosa." According to the New Testament myth, there are fourteen stations along the sacred route Jesus took as he walked towards crucifixion. The last five are located inside the church, including the spot on which Jesus is believed to have been crucified and the tomb from which he arose. Every Friday, led by Franciscan monks, Christian pilgrims from around the globe ritually relive Christ's mythic passion, following the Via Dolorosa and ending inside the Church of the Holy Sepulcher. Notice, once again, how a sacred site such as the Church of the Holy Sepulcher inspires our six dimensions of religion and illustrates their relationship.

Videotape Graphics

At this stage we suggest you watch the videotape. The graphics you will see on the screen are reproduced on the next page to save you the trouble of copying them down. You might like to add your own comments as you watch the tape.

The Doctrinal and Ethical Dimensions

Doctrine = Belief
Ethics = Behavior

$$\rightarrow \quad \frac{\text{Belief}}{+ \text{ Believer}} = \text{Behavior}$$

Class 14

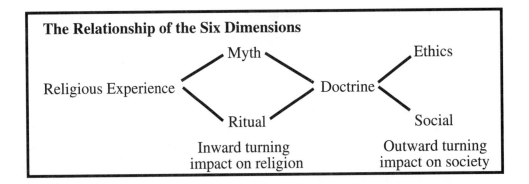

The Relationship of the Six Dimensions

Religious Experience

Myth

Ritual

Doctrine

Ethics

Social

Inward turning
impact on religion

Outward turning
impact on society

The Doctrinal and Ethical Dimensions
– Religious behavior impacts on the Social Dimension
– Religion is a *major determinant* of *human behavior*
– Religion is a *major determinant* of *cultural experience*

Review Questions

Answering the following questions will help you review key class themes and prepare for the examinations.

1. What is the relationship between the doctrinal and ethical dimension?

2. Please describe the relationship of the six dimensions of religions using the People's Temple as your primary example?

3. From the doctrinal and ethical perspective, how would you describe Reverend Cecil Williams' interpretation of Jesus' life and teaching? In other words, what is the most important thing a Christian can do to *be a Christian*?

4. Describe the relationship between religious doctrine, sacred texts, and sacred architecture using our examples from the Holy City in Jerusalem.

Sources and Further Readings

Chidester, David. *Salvation and Suicide: An Interpretation of Jim Jones, the Peoples Temple, and Jonestown.* Bloomington: Indiana, Indiana University Press, 1988.

Crossan, John Dominic. *The Historical Jesus: The Life of a Mediterranean Peasant.* San Francisco: HarperSanFrancisco, 1991.

Moore, Rebecca, Fielding McGeehee III, eds. *New Religious Movements, Mass Suicide, and Peoples Temple.* Lewiston, NY: Edwin Mellen, 1988.

BELIEFS AND BELIEVERS
Class 15 – Doctrinal Dimension: Conservative Christianity

Introduction

Reflection: *Should a person's religion make him or her angry? Should it make him or her hostile and militant towards human beings outside his or her chosen worldview? Is the taking of another human being's life ever justified in the name of religion? How does the doctrinal dimension fuel tensions between antagonistic religious groups?*

Never underestimate the power of religious doctrine. Someone once referred to this dimension of religion as "the institutionalization of answers about the unexplainable." From the dawn of consciousness, human beings have endured a gnawing spiritual hunger for the answers to life's profound questions. That much we have established in the first set of "Beliefs and Believers" classes. In review, *boundary questions* are questions such as: who am I, where did I come from, where do I go when I die, why must I suffer pain and disease, how can I find something permanent in a chaotic, constantly changing world? Death, suffering, and change are the stuff of human existence. Life's breaking points are forced upon us by sickness, hunger, disease, old age, frustrated desire, grief, loneliness, anxiety, despair, human destructiveness, evil, and failure. Certainly life offers us moments of extraordinary joy, peace, and pleasure. It is the negative side of life, however, that compels people to turn to religious doctrines for answers.

The primary reason for this is that death, suffering, and change are problems that, for the most part, cannot be resolved in terms of common sense or scientific knowledge. At least not to the satisfaction of most human beings. Science can tell us that when we die, our bodies will decompose. What a cheery thought! After seventy or so years of struggle, you end up as an afternoon snack for a tribe of worms. It is much nicer to contemplate an afterlife where you spend eternity flying from cloud to cloud strumming a harp.

Religious doctrines require a different kind of *knowing* than that demanded by common sense or science. Religions provide doctrines that must be *believed*. *Faith*, this fascinating way of knowing, rests on the authority of the religious institution that is providing a specific set of answers to life's disturbing questions. Authoritative doctrines are the lifeblood of major world religions like Christianity because they provide believers with the "correct" view of reality; define the theological, philosophical, and institutional boundaries of a given worldview; and by the very force of their presence, act to *weed out* heretical views that would besmirch the pure vision presented by the worldview in question.

In this session of "Beliefs and Believers," to illustrate all of the above, we continue our discussion of the *doctrinal dimension* by delving more deeply into the place of conservative, Protestant Christianity in American society. Of the three great branches of Christianity – Roman Catholicism, Eastern Orthodoxy, and Protestantism – the Protestant worldview has had the greatest impact on American self understanding. It is impossible to understand the history of the United States without recognizing that undercurrents of Protestant belief have had and continue to have a subtle, yet pervasive impact on public policy.

Protestantism was a 16th century "protest" with the Roman Catholic church aimed at reforming what were conceived to be doctrinal and institutional errors. Initially the great leaders of the movement, Luther, Calvin, and Zwingli, truly did wish to reform the church. But what, in fact, happened was that the inspired individuality of the movement – scripture not institutions became the authoritative source – led to a brand new Christian movement. The third child of the Christian family was born, but with a most interesting "birth-defect" – namely, the tendency to keep right on protesting and forming new Protestant groups according to the biblically-inspired consciousness of believers.

Thus, when we look at the world of Protestant Christianity we find there are about 900 or so different varieties of institutionalized Christianity including Lutherans, Reformed/Presbyterians, Methodists, Anglican/Episcopalians, Baptists, Pentecostals, Independent Fundamentalists, Amish, Mennonite, Apostolic Church of God, and any number of sectarian offshoots of this sparse listing. Since differences in interpretation of doctrine are as likely as not the cause of a schism within a particular Protestant group, Protestantism has much to teach us about the *doctrinal dimension*. Protestant Christianity will also help us understand the *doctrinal dimension* as it affects religious and social experience in the United States.

To put our interviews on Protestantism, particularly the Conservative or Fundamentalist expressions, into perspective, here are a few points to consider. For the first 100 years or so of this nation's history, the United States was a Protestant enterprise. This doesn't mean that everyone went to Protestant churches; in fact, there is a larger percentage of "churched" people today than in 1800. Nor does it mean that everyone believed in the tenets of Protestant Christianity. It simply means that the ideals expressed in the Protestant worldview were lived out, realized in the socio-political sphere of late 18th to mid-19th century America.

We have discussed how the American mythos reverberated with the Jewish story of the Jews' covenantal relationship with the Lord and conquest of the "promised land" He gave them. As one scholar, William McLoughlin, points out, the elements of this mythic drama provided a *biblical culture core* for the United States. During inevitable times of intense cultural change as the nation grew and prospered, the elements of the culture core guided national policy and grounded the country in the same Protestant Christian ideals. The four key elements of this Bible-inspired way of understanding reality for early American citizens are as follows: a) the United States is a covenant nation implying a special relationship with God; b) a manifest destiny, or sense that the land was promised as part of some greater Divine plan; c) a covenantal link between high moral standards and prosperity, in other words, just like the Old Testament saga, peace and prosperity depended upon meeting God's demands for moral behavior; and d) the "Protestant work-ethic," the particularly Protestant notion that success, progress and rewards on earth assured one that a place in the Heavenly realm was secure.

These are, of course, very weighty notions based on Protestant doctrinal interpretation of the biblical mythos. We obviously cannot enter into a long discourse on Protestant theology here. For our purposes, what is important to know is that in the early years of the United States, citizens lived out the successes and failures of the nation according to these religious precepts. In particular, *religious revivals, evangelism, witnessing to the Lord, getting saved* and *getting back into that covenantal relationship with God* became a powerful force for cleansing society, especially during times of high anxiety characterized by social change. What we now term as *evangelical conservative Protestant Christianity* was simply *religion* to the citizens of the United States up until approximately the last quarter of the 19th century when social changes became so overwhelming that the apparently seamless fabric of Protestantism tore in two.

In our interview with a representative of Conservative Protestantism, Pastor Walt Stowe, whom we met briefly in Class Eight as a major critic of the Ramtha School of Enlightenment, we will examine some of the reasons why Protestantism split into a liberal-mainstream camp and a conservative, evangelical camp. Naturally, the *doctrinal dimension* is at the heart of this split.

Background on Conservative Protestantism in America

As we discussed, for the first several generations of this nation, evangelical Protestant Christianity not only was religion for the citizens of this nation; it provided a *culture core* which governed and guided the political-social agenda of the people. In spite of the Constitution's precept of separation of church and state, Protestant ideas and republican ideas blended to form a single vision of America's destiny and purpose.

However in the latter years of the 19th century, enormous social and intellectual change conspired to disrupt this harmonious relationship and split American Protestantism into two distinct camps. Professor Martin Marty, whom we met in Class One, has referred to this religio-cultural event as the "Two Party Split" in Protestant Christianity.

Conservative Protestantism seized the name "evangelical" and took a doctrinal stand that emphasized salvation out of a corrupt world, the importance of a holy, moral life, the condemnation of drinking, dancing, card-playing, and sexual improprieties, and the *born again* experience. Christian Fundamentalism, as professed by Pastor Stowe, is one form of the conservative branch. Other forms include churches in the Pentecostal movement, Apostolic and Independent churches of various sorts and a constellation of "Holiness" groups with roots in the Methodist tradition (the Nazarenes, Church of God {Anderson, Indiana} and the Salvation Army).

Liberal or main-stream Protestantism took a decidedly "this worldly" focus. These churches concentrated on social reform, the building of a more perfect society here on earth. Their conservative cousins regularly accused them of what has come to be called "secular humanism." To the conservatives, especially Fundamentalists, liberal Protestants focused on the secular instead of the heavenly. They were driven by a "human centered" theology rather than a "God centered" one. To the Fundamentalists, liberal theologians seemed to equate the "Kingdom of Heaven" with human fulfillment rather than with radical spiritual transformation. Most of all, the evangelical, revivalist branch branded the liberals as heretics for *selling out* to modernity. New ideas emerging in science, theology, sociology and psychology seemed to undermine the authority of traditional Christian doctrine.

Let's examine the intellectual and social revolutions in America that caused this powerful doctrinal battle and the two-party split. By the 1880s two powerful revolutions had rocked the peaceful world of American Protestantism. A two-pronged attack came in the form of an intellectual revolution. First, new methods of scholarship threatened long-standing assumptions about biblical inerrancy. "In-errancy," the notion that the Bible contains no factual errors, along with "literalism," the claim that biblical events actually did happen – from the parting of the Red Sea to the resurrection of Jesus – were *fundamental* to a Christian's understanding of scripture. The new *Higher-Criticism,* developed in Europe and transported to the United States, used modern methods of historical and literary analysis to raise some serious doubts about the inerrance of sacred texts and undermine the taken-for-granted approach that biblical events were *literally* true.

If the *modernist* attack on Christian doctrine were not enough, the works of Darwin, Freud and Marx made claims for a kind of *material determinism*. Not only were we not made in the glorious image of an all powerful Deity, the combined perspective of these great late 19th century thinkers painted a rather grim picture of inexorable and often random control of human existence by biological, psychological and economic forces. Not only could God or Jesus not save man, man could not even save man. As you can imagine, good evangelical Christians were not about to take this assault on the authority of their faith lying down!

In addition, the nation was undergoing a radical social revolution. Increased immigration brought "new" worldviews, especially Roman Catholicism. A once quiet agrarian nation found itself caught up in a frantic industrial revolution. People moved from farm and family to the chaotic atmosphere of teeming urban areas. The simple values, most of which were drawn from the *ethical dimension* presented in ancient biblical stories, often were irrelevant in the rough, morally complex world of the cities. People began to long for those clear biblical answers to life's boundary questions. While the liberal Protestant churches embraced modernity and often re-adjusted Christian doctrine to *fit* new ideas such as those presented in Darwin's theory of evolution, the conservatives circled the doctrinal wagons in an all-out effort to protect the authority of their faith.

Of all the branches of conservative, evangelical Protestantism, no group responded more furiously to the call to do battle for the Lord than the Fundamentalists. Right doctrine was the key to righteous faith, and the Fundamentalists went about the process of attacking modern theology and culture with unabated zeal. The term "Fundamentalist" actually comes from a set of pamphlets that were published in the early years of the 20th century which attempted to define a *Christian* by what a person believed. In other words, with a thick, black magic marker, the Fundamentalists drew a doctrinal circle. You either believed in basic biblical teachings regarding Jesus – the Virgin birth, the miracles, literal death and resurrection, vicarious atonement on the Cross, the literal return of Jesus at the end of history – or you were not to be considered a true Christian. What made Fundamentalists different was, again, the willingness to debate, to argue, get down in the trenches and scrap it out whenever they perceived the threat of modernist ideas watering down fundamental Christian doctrines.

Key Class Themes

This lesson focuses on the following themes:

1. Conservative Protestantism
2. Protestant Christianity and the social dimension in the United States
3. The key functions of doctrine
4. Doctrine and interpretation
5. The Book of Revelation and social unrest in America

Videotape Synopsis

- Class discussion
- Video interview, Pastor Walt Stowe
- Class discussion
- Video-monologue on the Plain of Armageddon in Israel

Videotape Commentary

I suggest you read this section before you watch the videotape. You will find that it will help you organize your thoughts so that when you watch the tape it will be more meaningful. When you have finished viewing the tape, you may want to read this section again.

Classroom Discussion

In Class 15, our exploration of the important functions of the doctrinal dimension sparks a wide-ranging class discussion. The exigencies of human existence – death, suffering, and change – demand that clear answers be found to explain our shared predicament. Several students point out that science, in its own way, is involved in the all-important endeavor to explain the ups and downs of life. Interestingly enough, science and religion are becoming closer in their respective delineations of reality. As Karen, Jan, and Suzanne note, the new physics reveals unmistakable patterns in what was once thought to be random and chaotic material activity. However, science, as a way of knowing, necessarily has its own self-limiting boundaries.

Religious doctrines, quite naturally, offer explanations about the "unexplainable," and, for believers, these answers provide a sense of meaning, purpose, identity, and belonging. Faith, a way of knowing unique to religious expressions such as conservative Protestantism, is the energizer battery that keeps the doctrinal dimension ticking. Faith, supported by the authority of an institution, a sacred text, or a charismatic leader, doesn't take away the pain of sickness or the sting of death for believers; it simply puts suffering in a context that makes sense to believers.

Interview with Pastor Walt Stowe

Pastor Walt Stowe, spiritual leader of Calvary Baptist Church in Roy, Washington, is proud to be considered an independent, Fundamentalist Christian. As you view our interview segment, try to sense, not only in Pastor Stowe's words, but in his tone and demeanor, just how very much he embodies the Fundamentalist worldview.

For conservative Christians, the Bible is the bedrock of faith, the source of authority, the corner stone of religious doctrine, indeed, it is God's word. When fundamentalist Pastor Walt Stowe speaks of biblical inerrancy, he means that the Bible is without error and is to be taken as completely accurate whether the mode of inquiry is history, theology, psychology, geography or geology. He speaks to us of the Christian fundamentals which are the basis for his doctrinal interpretation of the life and teaching of Jesus. Notice how these fundamentals provide quite specific answers to those pesky boundary questions regarding meaning, purpose, life, and most importantly, what happens when we die? He also claims that he is not "interpreting" the Bible; rather the Bible, as God's word, is speaking directly to him.

Pastor Stowe is as genuine a religious person as I've ever met, but, from a "Beliefs and Believers" perspective, it is clear that this believer has adopted an *interpretation* of the Bible that "works" based on what we might call the *theology of exclusion*. The Bible speaks one truth. Pastor Stowe embraces and preaches that truth. If you or I don't agree with him, then we are excluded from the Christian community. In this Us v. Them, either/or, black/white worldview, "if you ain't with Jesus, you're with Satan and headed for hell." Dehumanized in this fashion, a "non-believer" becomes the target for verbal or even physical violence.

At this juncture in "Beliefs and Believers," we have to be very careful not to perpetuate the stereotype that all religious fundamentalists are prone to violence. As I say in our class session and would stress again here, I found Pastor Stowe to be an intelligent, caring gentleman within the confines of his worldview. To be a Christian, for Pastor Stowe, is to read the Bible as he reads it. Since the Bible speaks for itself, there is no room for doctrinal disagreements. You are either with him or against him.

This raises a provocative challenge for people trying to make sense of conservative or fundamentalist perspectives within any world religion. On one hand, the claim is made for an inerrant sacred text, in this case, the Bible. On the other hand, at least in terms of fundamentalist Christianity, believers tend to ignore the all-important cultural and historical context in which biblical passages are revealed. In the quest to formulate explanations for death, suffering, and change in the face of dire circumstances in the here and now, passages are taken out of context. Our discussion of the biblical book of Revelation catapults this disturbing tendency into the horrific headlines of the past several years.

In the latter years of the 20th century, both religious and secular groups have used the ancient visions in this apocalyptic book to justify violence in the name of God or ideology. Without some sense of cultural context regarding the Bible, what we end up having in America is a vast Christian majority that is biblically illiterate. A most sobering thought! Beware of the power of a sacred text unleashed indiscriminately according to any ideological or religious whim. The tragic results of an ahistorical/acultural interpretation of biblical doctrine are well-documented in the debacle at Waco in 1993 and the bombing of the Federal building in Oklahoma City two years later. Knowing the history surrounding a given biblical book or passage is an indispensible step in applying the Bible compassionately as believers deal with life's challenges in their own time.

Doctrine & Interpretation: Mt. Megiddo Monologues, with Background Material

During my monologue on Mt. Megiddo, I mention two types of *apocalyptic theodicies*, both of which draw heavily from the above symbols, to justify violent action – a *religious apocalyptic theodicy* and a *secular apocalyptic theodicy*. With all the media coverage that attended the disaster in Waco, Texas when *Armageddon = har megiddon* (Hebrew for Mountain of Megiddo) broke out between Branch Davidians and government agents, it isn't difficult to see how David Koresh transformed the Texas plains surrounding Waco into a biblical Armageddon. With tragic irony, the actions of the agents of the Department of Alcohol, Tobacco, and Firearms (ATF) and the Federal Bureau of Investigation (FBI) actually increased Koresh's status with the group because they played right into his prophetic hand.

Koresh taught his followers that *Babylon* meant the corrupt, secular society of the United States and that the *beasts* and *dragons* were represented by Justice Department agents. According to Koresh, *Armageddon* would actually occur on the plains of Texas and would begin with an attack on the Branch Davidians. He also prepared his Davidians to die willingly, using an interesting twist on the *tribulationist* theme. The Davidians were *mid-tribulationists* in that they fully expected to be slain by the forces of evil during the seven year period, which to those inside the compound, began with the February 1993 attack by ATF agents. However, death and suffering were good. The slain servants of the Lord would return with the Heavenly Host to vanquish Satan's minions at the final battle. Loyal Davidians would eventually live in a post-Armageddon paradise on Earth. So the idea of dying in a violent confrontation with government agents, far from being frightening, was actually welcomed as part of the overall divine, apocalyptic dream playing out on the fields of Texas. Tragedy was inevitable the moment government agents moved on the compound. It was not just the power of machine guns that the ATF and FBI agents faced; it was the power of a *religious apocalyptic theodicy*, the volatile mix of myth and doctrine, and, above all, a simple equation; B + B = B.

Religious apocalyptic theodices certainly caught the attention of the Justice Department following the Waco tragedy. However, recent violent events and current scholarship in religious studies reveal a much more nefarious form of millennial despair present in America today. That is a *secular apocalyptic theodicy*. A secular apocalyptic theodicy may discard the demonstrably supernatural elements present in the Armageddon-hungry visions of religious apocalypticists, but the goal they envision is equally violent, perhaps more so.

Extremists, such as white supremacists, more extreme members of various militias, radicalized members of the Patriot or Christian Identity movements and anti-government survivalists, reshape the symbols in the Book of Revelation in the following manner:

1. *Babylon* = Godless secular humanism; multiculturalism, globalism, cultural relativism, liberal America, in general

2. *Anti-Christ* = ZOG (Zionist Occupation Government, read, U.S. Government); United Nations, World Bank, etc.

3. *Beasts and Dragons* = FBI, CIA, IRS, EPA, Supreme Courts, United Nations, World Bank, etc. (include religious studies professors!!)

4. *Tribulationist perspective* = war, death, climatic disasters, invasion are imminent; prepare to survive by moving to remote areas and stockpiling weapons and food

5. *Armageddon* = the great battle to preserve American cultural (and racial) purity

6. *Millennialism* = apocalypse, Armageddon, then salvation in an America redeemed from the beasts and dragons of Babylon

7. *Messiah* = "self-salvation" through survivalism; violence becomes a kind of *messiah* in that violent acts may actually "hasten" the arrival of Armageddon

In fact, using this kind of extreme form of doctrinal interpretation, the images and symbols in *The Book of Revelation* can be transcribed onto any cultural situation a "believer" finds aberrant. One can only hope those who are inspired by *a secular apocalyptic theodicy* restrict the expression of it to prophetic tirades. Because as we have witnessed in our own culture, the potential for crossing the behavioral line into violence is very real. Once again, the *power* of religious belief pushes the *truth* about the religious belief to a distant and irrelevant corner of the cultural playing field.

Final Class Discussion

If we, as students of religion, can learn anything from our investigation of conservative Protestantism, it is the power of religious belief and its impact on human behavior. Once again, we encounter our second dimensional triangle; doctrine, as belief, ethics, as behavior, touching all of us in society. Chris' final comment following the Mt. Meggido monologue not only nicely sums up the class discussion but, in many ways, the entire course. Whether we believe the extreme doctrinal interpretations of a religious or secular group or not, it is of the utmost importance that we pay attention to these beliefs with at least enough respect to respond in a way that reduces the potential for violence. The volatile mixture of religious doctrine and the theology of exclusion is, unfortunately, an unavoidable threat in a free and religiously diverse society. The key is knowing how to "handle" the ingredients in any given crisis; a lesson the FBI learned the hard way on the plains of Texas in 1993.

Please note: in the heat of our lively class discussion your ever-excitable instructor inadvertently points us in the direction of Islam for Class 16. Actually, we will exlore Islam in Class 17. Our next class is Doctrinal Dimension: Sacred vs. Secular.

Class 15

Videotape Graphics

 At this stage we suggest you watch the videotape. The graphics you will see on the screen are reproduced on the next page to save you the trouble of copying them down. You might like to add your own comments as you watch the tape.

Religious Doctrines

Doctrines =
belief systems; they provide specific
answers to boundary questions

Religious Doctrines

Definition =
the institutionalization of answers about
the unexplainable (boundary questions)

Religious Doctrines

Death, suffering, change =
problems that cannot be resolved in terms
of common sense or scientific knowledge

Religious Doctrines

Faith =
a religious way of knowing the truth based on
the authority of the church, a sacred book, or
a religious leader

Functions of Doctrines

– bring order or focus to myth and ritual
– provide the institutionalization of answers
  to the unexplainable (death, suffering, change)
– control the boundaries of religious expression
– determine what is inclusive and exclusive
  in a given religion

Doctrine and Interpretation

The Book of Revelation
doctrine bringing order to myth
through interpretation

Apocalypticism
visions of the end time revealed by
God through chosen prophets

Theodicy
a mythic explanation for the existence
of evil and suffering

Revelation
a religious apocalyptic theodicy; cosmic
conflict explains Christian suffering
in the 1st century
Example today: Branch Davidians

Secular Apocalyptic Theodicy
a doctrinal interpretation that maintains
mythic power but lacks supernatural elements
Examples today: militias, patriots, survivalists,
Timonthy McVeigh mentality, anti-government groups

Myth and Symbol in Revelation

– Tribulation
– Dragons, beasts, anti-Christ
– Armageddon
– Babylon
– Messiah
– Redemption
– Millennium

Review Questions

Answering the following question will help you review key class themes and prepare
for the examinations.

1. What are the key functions of the doctrinal dimension? Using conservative Protestantism
   as an example, illustrate these functions.

2. Describe the two 19th century revolutions that challenged America's sense of identity, purpose, and destiny. What effect did this have on American Protestantism?

3. How do death, suffering, and change work as catalysts to the creation of religious doctrine? What does this tell us about boundary questions and rites of passage?

4. According to Pastor Walt Stowe, what does a Fundamentalist Christian believe?

5. What is an *apocalyptic theodicy?* How do current religious and secular American organizations use *The Book of Revelation* to justify violent acts?

Sources and Further Readings

Marsen, George. *Fundamentalism and American Culture*. NY: Oxford University Press, 1980.

Marty, Martin. *Righteous Empire*. NY: Harper Torchbooks, 1977.

McLoughlin, William G. *Revivals, Awakenings, and Reforms*. Chicago, IL: University of Chicago Press, 1978.

Robbins, Thomas and Susan J. Palmer, eds. *Millennium, Messiahs, and Mayhem: Contemporary Apocalyptic Movements*. NY: Routledge, 1997. (In particular, see the Introductory chapter and Chapter 5, "Secularizing the Millennium" by Dr. Philip Lamy.)

BELIEFS AND BELIEVERS
Class 16 – Doctrinal Dimension: Sacred vs. Secular

Introduction

Reflection: *Why do people believe and live by the most extraordinary descriptions of reality? Do people believe religious teachings because they are afraid of life's challenges? On the other hand, the pervasiveness of religions suggests that this is another way of knowing what life wants of us. Why is the everyday world so different from the ideal described in the world religions? From the perspective of the doctrine and ethics, belief and behavior, this is the tension that exists between the sacred and the secular in human experience.*

Throughout history, profoundly religious people have been locked in a struggle with the worldly, the mundane, the profane, the trivial. The ordinary has a way of smothering the extraordinary. Like a re-run from the vastly successful *Seinfeld* television series, we are always on the brink of sinking into the *infinite minutiae of life*. There is such a beautiful symmetry to the everyday pattern of human existence that it is often difficult to persuade people that there is a higher calling. Even the pain that inevitably accompanies life's joyous occasions, pain such as the Buddha identified, still makes more sense to the average person than the lofty visions of a prophet or a mystic.

In this class session, we want to explore how believers use doctrines, beliefs about the sacredness of reality, to create a religious life style that successfully keeps the secular world at bay. One strategy, that of the Old Amish, is to separate religious community from that which is deemed secular. Another, Mormonism, seeks to transform the secular into its own particular sacred story of *the way things really are*. As we examine these two different worldviews, keep in mind our B + B = B equation. The very different patterns of behavior exhibited by the Old Amish and the Mormons have a similar point of generation; rejection of the secular world in favor of the life within a cocoon spun from doctrinal filigree.

Historical Background on the Old Amish:

The Old Amish emerged out of one of the great doctrinal battles of all time – the Protestant Reformation of the 16th century. If you have had a course in European history, you are probably familiar with Reformation leaders such as Martin Luther, John Calvin, and Ulrich Zwingli. At least from the Protestant perspective, these men bravely led a "protest" against what they interpreted as corruption or repression in the Roman Catholic church. None of the reformation leaders orginally meant to form the new branch of Christianity we now call Protestantism. However, their reform efforts eventually cracked the doctrinal mortar holding the Catholic church together, and the stones that tumbled off that great foundation became the familiar Protestant denominations that make up the vast majority of Christian churches in America today.

Yet the "protesting" did not end with the doctrinal reforms initiated by "mainstream" Protestant leaders. The more radical reformers kept right on protesting. For these groups – which came to be called the Anabaptists because of their insistence on adult baptism – the key doctrinal debates were not so much focused on faith, the sacraments, or liturgy, but rather the most significant doctrinal argument concerned the relationship between the church and the state; the sacred and the secular.

Anabaptist groups, also referred to as the European Free-Church family, arose in Germany, Switzerland, and the Netherlands. Like so many "protesters" of that time, Anabaptists were regularly imprisoned and executed. That key function of doctrine, defining who is included and who is excluded in a given religion, as so often is the case, was being used as a weapon to wipe out dissent. Naturally, for believers, this type of sacrifice called for a clear understanding of the doctrinal position delineated by the leaders of the various Anabaptist movements. That position is best articulated in the Schleitheim Confession of 1525. A confession is, in actuality, a clear and concise outline of a given doctrinal position.

After the violent actions of even more radical Anabaptist leaders such as Thomas Muntzer brought the swift sword of restraint down upon the entire movement, Michael Sattler, leader of the Schleitheim Synod in Switzerland, set about to bring all the radicals into one mind on Anabaptist doctrine. Rejecting the state church in which citizenship and church membership were almost the same, the Anabaptists envisioned creating a church of true believers. The Schleitheim Confession set the distinctive doctrinal standard for what would become the worldview of the Old Amish. At the core of this stand is the creation of an impenetrable wall between church and state. Only converted, adult believers could be baptized and only those baptized could take communion. Since they no longer acknowledged the laws of the state, discipline on church members was enforced through the ban, or shunning for sinners. This was a form of excommunication for the fallen who were avoided until they repented their sins and mended their ways. Anabaptists were to separate themselves from the world. Anabaptists would not take part in any form of secular activity which included joining the military and fighting wars, voting, or swearing oaths.

Of course the doctrinal argument over the degree to which a believer should separate from the world continued to smolder throughout the Anabaptist communities. One of the major surviving Anabaptist traditions today, the Mennonites, takes its name from Menno Simons (1496-1561), a key participant in this ongoing discussion. Menno's views were similar to those of other Anabaptists on issues such as rebaptism, separation of church and state, opposition to holding office and taking oaths, and pacifism. However, in order to keep the church free of corrupt sects, he advocated "avoidance" or the shunning of any members who were banned because of aberrant behavior or doctrinal indiscretion. Later this strict disciplinary position of the Mennonites would be set forth in the Dordrecht Confession of 1632.

Jacob Amman, the founder of the Old Amish, embraced the practice of avoidance. He insisted on a strict interpretation of the Dordrecht Confession and appealed to the writings of Menno Simons in support of his position. According to Amman, a member whose spouse was under the ban was neither to sleep nor eat with him or her until the ban was lifted. Ultimately, his uncompromising position on avoidance ended up splitting the Mennonite church, and though Amman did attempt reconciliation with other Mennonites, his efforts failed and the Old Amish sect was born.

Also, in Amman's demand for strict separation of church and state, the quaint customs of today's Amish were instituted. Hooks and eyes were used instead of buttons, bonnets, and aprons. Broad-brimmed hats were the order of the day, and beards and long hair became identifying characteristics of church members. Today, Amish travel by horse and buggy rather than by car and strive in numerous ways to resist the technological culture of modernity. In many ways, a doctrinal battle between the secular and the sacred that began four centuries ago still rages in Amish communities in places like Lancaster County, Pennsylvania, Northern Indiana, Wisconsin, or Eastern Illinois. By their very presence in our secular culture, the Amish remind us just how much true believers are willing to sacrifice in the quest to keep secular and sacred worlds apart.

Historical Background on the Mormons

The Church of Jesus Christ of Latter-day Saints, commonly referred to as the Mormons, had its origins in the remarkable saga of its founder, Joseph Smith (1805-1844). Smith grew up in western New York state during an era of intense religious searching.

Tormented by the conflicting doctrinal statements proclaimed by the myriad revivalist preachers who "burned over" this district of western New York, Smith retired to the woods for prayer and was visited by heavenly personages who told him that all the creeds were corrupt. Shortly thereafter, another celestial visitor, the angel Moroni, directed Smith to the Hill Cumorah where, many centuries before, gold plates containing the *Book of Mormon* were buried. When the hieroglyphics were translated by Smith using two divining stones (Urim and Thumim), a fascinating historical account emerged that not only linked the young American nation with the biblical past but gave its inhabitants the possibility of playing the leading role in the "latter" days of God's great historical drama. For Joseph Smith's revelation called for nothing less than the gathering of "the Saints" and building of Zion – God's kingdom on Earth. Mormons, as the group came to be called, would *restore* the true Christian church on the North American continent.

The *Book of Mormon* relates a sacred history of the pre-Columbian inhabitants of North America. Among other astounding claims, the book explains that the Native American tribes were descendants of the lost tribes of Israel and migrated to this continent many years before the birth of Jesus. After Jesus' resurrection, He came to America to straighten out various doctrines and ritual practices. Eventually, an evil "dark-skinned" tribe wiped out the noble "light-skinned" peoples, but the sacred plates were preserved in the hills of upstate New York until Smith discovered them. Unfortunately, the racist overtones in the story spawned discrimination in the Mormon church. Not until the 1970's were African Americans allowed leadership roles in the church hierarchy.

Nevertheless, Joseph Smith's religious revelation immediately attracted fervent believers – and determined enemies. Settlers were attracted to the Mormon perspective because it injected the arduous pioneering process with divine elixir. A young nation, seemingly relegated to the backyard of civilization, suddenly was at the very heart of the divine plan. On the other hand, the exclusivity and intensity of the Mormons resulted in persecution. Until Brigham Young led "the Saints" to refuge in what would become the state of Utah, Mormons were driven from every settlement they established. Joseph Smith, in fact, died at the hands of a mob in Carthage, Illinois. Today, from their headquarters in Salt Lake City, Utah, Mormons direct a successful, worldwide, religious organization.

While our class discussion focuses on the Latter Day Saints (LDS) Church, it should be noted that several other Mormon groups, not connected to the LDS Church, emerged from the period of fragmentation following Joseph Smith's death. The largest of these surviving Mormon sects, the Reorganized Church of Jesus Christ of Latter Day Saints, maintains a membership of approximately 250,000 adherents and is headquartered in Independence, Missouri.

How New Religions Are Created

In a strange way, the secular world goads religious people into creating new religious expressions. From the perspective of the original founders and followers, the doctrinally defined set of answers to profound life questions is almost always described as a unique and ultimate revelation. Mary Baker Eddy of Christian Science reveals "Christ's true teachings." Mohammed delivers God's final revelation. Joseph Smith restores Christ's true church structure, and the Amish, guided by Jacob Amman, meld belief and behavior in a collective quest to achieve the holy in everyday life.

Why? What is the motivating force? So often it is the struggle people endure in a world without order, meaning, compassion, caring, love, or peace, in other words, the world most of us live in. The *real* answer to this mysterious cultural phenomenon is beyond the scope of this class. However, we can track the process of this ongoing *evolution* of religious expression through a set of *observations* which I call the "Five Ps." In order to create an alternative, new religious expression that tames the secular and brings the sacred back into cultural experience, individually and collectively, five ingredients are needed: a prophet, a promise, a plan, possibility and place. Using this model will help us understand the *beliefs and believers* motivation behind the Old Amish and Mormon *escape from the secular!*

Prophet

On the back of the common American one dollar bill, beneath the pyramid topped by a single staring eye, we find the Latin phrase *novus ordo seclorum*, in English, "a new order of things." Notice the *civil religion* implications! In the world of religion, where does the idea for a *new order of things* come from? Many religions claim that the inspiration to redefine the meaning of human life and recreate human culture comes through Divine revelation. Others say the call emerges from the purified vision of some spiritually evolved human being. Whatever the source may be, we know that the beginnings of all new religious movements require a prophet; a leader who is able to articulate his or her vision in a way that captures the imagination of other human beings and sets them on the path towards remaking the world.

Often prophets are described as *charismatic* leaders in that the power and intensity of their teaching attracts people like iron filings to a magnet. Once attracted these fervent believers radically transform themselves and, as much as possible, society according to the prophet's call for a *new order of things*. Prophets, like Jacob Amman or Joseph Smith, tend to be religiously minded people who find themselves at odds with the established religious institutions and doctrinal expressions of their time. Understandably, the process of challenging a pervasive view of the nature of reality and the meaning of life can lead to enormous tension in society and even persecution of those who advocate a *new order of things*. The story of the Old Amish and the grand saga of the Mormons contain as much violence and death as sublimity and divine exaltation.

Promise

Having met our prophets, we will want to explore what exactly it was they envisioned. What did they promise their believers that in each case prompted such zealous reaction? What did they teach? Jacob Amman promised his 16th century followers *noncomformity* with the secular world. He lived during the tempestuous doctrinal battles of the Protestant Reformation, and carried the *Anabaptist* banner of religious freedom into new doctrinal territory.

Plan

The Mormon *plan* spawned what is perhaps the greatest religious drama in the history of the United States. Joseph Smith was skillfully able to harness a new level of *protest* to the surging energy of a new nation with seemingly illimitable natural resources and untapped potential. Yet almost from the moment that this prophet proclaimed his vision of a restored Christianity on the North American continent, he and his ever-growing group endured constant harassment. They were run out of New York state, then out of Kirkland, Ohio.

Seeking solitude, a peaceful oasis where they might freely practice their religion, they moved to Missouri only to encounter armed resistance to their presence. Many died in what came to be called the "Mormon wars." Hostility drove them back across the Mississippi River to Illinois, where after building the largest city in the state at that time, Nauvoo, Joseph Smith was brutally murdered while being held in the Carthage jail. Yet again, always fulfilling the plan, Mormon men and women headed west, crossing the frozen Mississippi to begin their famous trek under Brigham Young towards a home in what is now called Utah.

The point is that being a Mormon in the 19th century meant being persecuted. And yet the religion never stopped growing, and the believers never gave up the struggle to see Joseph Smith's promise and plan realized in the world around them. Today, Mormonism is one of the fastest growing religious organizations in the world.

Possibility

Possibility may be nothing more than a little luck or it may rest on the Prophet's ability to adroitly handle the cultural exigencies of his or her time. In the case of the Amish, the *protesting spirit* present in 16th century Europe allowed Jacob Amman to convince his followers that radical non-conformity to the world was, indeed, a move towards an authentic Christian life. The eventual move to open frontier spaces of 19th century America allowed for some distance from secular intrusion, and the more liberal and open-minded attitude of Americans towards religious diversity has created a climate, if not optimal, at least conducive to the Amish promise and plan.

Joseph Smith's promise fit the cultural possibilities of his time. Change was in the air. The new nation was possessed of vast resources and endless opportunity in the unknown wilderness to the west. Hope combined with a pulsating anxiety about the destiny of the nation and the part that individual settlers were to play in the developing cultural drama. People were literally starved for a new vision; the possibilities were optimal for the emergence of a new religious movement. The Mormon religion not only answered every doctrinal query that smoldered in the hearts of Christian seekers in upstate New York but, at the same time, defined a divine mandate for the settling of the West.

Place

The struggle between sacred and secular realities is normally played out on secular turf. True, religious peoples have sought solitude in monasteries, rural communes, or even desert islands, but the most basic demands of human existence – food, shelter, clothing – always seem to find their way into the most austere religious setting. To be in the world, a person must deal with the world, no matter how much they wish to block out the essential secularity of meeting life's mundane demands. Establishing place, then, means creating sacred space. The Amish have managed to create sacred space through non-conformity. It is doubtful that such a radical approach to the sacred/secular battle would have survived without the *place* that became the United States of America. Religious tolerance, so hard for human beings to achieve, was built into the cultural infrastructure of the nation through the First Amendment to the United States Constitution which prohibits the establishment of a state supported religion and guarantees free exercise of religion.

Though the journey has not always been easy for the Amish, it has allowed them some respite from secular pressures while providing the opportunity to create sacred space in their rural communities. However, the struggle between sacred space and secular place is an ongoing one. The recent news, mentioned in class, that two young Amish men were arrested for buying cocaine from the Pagan motorcycle gang and distributing it during Amish youth meetings illustrates just how difficult it can be to practice *non-conformity* when the shadow side of secular society is just over the next hilltop. The movie, "Witness," with Harrison Ford, provides a stirring and accurate presentation of secular/sacred tension in Amish culture, and is highly recommended as background material for this class session.

The Mormons literally fought bloody battles in their quest to establish sacred space. Again, the vastness of the 19th century American West finally gave the Mormons what they needed – a place far enough away from doubters and detractors so that the religion could take root and grow. That place, of course, was Utah. Had most of the Mormons not followed Brigham Young out to the solitude of the American west, it is doubtful that the religion would have survived another generation. But in that critical period, the second generation, when most new religious movements either live or die, Utah became the place where the prophet's promise and plan could be realized.

Class 16

Key Class Themes

This class focuses on the following themes:

1. Sacred/secular tension
2. Old Amish response to the secular world
3. Mormon response to the secular world
4. The role of doctrine and ethics in human belief systems

Videotape Synopsis

- Class discussion
- Amish roll-in
- Interview with Elder Andrus
- Class discussion

Videotape Commentary

I suggest you read this section before you watch the videotape. You will find that it will help you organize your thoughts so that when you watch the tape it will be more meaningful. When you have finished viewing the tape, you may want to read this section again.

Fasten your seat beats and hold on to your hats! Our class discussion today is a wild roller coaster ride over the bumpy terrain of belief and behavior. And how could it not be? Sacred vs. secular tension always raises a challenge to Americans who, person for person, are one of the most religious people in the world yet live in a society that *constitutionally* separates church from state. While the remarkable cultural vision embodied in the First Amendment to the United States Constitution has created an atmosphere of religious freedom, it has never been easy for individual Americans to fully separate their deeply held religious feelings from the political process or the social structure of daily life. Consequently, I think people are actually *envious* of religious groups that manage to keep the sacred at the center of their daily lives and, by doing so, fend off the encroachment of secularism. Is it possible that we suffer from *Amish envy*?

I admit to purposely picking the Amish and the Mormons to highlight our investigation of sacred vs. secular tension in the doctrinal dimension. After years of teaching religious studies classes or giving lectures at some public gathering, I have found these two worldviews to be predictable catalysts to heated debate. In many ways, the discussion in today's class becomes *data*, illustrating just how real and how frustrating sacred vs secular tension can be. As you listen to the student's questions and comments, notice how tension rises in the classroom. Predictably, the conversation begins with "What about...?" questions. Jamie, our class professional photographer, questions why the Amish prohibit the taking of photographs. Annette wonders whether or not they are required to pay property tax on their extensive farmland. (Indeed, the Amish pay property tax like everyone else.) Karen, a nurse, asks if they rely on the medical establishment when serious illness or accidents break through their sacred cocoon. Barbara even seems to suggest that the "Amish" people seen in major tourist areas in northern Indiana or Lancaster County, Pennsylvania are just actors!

As the temperature rises in the classroom, the central issue seems to be *compromise*. How much compromise should a sacred people make in order to survive in a secular society? Like many of our students, the outside visitor to Amish country cannot help but notice a thousand strange little compromises the Amish seem to make with the modern world. For example, they want to avoid pesky visitors with their probing cameras, yet the country roads that connect their successful farms are dotted with signs advertising canned meats and vegetables, honey, pure-bred puppies, funiture and cabinets. They will ride in cars but refuse to drive or apply for a drivers license. They would never own a combine but are willing to let a non-Amish neighbor harvest their crops with a combine harvester.

But if the Amish, from time to time, strike a bargain with the secular world, and if their customs sometimes seem quaint or even silly, it is a bargain that has allowed them to preserve Amish culture. They might turn around and ask the "English," the term they use for anyone outside their group, what do your secular beliefs bring you? You shut your aging parents out of your homes, leave the towns and families you love to take jobs you hate, create political systems that exploit and oppress and produce weapons of mass destruction. While the Amish practice organic farming, the secular world supports a mega-agri-business that has consistently used chemical poisons that pollute the very land that gives forth sustenance. No wonder those of us on the "outside" suffer from *Amish envy!*

Several students noted that the Amish can be included in the *peace churches*, and in that conversation, comparisons with the Quakers (The Friends) arose. For the sake of clarity, it will be helpful to sort out some of the similarities and differences. Dr. J. Gordon Melton, author of the *Encyclopedia of American Religions*, clearly places the Quakers in the Free-Church family. Like the Amish, the Quakers took a strong stand against violence and war, embraced a simple, sacred livestyle based on biblical precepts, dressed conservatively, and avoided worldly distractions such as holidays, entertainment, and sports.

However, there are several significant differences. Rather than emanating from the European continent, Quakerism was founded in England by the mystic, psychic, and social activist, George Fox (1624-1691). For the Quakers, the baptism issue, so important to the Anabaptists, was resolved by doing away with water baptism altogether. Quakers believe in an "inner baptism" of the Holy Spirit. In general, on issues of faith, Quakers place spiritual experience over religious doctrine. Unlike other Free Church groups, women enjoyed the right of full participation in church activities and were accepted into the ministry earlier than most churches. While a *peace church*, Quakers became intensely involved in the political process as social activists for human rights and world peace.

While the Amish separate themselves from the secular world by constructing a doctrinal wall, the Mormons take another path. Mormons wish to transform secular culture or at least bring the spiritual insights they cherish to the attention of others. Few of us have missed young Mormon missionaries knocking on our door to share the faith. However, sacralizing the secular is never an easy process. As you listen to our interview with Elder Andrus at the restored Nauvoo site, see if you can detect the nature of the sacred vs. secular challenge for the Mormons. How do think the Mormons will wage the battle between the secular and the sacred in the future?

Doctrinal Battle: Polygamy

As Elder Andrus clearly states in our interview, polygamy, the practice of men having more than one wife, has been abolished in the mainstream Latter Day Saints (LDS) church ever since then Mormon President William Woodruff outlawed the practice in 1890. However, quite recent studies show that this original Mormon doctrine is still practiced by tens of thousands of Mormon fundamentalists scattered about the West in remote communes or in Salt Lake City. In fact, as mentioned in class, a recent *Chicago Tribune* article describes a women-led group called *Tapestry of Polygamy* that attempts to help Mormon women escape the trials and tribulations that may accompany the polygamous experience.

We are not focusing on polygamy to put the Mormon religion in a bad light or to gratuitously bring up controversy for the sake of sensationalism. Rather, the fact that polygamous Mormon sects still exist, clearly in violation of civil law, illustrates the ongoing tension between sacred and secular perspectives within this "made in America" religion. During his most theologically creative period while guiding the extraordinarily successful Nauvoo venture, Joseph Smith "received" a divine revelation that convinced him that polygamy was an appropriate model for his community. Biblical figures such as Abraham and Jacob were polygamous, and, combined with the Mormon doctrine that spirits are waiting to enter our world and prevented from reaching higher planes until they do so, it became the duty of every Mormon to bring as many children into the world as possible.

Put simply, polygamous Mormons today believe that the mainstream church erred in capitulating to secular pressures to abolish the practice. Indeed, in 1890, Woodruff abolished the practice only after the United States army threatened to invade the Utah settlement. If Smith's revelation were truly the word of God, then Woodruff's was not. Misguided or not, most polygamous Mormon believers are *behaving* in that fashion because they wish to maintain a sacred lifestyle, and, in doing so, keep the secular world at bay.

Videotape Graphics

At this stage we suggest you watch the videotape. Due to the lively class discussion, graphics not seen on the videotape are included below.

The Latter Day Saint Churches (Mormons)

Prophet

Joseph Smith, Jr. (1805– 1844)
Classic seeker, then charismatic leader
of the Mormon Church

The Latter Day Saint Churches (Mormons)

Promise

The "divine personage," Moroni, guides Smith
to ancient, gold plates on which the Book of
Mormon is engraved; published in March 1830

The Latter Day Saint Churches (Mormons)

Plan

RESTORATION of the "true Christian church"
in the "latter days" of God's great historical drama

The Latter Day Saint Churches (Mormons)

Possibility

– links (new covenant) the new American
  nation with the biblical past
– American citizens, as Mormons, are called
  to play the leading role in building God's
  kingdom on the American frontier
– combines millennial fervor with frontier
  spirit = powerful set of ideas

> **The Latter Day Saint Churches (Mormons)**
>
> *Place*
>
> – Latter Day Saints
>   Nauvoo, Utah, worldwide = 8,000,000 members
> – Reorganized Church
>   Independence, Missouri; followed Joseph
>   Smith III; 250,000 members

Review Questions

Answering the following questions will help you review key class themes and prepare for examinations.

1. What are the historic roots of the Old Amish? What is their primary response to the secular world?

2. In your opinion, is it selfish for Amish parents to deny their children the educational advantages of our society?

3. What are the Five Ps of alternative religions? Illustrate each of them with examples from the early Mormon movement.

4. Do you think polygamous Mormons should be permitted by law to practice plural marriage?

Sources and Further Readings

Arrington, Leonard and Davis Britton. *The Mormon Experience*. NY: Alfred A. Knopf, 1979.

Hostetler, John A. *Amish Life*. Scottsdale, PA: Herald Press, 1959.

Kloehn, Steve. "Mormon Women Uniting to Help 'Sisters-wives' Escape Polygamy." *Chicago Tribune*. Sunday, June 28, 1998.

Melton, J. Gordon. *Encyclopedia of American Religions*, 3rd Edition. Detroit: Gale Research, 1989. (See chapters on Mormonism and the European Free Church).

Miller, Timothy, ed. *America's Alternative Religions*. NY: SUNY, 1995. (See chapters on The Anabaptists and Latter Day Saints Churches).

BELIEFS AND BELIEVERS
Class 17 – Doctrinal Dimension: Islam, Part One

Introduction

Reflection: *If you are a citizen of the United States or its allies, you probably have been bombarded by negative media images of Muslims and the Islamic faith. In itself, this is an important worldview analysis lesson. If there are political tensions between two competing cultures, in this case the predominantly Christian industrial West and the oil-rich Muslim Middle East, the best way to denigrate your combatant is to attack their religiopolitical infrastructure. So the average American envisions a Muslim as either a romantic, incredibly wealthy Arab sheik or a religious fanatic, a terrorist ready to kill innocent people in the name of Islam.*

To some extent, there is truth in all stereotypes. However, more than 900 million of the world's population are Muslim and only a minority are Arabs, much less the stereotypical wandering desert dwellers out of Disney's "Aladdin." Actually, the majority of Muslims live in Indonesia, but we find Muslim farmers in Pakistan; Muslim businessmen in Turkey, Iran or France; Muslim herdsmen in sub-Saharan Africa and Muslims among prominent business, religious and political leaders in the United States. In fact, Islam embraces most of the world's cultures, a truly international religion. As you view this lesson and the next, put your worldview analysis skills to the test. Set aside any negative presuppositions you might be harboring about Islam and try to see the beauty, power and authenticity of this major world religion.

We have been discussing the tension between the sacred and the secular. This class begins with a provocative comparison of Joseph Smith, founder of the Mormon religion, and Muhammad, the prophet who received the divine revelations that became Islam. Though approximately 13 centuries separate the two, not to mention custom, culture and geography, both religious leaders have something to tell us about the inseparable relationship between the *doctrinal, ethical* and *social dimensions.*

Both men were energized by an overwhelming need to know God and to understand how God wished human beings to live. Both received, through divine revelation from angelic beings, specific doctrines that explained the relationship between God and humans in terms of ethical demands and the building of a just and holy community. Both men transmitted this divine guidance to their faithful followers in a holy book. Thus, when we look at these two worldviews, Islam, the enormously successful world faith and Mormonism, perhaps the next major world religion, we see religious *doctrines* defining *ethical* behavior which, in turn, undergirds a holy, sacred community.

In fact, what may be the model or paradigm for success that is shared by these two otherwise diverse worldviews is the ability to overcome the sacred versus secular tension. The potent dimensional mixture of doctrine and ethics in each case creates a *social dimension* that is essentially sacred. The secular becomes *sacralized* as all of life's activities, from the most trivial to the most profound, are conducted according to divine command. In this religious system, ideally, everything is holy.

Of course the secular may scurry under the rug like a wounded rat in Iran or in 19th century Utah. But what happens to these sacred worldviews in a predominantly secular setting, like the United States, or a secular setting where there is, nonetheless, fierce competition between faiths, as in Israel? One of the reasons we are focusing on Islam in this class is to explore what happens to this *dimensional symmetry* when the religion is practiced in a religiously diverse, secular society characteristic of the United States and Israel. Our visits with Dr. Aasi at the American Islamic College, Chicago, with a Muslim family in Cana, Israel, and a Sufi sheik in Nazareth afford us the opportunity to meet real *believers* who will help us sort out this important relationship between *doctrine, ethic,* and the *social dimension*. The following short summary of key elements in Islam put into our dimensional framework may be useful as we journey through the world of Muslim believers.

Doctrinal Dimension

At the heart of Muslim faith is Allah, the creator and sustainer of the universe. God is supreme and He is one. He alone exists absolutely; everything else exists only according to His will. The will of God is revealed in the holy Koran (Qur'an) given to the prophet Muhammad by the angel Gabriel. Muhammad is the last of a long line of prophets, *the seal of the Prophets*, extending from Abraham to Muhammad. It is important to note that, unlike Jesus for Christians, Muhammad in no way shares in God's divinity. Only God is God in Islam. For Muslims, Moses was a prophet as was Jesus; both are revered. God also spoke to Moses and Jesus but, according to Islamic doctrine, Jews and Christians garbled the divine message. He then decided to speak one last time. Thus, in the Qur'an we find the final, complete, unalterable word of God. Having defined *identity* and guided *relationship once and for all*, He will not speak again.

Ethical Dimension

Human beings are to submit to the will of Allah. The word "Islam," in fact, means something like "submission" in Arabic. Islam presents a complete guide to the holy life, defining God's relation to human beings and presenting ethical codes, most noticeably present in *The Five Pillars of Islam*, which guide human relationships. The Islamic law, known as *Shari'ah*, is derived from four main sources: a) the Qur'an, which Muslims believe has existed eternally in heaven; b) the *sunna* or the countless traditions of what the Prophet Muhammad did or said; c) the *ijma* or consensus of the Muslim community or its leading scholars; d) *qiyas* or deductions, through analogy, from the first three sources. Thus, *Shari'ah*, across time and culture, has been able to cover every situation in the human social arena including family concerns, business, education, criminal law and so on. Though rights may vary with men and women, obedience to God's law should lead to the recognition of human equality and the establishment of a just and fair society. One of the appeals of Islam for African Americans is equality before God regardless of color or place of origin.

Social Dimension

As we have already mentioned, Islamic doctrines and ethical practices work together to make Islamic society. Consider, for example, the Iranian revolution in the late 1970s. The driving force behind it was the desire to re-establish authentic Islamic society in a country that, under the Shah who was supported by the "satanic United States," had turned to secular values. During our trip to Israel the United States and Iraq were once again on the brink of a "one-sided, missile-tossing contest." Over and over again, we heard from Muslims in Israel that, while they had no great love for Saddam Hussein, the real enemy was Western secularization because it presents such a threat to the Islamic way of life.

The *Umma*, or total community of Muslims, is a society not unlike orthodox Jewish society that moves, lives, and breathes according to Islamic doctrinal and ethical precepts. We might say that the *Five Pillars of Islam*, also known as the Five Articles of the Islamic Faith, hold up Islamic society. They are identified in our class discussion, but quickly for review, they are: a) the profession of faith that Allah is God and Muhammad is his Prophet; b) performance of the five daily prayers; c) giving of alms which amounts to the payment of a religious tithe called Zahat; d) fasting from dawn to dusk during the ninth month of the lunar calendar called Ramadan; e) the *haji*, going on a pilgrimage to the holy city of Mecca once in a Muslim's lifetime. In the Five Pillars, we can detect a fascinating process whereby society is bound together on a daily, monthly, yearly and generational basis. Once again, we observe a cyclical pattern designed to turn the mundane, the secular, into the sacred.

Key Class Themes

This lesson focuses on the following themes:

1. Doctrine/ethics/society connection in Islam
2. Secular versus Sacred tension in Islam
3. The Five Pillars of Islam
4. Islam in the United States and the Middle East

Videotape Synopsis

- Class discussion
- Video interview with Dr. Aasi at the American Islamic College, Chicago
- Dome of the Rock video
- Video interview with Muslim family in Cana, Israel
- Video interview with Sufi sheik in Nazareth, Israel

Videotape Commentary

I suggest you read this section before you watch the videotape. You will find that it will help you organize your thoughts so that when you watch the tape it will be more meaningful. When you have finished viewing the tape, you may want to read this section again.

Classroom Discussion

Though Islam is the subject for today, we open the class with a more general discussion of " 'Beliefs and Believers' sightings." At this point in the development of *worldview analysis skills*, students really begin to notice the pervasiveness of religion and religious ideas in our shared daily experience. I like to call these observations "'Beliefs and Believers' sightings." As we've mentioned several times already this semester, one of the most troublesome misconceptions about religion, at least in the United States, is that religion is a private affair that rarely impacts on the social dimension. That is why people are so *shocked* when extreme acts motivated by religion explode on the scene like a brush fire in California. Because religion deals with the most fundamental aspects of human existence, it has been, is, and always will be a primary motivator for human behavior. Though secular humanists might argue otherwise, the notion of a completely secular society is a human impossibility. Once you become *attuned* to religious activity, the blinders are lifted, and you begin to notice how large a role religion plays in shaping our individual and collective lives. As you listen to the student's stories, you might want to jot down one or two of your own recent "'Beliefs and Believers' sightings."

With no prompting from me, Virginia says that she is beginning to see "religious things" everywhere, from comics in *The New Yorker* magazine to bumper stickers and road-side billboards. Margaret pulls out a copy of *The Wall Street Journal*, bastion of secular economic supremacy, and reads a bit of a heart-warming story about a terminally ill woman who asks her doctor to pray with her. The doctor thoroughly enjoys the experience and ends up wondering why he has never prayed with his patients before.

As the field of medicine became more *scientific* in the latter years of the 19th century, doctors went out of their way to establish secular boundaries. Healing was to be conducted apart from the unscientific, non-rational claims of religious superstition. As we move into the 21st century, how interesting it is that more and more doctors are shedding their secular skin and openly embracing human spirituality as an effective catalyst towards healing physical and emotional woes.

Jo Ann's account of her experience in witnessing a terrible traffic accident involving two trucks underscores another key class theme. Ego, the illusion that we lead separate, unconnected lives, keeps us apart, makes us feel less than we are, contributes to an oppressive sense of alienation and loneliness, and generally limits our existence. All the world's religions, in one way or another, work to divest us of this self-limiting perception. In one of life's eternal ironies, it is often tragedy that cracks the encrusted layer of ego-consciousness and forces us to deal with other human beings, usually strangers, in a genuinely caring and compassionate manner. That uplifting experience, which is essentially spiritual in nature, is exactly what Jo Ann describes when she and her daughter, along with many other "strangers," saved the lives of the people involved in the truck accident. Answers to the profound questions of life, our *boundary questions*, can of course be found by attending a religious organization. But life, itself, is a great teacher. If you're attuned to the *pervasiveness of religion*, "church" is just as likely to happen to you on a highway returning home after a dinner in Peoria as any place else in the world.

Moving on to our exploration with Islam, the students do an excellent job of creating an atmosphere of appreciation for religious diversity. As we move through our various video interviews, especially the interview with Dr. Aasi in which he explains the *Five Pillars of Islam*, notice how the general tone of the in-class discussion resonates with an openness towards accepting the traditions, ritual practices, and holidays of Muslims in America. In fact, Islam is one of the fastest growing religions in the United States, recently overtaking Judaism as the "number two" world faith in this country. So there are practical reasons for coming to an understanding and appreciation for Islam. Your next door neighbor, boss, golf partner, or school board member may turn out to be a Muslim. Please pay particular attention to the discussion involving fasting (going without food or water) from dawn to dusk during the holy month of Ramadan. The students relate a number of "down to earth" experiences in their own interaction with Muslim friends and associates during Ramadan.

Towards the end of the class, Mary nicely sums up our brief encounter with Islam. She describes her Muslim neighbors as the most gracious, hospitable people she had ever met. Once again, the key to successful "moccasin-walking" is to set aside media-generated stereotypes, resist the temptation to label people and stick them in some cognitive cubbyhole, and meet other human beings face-to-face on the playing field of life. When interacting with a person from a different religious tradition, it is always helpful to recall one of our key "Beliefs and Believers" axioms, suitable for needle-point wall-hangings; "It is not the religion that defines the person; it is the person that defines the religion." Now on to our interviews.

Interview with Dr. Aasi at the American Islamic College

Recently, Islam surpassed Judaism as the "number two" faith in the United States. Islam is growing in this country, and the American Islamic College is typical of the institutional expression of Islamic expansion. The American Islamic College is a four year liberal arts college, opened in 1983, which combines religious instruction (in Islam, of course) with a fully-balanced educational program. Students living on campus have the opportunity to pursue an education in an Islamic environment much as Roman Catholic students would experience a Catholic environment at Notre Dame. The cafeteria serves food made according to dietary requirements of Islam, and regular worship is an important part of campus life. We arrived just as the *muezzin* was calling the students and other community members to noon prayers.

The very fact of the college's existence tells us something about the changes in the religious demographics of the United States. The college edifice previously served as a Catholic girls school. With the move of Catholics to the suburbs and the increase in the Muslim population in the Chicago area, the building has been transformed into Muslim educational and sacred space.

Dr. Aasi does an excellent job of explaining the Five Pillars of Islam and providing us with a *believer's* insight into various ritual aspects of daily prayers. From our perspective, we might say that the first *pillar*, the call to proclaim one's faith in Allah and His Prophet, Muhammad, acts like a *doctrinal power-center* which then drives the other four *pillars*. The first pillar concerns foundational *belief*. The subsequent four pillars are *ethically-grounded*. In other words, once a believer declares his or her faith in Allah, certain *proper patterns of action* are required to demonstrate this faith. Note that praying five times a day, giving alms to the poor, fasting during the month of Ramadan, and making a pilgrimage to Mecca are all types of *behavior*. When you consider that almost a billion Muslims are following the same ethical *patterns of action*, the impact on the Islamic *social dimension* is obvious. What genius to have all the Muslims all over the world facing the same direction when they pray! Once again, the Five Pillars of Islam, as described by Dr. Aasi, offer us a wonderful window into the dynamic relationship of the *doctrinal, ethical* and *social dimensions*.

El Aqsa Mosque and Dome of the Rock Roll-in

As anyone knows who has visited the Holy City in Jerusalem, secular versus sacred tension is palpable. When you have three of the world's great religions – Judaism, Christianity and Islam – struggling to share the same sacred space, it is like a close family celebrating a holiday meal; a collision of myths is inevitable. It took us at least two hours to get permission to even enter the sacred Muslim ground of the Temple Mount. As we were negotiating with guards and Muslim officials who are keen to protect their sacred space from any form of desecration, the police dragged a young Jew out of the Muslim area, who had supposedly been taunting the Muslims. Ultra-Orthodox Jews believe that the Dome of the Rock and El Aqsa mosque should be torn down and the Jewish Temple rebuilt in order to initiate the *messianic event*, that is, the coming of the promised messiah. Even some conservative Christians find common cause with Jews on this potentially disastrous agenda, believing that a re-constructed Temple is a necessary step for the end-time events leading to Jesus' Second Coming.

In any event, we were finally allowed into the sacred area, but with minimal video-taping rights. Nevertheless, this short visual piece affords us the opportunity to visualize the relationship between the mythic, ritual and doctrinal dimensions. According to the grand mythic saga in Islam, the *rock* is the spot where Muhammad, after taking a whirlwind night journey on his winged horse Buraq, ascended into the seventh heaven. On his way, he confided with great prophets such as Moses, Abraham and Jesus. The *five daily prayers*, the heart of the ritual dimension, were revealed to Muhammad on this journey.

The Temple Mount is graced with two of the most beautiful and sacred structures in all of Islam: the El Aqsa mosque and one of the wonders of the modern world, The Dome of the Rock. To enter these sacred shrines is to be overwhelmed by two of Islam's foundational doctrines: Allah is one and His creation is beautiful. The typical architecture of the mosque was originally inspired by the Arab house with its large courtyards and cool inner spaces. The courtyard will usually contain water for ablutions before prayer and is a favorite meeting place of the community. A feature that first attracts the attention of visitors to the Islamic world is the minaret, the high tower from which the muezzin calls the faithful to prayer five times a day. Atop the tower is usually found the star and crescent moon, the symbol of Islam, which according to the myth, lit the Prophet's way on his journey from Mecca to Medina.

Class 17

Inside the mosque, the austerity and majesty of Islam and its God, Allah, are strikingly evident. Unlike other faiths, the Islamic tendency in decoration is to avoid visual representations of God's creation, including human and animal forms. Geometric abstractions are the preferred form of sacred art in Islam. These designs express the perfection and beauty of Allah as well as celebrate the fact that he transcends His creation. Calligraphy, highlighting passages from the Qur'an, grace the walls, and elaborate Arabesque tile and grillwork speak of a beauty in life that can only be experienced through submission to Allah. For the devotee Muslim, Allah is the source of beauty, the world created by Him is beautiful, and the ritual activity that takes place in mosques around the world nurtures the believer's awareness and appreciation of this beauty.

Whether it serves as a sacred shrine for all of Islam or is simply the local community mosque, these sacred structures provide Muslim communities with their sacred center, guiding all other aspects of Islamic life. At El Aqsa, Muhammad learned, through divine revelation, to pray five times a day. And so, to this day, this central ritual activity, inspired by myth and guided by doctrine defines identity and relationship in the Muslim world.

Muslim Family in Cana, Israel

Having had a glimpse of how the *Five Pillars* work amongst the Muslims in a major metropolitan area of the United States, we turn to "small town" Israel for a look at the relationship between the *doctrinal, ethical* and *social dimensions* as it plays out in the everyday lives of Arabs living in a Jewish state. Later in the semester when we explore ethical conflicts in the Middle East, we will focus on the struggle Muslims endure in maintaining the integrity of their faith in the midst of an often hostile social environment.

In this class, we simply want to absorb the Muslim life as it is defined by the *doctrinal* and *ethical* dimensions. A wonderful Muslim family invited the entire video crew into their home for dinner, friendship and cultural exchange. We, in turn, would like to invite you to listen to their explanation of how Islam defines and delineates every aspect of their daily lives. Enjoy!

Sufi Sheik in Nazareth, Israel

This short interview must stand as one of the most remarkable video excursions in the entire teleclass. We have been focusing on the outward dimensional thrust of Islam, but what of the *experiential dimension*? The history of Islam includes another path, perhaps an inevitable tributary from the flowing river of submission to Allah. To love Allah is to *be Allah*. This is the mystical path in Islam, the *Sufi path*.

Sufism began as an experience of oneness with Allah. Sufi groups would gather to cultivate the deeply mystical experience of the presence of God, and it was not surprising that mainstream Islam resisted such radical ideas. From our study of religious experience, it would be fair to say that the Sufi experience began as a *numinous* experience leading towards *theist mysticism*. Through meditation, ascetic practices, dance, song and poetry, Sufis experience a loss of ego and the accompanying union with the divine. Sufis believe their mystical path is grounded in the inner experience of the Prophet, Muhammad, who clearly prayed deeply and knew God intimately. If God is all, and God is everywhere, then the Sufi *experientially* participated in this *oneness*. The path of Muhammad, for the Sufi, is the eternal path of all wise seekers in all generations and in all religious expressions.

One famous Sufi, al-Hallaj, had taken Jesus, son of God, as his exemplar of inward mysticism. In public, he proclaimed, "I am the Truth." Truth is an attribute of Allah, and for his heresy, in 922 c.e., he suffered the same fate as Jesus – crucifixion. However, these "friends of God," as the Sufis called themselves, were simply too valuable to be sacrificed by mainstream Islam. The great philosopher, al-Ghazali, constructed a potent defense of Sufism. In particular, he pointed out that the ultimate Sufi experience, ecstatic love of God, rendered the believer "intoxicated," and statements about oneness with Allah should not be taken literally. In any event, Sufism has survived in Islam, and we are most fortunate to have the opportunity to hear the words of a real life Sufi atop a building in Nazareth, Israel.

Videotape Graphics

At this stage we suggest you watch the videotape. The graphics you will see on the screen are reproduced below to save you the trouble of copying them down. You might like to add your own comments as you watch the tape.

Islam

Identity

"God (Allah) is great! God is great!
There is no god but God, and Muhammad
is his prophet!"

Islam

Relationship

Islam = "submission" = Muslims believe
in total submission to the will of Allah (The God)

Koran (Qur'an) = sacred text; God's will for
humanity revealed to Muhammad

Shirk = idolatry, putting anything else in the
place of Allah; ultimate sin in Islam

Umma = the whole Muslim community

Islam

Relationship

Sharí'a = Islamic law

Salat = prayer, 5 times a day

Zakat = giving "alms" to the poor

Suam = fasting during Ramadan

Hajj = pilgrimage to Mecca

Jihad = struggle for Islam; spiritual striving

Sunna = the body of established Islamic faith,
morals, and practice established by consensus
  – Sunni Islam
  – Shi'a Islam (leadership by Imams)
  – Sufism = the mystical tradition

Class 17

> **Islam**
>
> *The Five Pillars of Islam*
> Religious doctrine defining ethical behavior;
> impacts on the social dimension

> **Islam**
> 1. Profession of Faith = Allah is God Above all
>   and Muhammad is His Prophet
> 2. Prayer five times a day
> 3. Almsgiving/charity for the poor
> 4. Fasting during the Holy Month of Ramadan
> 5. Pilgrimage to Mecca (The Hajj)

> **Sufism in Islam**
>
> Sufism = the mystical tradition
> Suf = the coarse wool worn by ascetics

> **Sufism in Islam**
>
> Sufi practice = meditation, spiritual practices,
> and love for God can lead to a mystical union
> with the devine
>
> Sufis become "God intoxicated"
> – leads to ecstatic experiences

> **Sufism in Islam**
>
> *al-Hallaj*
> executed in 922 c.e. for declaring, "I am God!"
> *al-Ghazali* (1058-1111)
> provides philosophical defense of Sufism;
> legitimizes the practice in Islam

Review Questions

Answering the following questions will help you review key class themes and prepare
for the examinations.

1. What parallels can we discern between Joseph Smith, the founder of Mormonism,
   and Muhammad the Prophet who revealed Islam to the world? What are some of
   the differences?

2. Describe the inter-relationship of the *doctrinal, ethical* and *social dimensions* in Islam.

3. What are the Five Pillars of Islam? How do they illustrate the relationship between the *doctrinal, ethical* and *social dimensions* in Islam?

4. What is *Sufism*, and why might the Sufi perspective be offensive to the traditional, orthodox Muslim?

Class 17

Sources and Further Readings

Geetz, Clifford. *Islam Observed*. New Haven, CN: Yale University Press, 1968.

Martin, Richard. *Islam: A Cultural Perspective*. Englewood Cliffs, NJ: Prentice Hall, 1982.

Porterfield, Amanda. *The Power of Religion*. NY: Oxford, 1998. (See chapters on Islam)

Rahman, Fazlur. *Islam*. second ed., Chicago: University of Chicago, 1979.

Smart, Ninian. *The World's Religions*. Englewood Cliffs, NJ: Prentice Hall, 1989.

BELIEFS AND BELIEVERS
Class 18 – Doctrinal Dimension: African American Islam

Introduction

Reflection: *As we discovered in the previous class session, Islam presents its believers with a unified worldview guided by Divine Will as revealed in the holy Qur'an. Certainly the power of the doctrinal dimension and its effect on the ethical and social dimensions are obvious. But what happens when a group takes these doctrines and reinterprets them according to their particular social/cultural situation? This is exactly what happened in the case of African American Islam in America, particularly in its manifestation as the Nation of Islam. During this fascinating class session, reflect on what the African American experience of Islam tells us about the dynamics of worldviews in general and the relationship between the doctrinal, ethical, and social dimensions.*

The following session on African American Islam is one of the most entertaining and provocative in the entire course. Most of the credit goes to our articulate guest, Imam W. Deen Mohammed, one of the most influential religious leaders in the African American Muslim movement today. We also have a roll-in interview with an eloquent spokesperson, Dr. Abdul Salaam, at the Al-Faatir mosque in Chicago. Before we analyze these interviews and accompanying discussion, it will be helpful for you to have some historical background on the Black Muslim movement in America.

Right at the start, we should note that there are many different Muslim groups functioning in African-American communities in the United States. If, as we discuss in class, *identity* is about s*elf-esteem* and *relationship* is about *empowerment* in the religiopolitical experience of African-Americans in the United States, then the simple matter of "labeling" religious or cultural activity becomes problematic. Naturally, African Americans are sensitive about labels that tend to perpetuate racist attitudes and undermine their quest for self-esteem and empowerment. What a person is "called" impacts on his or her self-understanding. Thus we have moved from using the term *colored people* to *Negro* to *Black* to *African American* to *people of color* in describing American citizens with African roots who typically ended up in North America as part of the slave experience of the 18th and 19th centuries.

Having acknowledged this ever-present *labeling problem* when we use the term "Black Muslim," we are referring to the Nation of Islam, founded by Master Wallace Fard Muhammad (known variously as Wallace D. Fard, Farrad Mohammad, or Wali Farrad) and led for many years by Elijah Muhammad (1897-1975). Without a doubt, this group has been the most successful of the *Black Muslim* movements in America.

The early history of the organization is somewhat sketchy. A mysterious peddler by the name of Wallace D. Fard (Wali Farrad) emerged in Detroit around 1930. Thought to be of Arab extraction, he won the confidence of his listeners by proclaiming that he taught the *true religion* for African Americans. Fard and his followers rented a hall, named it the Temple of Islam and the movement known as the *Black Muslims* had begun. He taught a life of self-discipline and family solidarity that *empowered* African Americans when racist oppression was their daily fare.

W.D. Fard soon dropped out of sight, but his chief minister, Elijah Poole, renamed Elijah Muhammad, became the leader of the second temple in Chicago. He claimed, like Muhammad, that he was a Prophet who would lead his people out of bondage. The voice of Allah was thought to speak through Elijah Muhammad, regardless of the key Muslim doctrine that Muhammad, 13 centuries earlier, was God's final spiritual conduit. Under his direction, the Black Muslims developed into a cohesive religious movement.

One of the questions that arises with respect to the Black Muslims concerns the nature of the Islamic religion they claimed to embrace. While African Americans really had little contact with worldwide Islam, it was true that quite a number of slaves had been Muslim. In addition, many African Americans equated Christianity with their white oppressors and, thus, could not feel entirely comfortable in that worldview. Our guest, Abdul Salaam, tells a story of growing up in Alabama in the 1940s. Churches were segregated, and at 11 a.m. on a given Sunday morning, his first vision upon entering the local black church, was a picture of a blonde, Caucasian Jesus. Under the picture was an inscription, "Jesus Christ, My Lord and Savior." Down the road, white people were gathering in their own churches, and it wasn't a rare occasion in that time and place, that a black person in his community was beaten or lynched by a white mob. Yet he had to look up at a *white savior* when entering into the place of his communion with God. In his understandably self-protective, wry humor, Dr. Salaam remarked, "If we ever do get to heaven, the white folk will have us sweeping them golden streets!" See how *self-esteem* and *empowerment* are, inevitably, catalysts in the Black Muslim movement.

This explains why Elijah Muhammad's teachings exhibited a kind of *reverse-racism*. Mythically, he needed to cut down the Caucasian cultural *hegemony* in order to uplift the black community. If Elijah Muhammad's doctrines were those of the Islamic faith, then to be sure, he had taken some unorthodox twists and turns. He taught that human beings were originally black, but a mad scientist, Yakub, created an evil race of white devils. The whites were allowed by Allah to rule for 6,000 years, after which civilization would collapse in chaos and a new world order would emerge governed by blacks. The year World War I began, 1914, signified the end of white rule; the 20th century would be the time in which blacks would regroup and regain control.

Elijah Muhammad taught that not only should blacks separate themselves from whites, they should also purify their minds. Schools and other educational institutions became an important, positive focus of the movement. Members were to abstain from alcohol, tobacco and drugs, pork, movies and cosmetics. Economically, the movement stressed work ethic and business development, so that blacks could control their own economic destiny apart from whites. Politically, the Muslims aspired towards a black nation on the North American continent – a *Nation of Islam*. Whites, of course, were excluded from the movement.

Beyond a cursory mixture of Islamic terminology, custom and ritual practices, there was little else in the Nation of Islam that reflected traditional Islamic teachings. But that hardly mattered to oppressed African Americans who longed for a spiritual vision that would boost self-esteem and deliver empowerment. Under Elijah Muhammad, the Black Muslims instituted a far-reaching evangelizing effort, and by the time of the leader's death in 1975, there were approximately 100,000 adherents in 70 temples across the nation.

Of course nothing comes easily in the world of religion. Other African American Muslims resented the Nation of Islam for its success and criticized the movement's departure from orthodox Islam. Occasionally this tension led to violence, which was the case in the death of the group's most articulate spokesperson, Malcolm X (1925-65). In the increasing racial tensions of the 1960s, Malcolm X struck fear in the heart of the white establishment with his powerful oratory calling for blacks to use violence in order to further the vision of a black nation. At one point, he seemed to be the alter-ego to Martin Luther King Jr., rejecting that great leader's non-violent approach.

However, during a pilgrimage to Mecca in 1964, Malcolm X realized that Elijah Muhammad's teachings were incompatible with those of traditional Islam. Islam's foundational stand is for equality, justice and unity of all peoples. He came to see the message of Islam as universal human solidarity. Caucasians could not be excluded. When he returned, he could no longer support the radical separatism of the Black Muslims. He broke with the Nation of Islam movement over these doctrinal differences, formed the Muslim Mosque, and began moving blacks closer to orthodox and universal Islam. Shortly afterwards he was assassinated.

Ten years later, upon the death of Elijah Muhammad, the movement was take over by his son, Imam W. Deen Muhammad, who moved the group in the direction preferred by Malcolm X. The Nation of Islam changed its name to the World Community of Islam in the West then to the American Muslim Mission. In addition, during the decade of Imam Muhammad's leadership the group began a process of reformation. His father's claim to Prophethood, a teaching that offended all the rest of the Muslim world, was abandoned; racial prejudices were relaxed thus allowing Caucasians to join the movement, and legitimate Islamic doctrines and ritual practices were instituted. Even the temples underwent changes; they were now referred to as mosques; chairs and pews were replaced with traditional prayer rugs; the leaders were no longer called ministers but Imams, again, a move towards the more traditional. We are indeed fortunate to have Imam W. Deen Muhammad in today's class, to further our understanding of African Islam.

Of course, not all Black Muslims accepted W. Deen Muhammad's reforms, the most notable exception being Louis Farrakhan. Farrakhan emerged as the leading voice among Black Muslims who wished to remain faithful to the pre-1975 Nation of Islam. He left the group in 1978, started a new Nation of Islam, established mosques, and developed an outreach to the African American community on radio. He rose to national prominence during the 1984 presidential campaign when he supported the Reverend Jesse Jackson. Though he has done much to improve the lives of African Americans, especially in gang-ridden, impoverished neighborhoods, he continues to be a thorn in the side of the white establishment for the same reason the Nation of Islam always has disturbed Caucasians – white fear of black empowerment.

Key Class Themes

This lesson focuses on the following themes:

1. Doctrine and cultural change
2. History of the Black Muslim movement
3. Racism and religion
4. Identity and relationship
5. Self-esteem and empowerment

Videotape Synopsis

- Class discussion
- Video interview with Dr. Abdul Salaam
- Guest – Imam W. Deen Muhammad

Class 18

Videotape Commentary

I suggest you read this section before you watch the videotape. You will find that it will help you organize your thoughts so that when you watch the tape it will be more meaningful. When you have finished viewing the tape, you may want to read this section again.

Interview with Dr. Abdul Salaam, Al-Faatir Mosque

In order to illustrate our *identity = self-esteem, relationship = empowerment* comparison, we move to our first roll-in with Dr. Abdul Salaam, a successful dentist who converted to Islam – at least the Nation of Islam variety – upon meeting Elijah Muhammad in 1957. In addition to being a most articulate spokesperson for the African American Muslim community, he has been a personal friend of Elijah Muhammad and is a close associate of both Louis Farrakhan and Imam W. Deen Muhammad. The Al-Faatir mosque is within the American Muslim Mission branch of the movement, but one gets the impression that Dr. Salaam, personally, resides somewhere between W. Deen Muhammad and Louis Farrakhan in terms of his own view of the African American Muslim movement.

Notice his interpretation of the inclusiveness of Islam. He seems to suggest that the version of Islam taught by Elijah Muhammad is authentically Muslim because it is applicable to the African American experience in America. This raises another of our key class themes when considering the *doctrinal dimension*. Can doctrines be dynamic, opened up to make sense in a variety of cultural settings? There is no easy answer to this question. As we have seen, even within the Nation of Islam, there has been a sharp difference of opinion regarding the identity of African American Muslims. Is a person African American first and Muslim second; or does religious tradition overcome race and culture?

A theme that inevitably arises in this session is the relationship between religion and racism. In another interview I enjoyed with Dr. Salaam for my *Religion in America: a Historical Perspective* teleclass, he accurately pointed out that Christianity was the religion of Caucasian oppressors, and even though many African Americans stayed with Christianity while giving it their own cultural coloring, many could not accept a worldview that once condoned slavery. He also contends that traditional Islam, perhaps brought to the United States by an Arab or Iranian Muslim, would have had little impact on African Americans. It was the doctrinal interpretation upheld by Elijah Muhammad that caught the religious imagination of searching African Americans. Given our study of Islam, it would be interesting to consider why this might be; why Islam? Why not, say, Buddhism? And for that matter, why not a re-interpretation of Christian doctrine such as we might find in revolutionary *liberation theology* as practiced in Central and South America? Again, there are no easy answers but fascinating material to help us consider our B+B = B equation.

As Dr. Salaam notes, classic Islam speaks of inclusiveness and seeks peace. But the world is neither a peaceful nor an inclusive place. African Americans know this as well as any other repressed peoples around the world. So the world needs its Farrakhans to light a fire in the hearts of the oppressed as well as under the toes of the oppressors. Dr. Salaam seems to see this as a political necessity in any religious worldview, an interesting insight that reveals the powerful relationship between religion and politics. We have said many times in this course that religion and politics are inextricably linked. Just as the *doctrinal, ethical,* and *social dimensions* function as worldview-defining, behavior-guiding forces in human cultural experience, so do the parallel forces of *ideology, public policy,* and *governance.* Perhaps there is no better example of the link between religion and politics than the African American Muslim movement in the United States. Political oppression of African Americans created the need for a religion that would define a black society that was beyond oppression. Elijah Muhammad articulated this vision, raised the self-esteem of African Americans, showed them the path to empowerment, and with this social ideal in mind, the Nation of Islam had gone about the business of *realizing it in the world!*

Interview and Class Discussion with Imam W. Deen Muhammad

All of us involved in creating the "Beliefs and Believers" teleclass, the production crew, the students and myself were absolutely thrilled when we heard that Imam W. Deen Muhammad would be joining us for our session on African American Islam. Never has it been more important to have a legitimate spokesperson, a *believer*, explain the nuances of his beliefs in the classroom studio and on camera. There is so much misinformation surrounding the history of the Nation of Islam, it is really impossible to develop and present an accurate portrayal of the movement from secondary sources. True, Dr. Salaam is a most articulate spokesperson, but he was not in the studio to answer questions or defend his point of view. We needed an *insider*, so we arranged to have a local Imam as an in-class guest. Not until the day before the class taping did we get a hint that Imam Muhammad might attend in his place. And we weren't sure he could take time from his busy schedule to be with us until just minutes before the class began when he indeed did arrive with his entourage.

It would be fair to say that Imam Muhammad is just a bit more than "a legitimate spokesperson." He is recognized as *the* Muslim American Spokesperson and is the spiritual leader of an estimated 2.5 million American Muslims. The fascinating discussion that occurs between our honored guest and the students really needs little elaboration here. However, two issues that arose in discussion are worthy of broader consideration.

In response to Chris' request for clarification on the history of the Nation of Islam and its relationship to traditional Islam, Imam Muhammad makes a rather astounding statement. Having stressed that his father's teachings were not his own but were the teachings of Wallace D. Fard (Mr. Farrad), Imam Muhammad says that Farrad purposely used religion to "trick the black man." In order to raise up African American self-esteem and begin the process of empowerment, Farrad created a religion based on a mythology that, in Imam Muhammad's words, was necessarily "absurd." But it worked. Now, according to the Imam, it is time for African Americans to move on to the "true Islam." Thanks to Farrad's teachings as passed on by Elijah Muhammad, the African American is ready to grow spiritually, economically and personally as a full member of the international Islamic community.

This may well be, but what an extraordinary take it has on the power of belief and its impact on behavior. Is it acceptable to "trick" followers in order to raise their consciousness so that they can self-actualize spiritual truths? Does a charismatic religious leader have a free hand to use the mythic dimension in any way he or she desires in order to inspire followers? We are obviously moving into some very controversial ground here. Do you see the implications of this dimensional tangle? True or not, does JZ Knight have the "right" to claim to channel a 35,000 year old ascended master in order to pass on her message of self-esteem and empowerment, which the Ramtha School of Enlightenment certainly is in the business of doing? True or not, does Joseph Smith have the "right" to "find" the Book of Mormon and, in doing so, ignite the fires of religious zeal in his followers? True or not, do the leaders of the early Christian church have the "right" to insist on the physical resurrection of Jesus? In the world of beliefs and believers, is it acceptable to create viable, positive, nurturing doctrines that benefit a religious community out of myths that may be fabrications? Do the ends, in religion, justify the mean? What of Jim Jones' "mythic dimension," and its ultimate impact on his community? No answers will be forthcoming from this author, but what a sizzling topic for your next 3 a.m. philosophical-discussion!

Suzanne tactfully raises another thorny issue; why do women appear to have less status in the world of Islam? She notes that other traditions, particularly Judaism and Christianity, are making a concerted effort to overcome the cultural residue of androcentrism and patriarchal attitudes. If African American Muslims have gone to such trouble to re-arrange Islamic doctrines to fit their cultural needs, why not open it up further now that people have been sensitized to sexism? In response, Imam Muhammad offers the explanation that in Islam men and women are equal spiritually, but physical differences demand different roles in human society. In addition, he points out that women in the Western secular world are denigrated, preyed upon, and treated as sex objects while Muslim women are honored and protected. In fact, the majority of traditional Muslim women agree with this assessment of their place in society. Should the Nation of Islam, which reacted violently to institutionalized racism, tackle the issue of institutionalized sexism? Or are we back to the familiar difficulty of trying to interpret the ethical precepts of a sacred worldview from a decidedly secular stance? Again, our conversation with Imam Muhammad has generated exciting material for future discussions.

No doubt, other points that I may have missed will strike you as important. The more the merrier, when it comes to lively topics for "Beliefs and Believers" discussions. As you view the tape and ponder Imam Muhammad's remarks, keep in mind our primary class theme for this segment of the course, the powerful relationship between doctrine, as belief; ethics, as behavior; and the impact of both dimensions on society. Enjoy!

Videotape Graphics

 At this stage we suggest you watch the videotape. The graphics you will see on the screen are reproduced below to save you the trouble of copying them down. You might like to add your own comments as you watch the tape.

African American Muslim Movement

Religion = identity and relationship

Identity = self-esteem
Relationship = empowerment

African American Muslim Movement

Nation of Islam =
the re-interpretation of traditional Islamic (Muslim) doctrine in order to meet ethical challenges in a society that is perceived to be racist by many African Americans

Nation of Islam = new "ethno-religious" identity for African American believers

Goal = remaking the social dimension according to the new ethno-religious identity

---

> **Nation of Islam**
>
> Key Players
>
> *Wallace D. Fard*
> – first prophet of the Black Muslim Movement
>
> *Elijah Muhammad* (1897–1975)
> – founder of the Nation of Islam
>
> *Malcolm X* (1925–1965)
> – key leader, assassinated in 1965
>
> *W. Deen Muhammad*
> (Wallace D. Muhammad) Son of Elijah Muhammad;
> after doctrinal disagreement with his father, he
> founds American Muslim Mission
>
> *Louis Farrakhan*
> – current leader, Nation of Islam

Review Questions

Answering the following questions will help you review key class themes and prepare for the examinations.

1. Describe how *identity* and *relationship*, our two key elements in any worldview, function in the teachings of Elijah Muhammad. What cultural forces motivated Elijah Muhammad to found the Nation of Islam?

2. What are some of the major differences between traditional Islam and the Islam practiced by Nation of Islam believers?

3. Why did Imam W. Deen Muhammad come to disagree with his father's teachings? What is his explanation of why the Nation of Islam movement was so attractive to African Americans?

4. What does our study of the African American Muslim Movement tell us about the dynamic relationship of the *doctrinal, ethical* and *social dimensions?*

Sources and Further Readings

Albanese, Catherine L. *America: Religions and Religion,* second ed. Belmont, CA: Wadsworth, 1992. (See section on "Black Center: African American Religion and Nationhood")

Lincoln, C. Eric. *The Black Muslims in America.* Boston: Beacon Press, 1961.

Melton, J. Gordon. *Encyclopedia of American Religions,* third. ed. Detroit: Gale Research, 1989. (See section on Black Islam)

Muhammad, Elijah. *Message to the Blackman in America.* Chicago: Muhammad Mosque of Islam, No.2, 1965.

Muhammad, W. Deen. *As a Light Shineth from the East.* Chicago: WDM Publishing Co., 1980.

BELIEFS AND BELIEVERS
Class 19 – Ethical Dimension: Ethical Conflicts, Part I

Introduction

Reflection: *Most people want what is good, what is right to characterize their lives. Most people want to be happy. Why is it then, that we cannot agree on the proper course of action to achieve the good life? Instead of arriving at some agreed upon system of ethical behavior, people usually end up taking sides on some difficult issue, arguing and even shedding blood, in defense of their position. The end result is discord in society. During this class, reflect on the role religion plays, both positively and negatively, in defining proper ethical behavior in society.*

Recently, a mother and father were found guilty of involuntary manslaughter in the death of their child. The parents were Christian Scientists, a religion with doctrines that stress prayer as the only legitimate source of healing. Christian Scientists do not rely on the medical profession, but solely upon God, or in some cases on Christian Science practitioners, to pray with believers who confront life's difficulties.

From the secular, legal point of view, the parents were obviously wrong. Their son had a simple bowel obstruction which could easily have been dealt with by the medical establishment. According to the court, the parents were guilty of "wanton and reckless conduct" in not seeking medical help for their child. The jury had no choice but to convict them. Yet they were so sad about the result that several jury members sobbed loudly when the verdict was read. What we have here is an *ethical conflict* between secular patterns of behavior and sacred patterns of behavior. The parents firmly believe the doctrines in Christian Science which provide an ethical *pattern of action* in the case of illness. Prayer always heals. So they turned to prayer. They could be convicted a thousand times and it would not change their *obligation* in response to illness with prayer.

On the other hand, secular society has adopted a different pattern of action. Society cannot conceive of any other possible source of healing except through the medical establishment, even in the face of the fact that people die regularly in hospitals from unknown causes. From the secular perspective, the pattern of action chosen by the Christian Science parents was unethical. The focus here is on the child's illness and death which, from a legal perspective, pits secular and sacred ethics against each other. Other ethical questions arise from this sad situation. Do parents have absolute control over their children's lives? Or can the state take away that liberty when it considers a child's life to be in danger? Do deeply held religious beliefs and their accompanying ethical obligations and responsibilities necessarily have to take a backseat to those of secular society?

This deeply troubling case of the Christian Science family is just one illustration of ethical conflicts. If you are developing your *worldview analysis skills*, and we certainly hope you are, at this point in the course you are aware that ethical conflicts pepper our daily fare of news items offered up by a user-hungry media machine; ethical stands on abortion, assisted suicide, capital punishment, birth control actually define the public policy statements of our major political parties and in doing so, illustrate, once again, the impact of religious sentiments on the social dimension.

Class 19

In this class session we go to the heart of the B + B = B equation. Believers will behave according to their cherished beliefs. If we really want to know what motivates believers to devoutly pray five times a day, have their young sons circumcised, build pyramids and cathedrals, or blow up hundreds of innocent people in a terrorist act, we have to enter the world of the *ethical dimension*. Onward!

Key Class Themes

This lesson focuses on the following themes:

1. Ethics as *patterns of action*
2. The pervasiveness of the ethical dimension in society
3. The ethical process
4. Ethical rules: law, custom, morals

Videotape Synopsis

- Class discussion
- Video interview with Harrison Sheppard, lawyer
- Video interview with Professor Robert Moore

Videotape Commentary

I suggest you read this section before you watch the videotape. You will find that it will help you organize your thoughts so that when you watch the tape it will be more meaningful. When you have finished viewing the tape, you may want to read this section again.

Our inevitably lively class discussion brings out a rather *timeless* perspective on the ethical dimension. Ethical conflicts may arise over issues that may topple a civilization or over the most mundane disagreement. Jeff, quite accurately, points out that the "definition" of *proper patterns of action* is vague and, thus, is based on the cultural mores of those doing the defining. He asks, "What of the religious radical who believes he is doing God's will by blowing up a building?" "What of the Chinese mother who, in response to a governmental *ethical* edict that a family may only have one child, smothers her new born daughter in hopes of eventually having a son?" Indeed, defining "proper patterns of action" is no easy task.

Ethical disagreements need not be centered on "weighty" conflicts. In an almost humorous interchange, Jeff and Suzanne have a *slight disagreement* over the weight of a can of tomatoes! Suzanne has observed that, over time, what was once a one pound can of stewing tomatoes has shrunk to 14.5 ounces. For Jeff, that is an appropriate competitive move if tomato canning companies are to stay afloat in a free-market economy. For Suzanne, it is an ethical failing of biblical proportions. She accurately points out that the great prophets of the Hebrew Bible regularly condemn cheating in the market place. If intelligent, caring people can disagree over a can of tomatoes, no wonder we live in a world of ethical conflicts!

Our class discussion is especially lively in this class session because of the very nature of discourse when considering the ethical dimension. To explore religious ethics is to engage a set of questions that have challenged human beings throughout history and in all human cultures. The search for answers to these questions has ignited the creative fires in the great names of history just as it has perplexed the most common person. Grand civilizations have arisen then disappeared depending on who held the power generated by answers to these questions. Great texts have been written; philosophies of life have sprung from the minds of profound thinkers; art, architecture, poetry, and music have sometimes soothed and sometimes inflamed the intense emotions that arise during this questioning process. And of course the great religious leaders of all time have, in part, staked their authority on ethical precepts.

Ethical questions are fundamental. What are we to value? What is the good? How do we achieve the good life? How should we behave towards one another? What are our responsibilities and obligations in relationship with *the other*, be it Divine, nature, other human beings, society or our own inner-selves? How should wrongful acts be punished, and how should noble accomplishments be rewarded? What are the ritual mechanisms needed for resolving or harmonizing dissonant activity? How might we transform ourselves? In a nutshell, what are the *proper patterns of action* that will lead us towards the enduring, the-good-and-the-true and help us sustain that reality?

As is so often the case in our dimensional adventure, ethical rules exist outside the realm of religion. Laws are the most common form of ethical guidance backed up by the authority of society which by force or threat of force defines the parameters of human behavior. From parking tickets to maximum security prisons, laws permeate our cultural experience. As Virginia notes, politics and economics play as much of a role as religion in engendering ethical conflicts.

Custom is a more amorphous but no less effective form of ethical guidance, including lifestyle choices, manners, mores and habits. Authority, in this case, is generated by repetition over time and collective agreement that the behavior is acceptable. Christianity, one would suppose, has little to do with suits and ties, dresses and lipstick, shiny Buicks and bean suppers, but one would be hard put to find a Methodist Sunday service in a rural hamlet in which these and other custom-generated symbols were not prominent.

Moral rules imply a certain kind of behavior based on both intellectual and emotional assent. In a free society, moral rules understandably generate a good deal of tension as most people tend to display emotions on issues such as abortion, suicide, marriage rules, gay-lesbian rights and a host of other moral issues. Humans in a given society are especially prone to violent action when laws governing human behavior are vague on moral issues. Since disagreements are so often based on differing interpretations of religious doctrines, resolution is almost impossible within the secular arena. Nevertheless, in a democratic society, laws are passed in an ongoing struggle to bring some clarity to moral issues. This fact brings us to our first interview with Harrison Sheppard, a prominent lawyer in San Francisco.

Video Interview with Harrison Sheppard

Lawyers, who are not adverse to enjoying a joke at their expense, delight in repeating one of Shakespeare's classic quotations, told with respect to making the world a better place, "The first thing we do, let's kill all the lawyers!" (Henry VI, Part 2) To be sure, the legal profession is much maligned and for the most part, deserves the criticism. The image most of us have of lawyers is about on the level of circling vultures; like birds of prey, they survive off the misery of others.

However, from the ethical perspective, the legal profession *should* be one characterized by integrity and honor. Harrison Sheppard has developed a national reputation by calling for a radical overhaul of the legal profession starting in the law schools of the nation where lawyers should be trained to be peacemakers not conflict instigators. As he so eloquently puts it, lawyers should be the "secular ministers" of a democratic society. According to Harrison, lawyers have one of the highest callings in all the professions. They should be the guardians of the ethical standards in society that lead to *proper patterns of action*. As you view this segment, notice how Harrison envisions the ethical dimension within the legal profession as an essentially spiritual bond between the individual and society. If Harrison's noble ideas catch on, we might have to give up all those nasty lawyer jokes!

Warren, who is a career nurse, would raise a challenge to Harrison Sheppard's antilitigation stance. What of the people who really have had their rights violated? He remembers several instances where patients clearly were the victims of medical malpractice, but, for whatever reason, chose not to exercise their right to legal protection. Perhaps the key to the expeditious use of our legal system in the quest for ethical harmony is discrimination; knowing when it is or is not appropriate to enter into a legal entanglement for the sake of justice.

Interview with Professor Robert L. Moore, President of the Institute for World Spirituality

Professor Moore's sentiments on the power and importance of the ethical dimension mirror those of Harrison Sheppard. Only Professor Moore, as President of the Institute for World Spirituality located on the campus of the Chicago Theological Seminary, seeks to do more than just heal the legal profession. He looks to healing the world. His institute serves as a think tank and policy-making center with the goal of uniting the world's religious leaders and using their considerable collective insight to work towards world peace. Now that may not seem like a new idea, but the urgency he expresses as we move into a new millennium is starkly accurate.

Religious leaders, guardians of the highest and most noble manifestations of ethical standards, need to overcome their differences and work with scientists, doctors, lawyers and politicians to create a global ethical transformation. According to Professor Moore, unless we overcome our differences and petty animosities and finally work towards peace and a sustainable future on planet Earth, we can look forward to cultural and environmental chaos in a mere 15 years. Whether you agree with his meager time-table or not, our interview with Professor Moore clearly illustrates one of our most important "Beliefs and Believers" class themes – religion is not a private affair. The *ethical dimension*, as is the case with all our dimensions of religion, is critical to human self-understanding as well as the harmonious evolution of human cultures.

Our interview with Professor Moore, along with a somewhat heated class discussion, helps us develop an accompanying key class theme; the *pervasiveness* of the ethical dimension. We do this in a number of ways. First, *ethics*, quite simply, provides human beings with a connection between right beliefs and right actions. To put it in our dimensional framework, right doctrines specify correct ethical activity. And, of course, we cannot forget the importance of the *ritual dimension*. Particularly during life's rites of passage, ritual activity calls for proper ethical behavior which guides a person through a transitional stage and on into a new level of identity and relationship. For example, when a young Native American participates in a *vision quest* on life's journey from adolescence to adulthood, ethically, the traveler must maintain the highest standards of behavior.

The *ethical dimension* is also pervasive in that ethics direct human beings toward the good by providing proper patterns of action. Since you were a child, your parents, your teachers, your older role-models stressed above all proper behavior. Early on, you learned right patterns of action. Over time, you began to feel obligated to act in a certain manner. When you meet an adult, without thinking, you extend your hand and say something like,"Nice to meet you." In a religious context, the obligation to say grace before a meal may have been instilled in you. Even something like "good sportsmanship" represents a pattern of action designed to direct young athletes towards proper behavior on the playing fields.

Yet another place where we encounter the pervasiveness of the *ethical dimension* is in what we call the four-stage ethical process: obligation, responsibility, dissonance and harmony. We spend a good deal of time illustrating this process in class, but, the point is, it is part of the human condition to go in and out of this process on a regular basis. In society, the process is governed by laws. For example, you have an obligation to operate a vehicle safely on public roads. One way of behaving irresponsibly, given that obligation, is to drink excessive amounts of alcoholic beverages before driving your car. "Driving under the influence" is against the law and, if you behave in this unethical manner, you are in dissonance with the laws of society. If you are caught by a state patrol officer, or worse, cause an accident, you rightfully must endure some mechanism designed to bring you back into harmony or "pay your debt to society." The laws of society determine the level of punishment that will balance your ledger sheet.

The ethical process functions the same way in the sacred world. Major religious traditions set out ethical patterns of action that must be observed by believers – the Ten Commandments or the Eight-Fold path, for instance. Adherents are obligated to respond to life according to these patterns. Straying from the ethical path cuts one off from the religious community and thus, is a source of shame, guilt, distress and tension. Religions, then, provide mechanisms for re-alignment and reconciliation such as the ritual of confession in the Roman Catholic church. Ritualized reconciliation, whether as a fine or a prison term or confession and prayer, plays an enormously important role in this final stage of the ethical process.

During class discussion, an important, if frustrating, topic emerges. What happens when there are a number of competing ethical standards of behavior? What happens when a dominant religious system imposes its *patterns of action* on those less powerful, all within the same social environment? In particular, how do you determine proper patterns of action when religious ethics and secular ethics conflict? In our next class, *Ethical Conflicts: The Middle East*, we will wade into these difficult questions with the help of real believers – Jews, Christians, and Muslims – living in Israel and Egypt.

Videotape Graphics

 At this stage we suggest that you watch the videotape. The graphics you will see on the screen are reproduced to save you the trouble of copying them down. You might like to add your own comments as you watch the tape.

Ethics
– Key to values/behavior relationship in any worldview
– Provides link between beliefs and right action

Definition
Religious ethics is that aspect of religion concerned with proper patterns of action in the situation and circumstances of the human life cycle and social relations

Patterns
– a pattern of *obligation* that sets standards for *proper* action
– a pattern of *rules* (laws) that sets standards for *right* action
– a pattern of *values* that sets the standard for *good* action (morality)

Class 19

> **Ethical Behavior**
>
> Ethical behavior is guided by *laws*, *customs* and *morals*.
>
> Religious doctrines inform or guide *laws*, *customs*, and *morals*.
>
> *The Ethical Process*
>
> – obligation
> – responsibility
> – dissonance = doing what is wrong;
>   guilt, anxiety
> – redemption/harmonizing mechanism =
>   returns person to *proper patterns of action*

Review Questions

Answering the following questions will help you review key class themes and prepare for the examinations.

1. How do law, custom, and morals guide ethical *patterns of action* in a given society?

2. Using our definition of ethics as a basis for your answer, why does Harrison Sheppard believe that lawyers should be the "secular ministers" of American democracy?

3. Identify the four steps in the ethical process? What does this process tell us about the pervasiveness of ethics in human experience?

4. The sad story of the Christian Science parents convicted of involuntary manslaughter in the death of their child reveals much about the conflict in our society between religious and secular ethics. Do you think they are guilty as charged? If not, why not? Please elaborate.

Sources and Further Readings

Chidester, David. *Patterns of Action: Religion and Ethics in a Comparative Perspective.* Belmont, CA: Wadsworth Press, 1987.

BELIEFS AND BELIEVERS
Class 20 – Ethical Dimension: Ethical Conflicts, Part II: The Middle East

Introduction

Reflection: *If the ethical dimension is supposed to prompt believers to seek the good, the enduring and the true, why is it that deeply religious people from different faiths feel justified in using political power to oppress, humiliate or kill other human beings in the name of their religion? What is it about the volatile mixture of religion and politics that seems to undermine religious ethical systems and bring out the worst in people?*

The story of the Middle East is the story of the inseparable relationship between religion and power. Religion is the collective expression of an idyllic human vision or worldview. It is the creative description of how life should be. Power, expressed primarily in political activity, represents the natural drive to see that ideal vision of reality *realized* in the social arena.

Religion in its most fundamental form is about expansion, transcendence, transformation and change. Power, on the other hand, is about control, self-assertion, structure and the setting forth of boundaries. The dynamic relationship between these two complementary cultural forces plays havoc on ethical systems. Perhaps no place else on earth is that more obvious than in the Middle East.

In our "new and improved" edition of "Beliefs and Believers," we wanted to visit a cultural setting in which there was palpable religious tension. The motivation was certainly not to cast religion in a negative light. Rather it was to find a cultural environment in which ethical conflicts, based on differences in religious perspective, were a very real part of the daily lives of the nation's citizens. Though the circumstances differ in Israel and Egypt, both countries seem caught in a whirlpool of religiopolitical tension. During our journey through the Middle East, we observed how *identity* and *relationship*, our fundamental elements in any religious system, are intertwined with the quest for political sovereignty which is in turn linked to ownership of land. We learned that ethical *patterns of action* often conflict because of a tension we have already explored in Class 16, the natural tension that arises between secular and sacred worldviews. And it was impressed upon us how appreciation of religious diversity is only possible when justice, freedom and equality are foundational principles characteristic of the political environment. Unfortunately, this is not the case in either Israel or Egypt, and citizens of these great nations suffer accordingly.

In our class sessions on the *social dimension*, we will primarily be focusing on the cultural environment of the United States. In this country, religious pluralism seems to work, if for no other reason than that the incredible number of religious organizations that exist prevents any one religion from gaining the upper hand. Two hundred years or so after the first amendment to the United States Constitution guaranteed religious freedom and prohibited the establishment of any single religious system as a dominant political force in society, the United States continues to provide an ideal social environment for diverse religious expressions. By some estimates, more than 1,500 different religious organizations exist within the

Class 20

cultural and geographic boundaries of this country. It may be a sad statement about religion in general, but the very fact that there are so many religious groups in this nation prevents any one group from oppressing another, at least at a threatening level.

In the Middle East, however, the situation is obviously different. Jews, Christians and Muslims in Israel, and Muslims and Christians in Egypt are locked in an always painful, sometimes deadly struggle to survive. Our journey to the Middle East wasn't always pleasant, and, accordingly, you may find this class a bit frustrating, even disturbing. Nevertheless, it is a key class objective in "Beliefs and Believers" to take an unadulterated, unprotected look at the power of religion and its impact on society. In Israel and Egypt, power and impact are glaringly evident!

Key Class Themes

This lesson focuses on the following themes:

1. Ethical conflicts in Israel
2. Religion and politics in the Middle East
3. Ethical conflicts in Egypt
4. Land, sovereignty and ethical conflict
5. Secular/sacred tension in Egypt

Videotape Synopsis

- Roll-in; Ethical Conflicts in Israel
- Roll-in; The Struggle for Land and Sovereignty
- Roll-in; Interview with Rev. Menes Abdul Noor in Cairo
- Roll-in; Interview with Akmed, a young Muslim student in Cairo

Videotape Commentary

I suggest you read this section before you watch the videotape. You will find that it will help you organize your thoughts so that when you watch the tape it will be more meaningful. When you have finished viewing the tape, you may want to read this section again.

In class discussion, Jeff raises a provocative question. Is there such as thing as a "religious ego?" In many ways, his question sets the tone for our entire class session. Ideally, religion should work to relieve believers of the oppressive and often destructive tendency to think of ourselves as separate entities, alone in the universe, locked in a struggle with other ontologically autonomous beings for the scarce resources that sustain our meager existence. Religion is supposed to make what is a part apart. As we mentioned in one of our earliest classes, the root of the word religion, "religare," is to re-unite.

Not so in Israel. Jeff is right on the money in that the vagaries of religious ego are everywhere present in that troubled land. It is almost as though the individual human struggle to form ego by differentiating between what is me and what is not me is expanded to the collective level. Consequently, the power of a religious ego is multiplied by the number of individual egos that plug into this identity-forming energy source. When individual egos clash, the resulting violence can be disturbing. However, when religious egos clash, the results can be devastating. Proper patterns of action are reduced to chaos. Janet points out the irony that often in the Middle East it is the people who work for peace – the reduction of religious ego – that are murdered. Mr. Fahoom, a Muslim living in Nazareth, Israel, laments that he is 68 years old and has never lived "one happy day." A sad lesson we learn in Class 20 is that when religious egos roam the social environment, a "happy day" is like dust in the wind.

Background on Ethical Conflicts in Israel

Before viewing this class segment, I thought it might be helpful if I shared some of the historical background on the Middle Eastern/American-Western relationship. Having some sense of the historical/cultural context out of which a growing animosity has emerged will help put our various interviews into perspective. Most Americans are unnerved by the hatred that Middle Eastern Muslims have for the West, particularly the United States. Muslim extremists have attacked American military and diplomatic facilities in the Middle East and Africa and have even brought their "holy war" to the shores of this nation with the bombing of the World Trade Center in New York City.

As I mention in the opening segment of this class, our trip to Israel and Egypt found us smack in the middle of yet another crisis situation, part of the tangled mess between Iraq and the United Nations, and hatred for Americans was indeed palpable. The State Department had issued a warning that Americans should not travel to the Middle East, and we later learned that a local Imam had declared attacks on American civilians justified according to his interpretation of jihad, the Muslim term for the inner and outer struggle against all enemies of Islam.

A six person camera crew sticks out like the proverbial sore thumb, and were it not for the caution and cultural expertise of our Arab Christian guides, we might have ended up as data on some State Department casualty page.It was a bit of a shock to realize, in conversations with otherwise friendly and hospitable local Muslims in the towns and cities of Israel, that they uniformly took Saddam Hussein's side over that of the secular West. Though Muslims are well aware of Hussein's despotism, the secular West represents more of a threat to the ethical patterns of action deeply rooted in the Muslim way of life.

There are probably two major reasons for Muslim animosity towards Americans and the United States: a) U.S. support of Israel; and b) a long history of perceived humiliation of Muslims by the West. Let's take on the historical challenge first. Since the birth of Islam in the 7th century, the Islamic world has enjoyed grand periods of cultural and geographic dominance on the world stage. As recently as 1683, the Muslim Ottoman empire had risen through its conquests of land formerly belonging to the Byzantine empire to a power that stretched from Central Europe to Kurdistan and south to Egypt. However, when Turkish forces failed to take Vienna in that year, a downward spiral ensued. By the end of World War I in 1918, the Ottoman empire was broken up. Virtually the whole of the Arab world found itself occupied by Britain and France through a League of Nations mandate. It was a traumatic experience for this once proud and mighty civilization. Since the United States has emerged as the Western political power in the global arena, all the festering anger generated by almost a century of humiliation is aimed at this nation. Like it or not, if your passport says you are an American, for the Arab Muslims, you are part of the problem; not part of the solution.

Muslim anger at the West was exacerbated by Britain's seemingly contradictory promises about a Jewish homeland in Palestine and the subsequent creation of Israel in 1948. A raging sense of injustice sharpened Arab nationalism and a sense of solidarity with Palestinian Arabs who were displaced from their land. As Dr. Lorberbaum explains in his precise and eloquent explanation of ethical complexity in Israel, "the argument" over a Jewish state in Palestine has erupted into bloody conflict in 1948, 1956, 1967, and 1973 and has definitely fanned the flames of hostility between Muslim and Jew. Palestinian Arabs hold the mostly accurate perception that Israel could not continue to exist, at least at its current level of political power, if the country were not "propped up" financially and militarily by the United States. Thus, the U.S. becomes the "Great Satan," supporting a "cancerous growth" in the midst of Arab lands.

Class 20

Roll-in: Ethical Conflicts in Israel

The key ethical question – "how should we then live?" – is never easily answered. In Israel, however, finding an answer to that question may well mean the difference between life and death. As you view this unique set of interviews with Jews, Christians, and Muslim citizens of Israel, notice how each person, with obvious integrity, struggles with ethical conflicts. On one hand, their respective religions call for peace and love. Yet the political playing field in Israel is not even. Political power, held by the Israelis, generates a constant stream of complaints regarding justice and equality. Religion, as we have noted many times, is about reconciliation and the quest for unity. In Israel, religion, by the very fact that it defines identity and guides relationships, divides Arab from Jew, Christian from Muslim, and human beings from the ethical ideals they cherish. The same is true in Northern Ireland, Serbia, Sri Lanka, and other hot spots around the world where religious and political agendas collide.

Roll-in: The Struggle for Land and Sovereignty

Imagine, if you can, you live on a farm in Wisconsin. Your great-grandfather, your grandfather, your father, and now you farm the land. Your daughter and son and their children will one day walk the land and draw their livelihood from the cherished earth that has supported generations of your family. The land is enriched by their blood and bones drawn from the family grave site beneath an ancient elm tree.

One fine spring morning, government agents arrive at your farm with an eviction order. By federal edict, you no longer own this land. The political powers within the United States have decided that the moral and ethical response to the displacement of Native Americans is to return their lands to them, and there is nothing you can do about it. You have no power to stop the transfer of land, so you pack up and leave. How would you feel? This situation is obviously hypothetical, but it raises similarly intense emotions that are daily fare for Palestinian Arabs in Israel who have been displaced from what they consider to be their ancestral land. As Dr. Lorberbaum accurately describes the situation, sovereignty presumes territory. Without land there is no sovereignty. Without sovereignty, there is no line of defense against injustice, humiliation, and exploitation. This is the story of land and ethical conflict in Israel.

In order to understand land, religion, identity, and the accompanying ethical complexities in Israel, it is necessary to have some background on Zionism and the Zionist Movement. As you know, in the *Holocaust*, the planned extermination of the Jews during World War II, some 6 million Jewish men, women, and children died in the Nazi extermination camps. As horrifying as this pivotal event is for Jews, it is only the ragged tip of a twisted and tormented historical iceberg. For centuries the Jews have contributed to the social and economic well-being of non-Jewish cultures, only to be attacked and stripped of their belongings, their livelihood and often their lives when events took a negative turn. Always the convenient scapegoat for political, economic, and even biological disasters like the Great Plague of the 14th century, Jews have endured unspeakable hardship and oppression. It is one of the miracles of history and a testament to the strength of Jewish traditions that we even have a people we can call Jews today.

Finally, enough was enough. Land equates with sovereignty, and sovereignty with power. The Israel we know today is the realization of a "one hundred year discussion," as Dr. Lorberbaum "gently" puts it, that began with a Zionist program formulated in the first Zionist Congress in 1897. The origin of the word Zion is unclear. It may originally have meant something like "rock" or "stronghold." Nevertheless, from biblical times, Zion, or the "holy land" has captured the Jewish religious imagination, but not without engendering a peculiar tension in the Jewish quest for identity. On one hand, Zion is the land promised to the Hebrews by God. According to this perspective, God can only be worshipped on this sanctified territory which is the place of the state of Israel in Palestine today. On the other hand, since the Babylonian exile of the Jews in the 6th century b.c.e., a strong universalist tendency has existed which holds that God rules over the entire world and can be worshipped anywhere.

These two complementary ideas about the nature of God and necessity of a particular sacred place account for the somewhat conflicted self-understanding of the State of Israel. During our interview, Dr. Lorberbaum does a terrific job of sorting out the intra-Jewish dialogue on the meaning of the land known as Israel. The Zionist movement was originally led by Jews who were inspired, not so much by religion, but by nationalism, the Socialist idealism of their time. Israel was to be a secular state, a place where Jews could achieve sovereignty and, thus, a line of defense against the exploitation and cruelty that had stalked them for centuries. At the same time, religious Zionists called for a "redemption of the land in Israel" as a step towards the coming of the Messiah, the defining eschatological event in Judaism's mythos. To make matters more complex, there are religious Jews in Israel today who consider themselves exiles. They are anti-Zionist, represented by ultra-Orthodox Hasidic Jews who see their role as "enforcing" Jewish law in a supposedly secular state. They live in a close community, govern themselves, pay no taxes, do not join the army, wear traditionalist clothes, and have even been known to stone cars that attempt to travel through their community on the Sabbath. Though Israel is a secular state, by self-definition, family and personal law which define ethical patterns of action are determined by an Orthodox rabbinate. Since the rabbinate is Orthodox, it means that Reform and Conservative Jews have no say in matters such as marriage or divorce. In effect, we have a secular state governed, in part, by the ancient sacred Jewish law or halakhah. Could it be that Israel is a secular theocracy? Once again, Dr. Lorberbaum helps us sort out these complexities. However, even his frank assessment of the situation, that the only solution for Arab-Jewish relations in Israel is a partition of the land into two sovereign states, leaves Christian Arabs without land or sovereignty. The strategy for achieving peace in Israel seems to elude even the most intelligent and insightful experts.

In any event, the horrors of the Holocaust and the changing balance of power among the survivors of World War II created a global social environment conducive to the establishment of a Jewish state in Palestine. Depending on your point of view, when the United Nations recognized Israel as a sovereign nation in 1948, a long-suffering people were finally given a chance to return to a sacred and safe haven or a huge injustice had been perpetrated upon the Palestinian, Arab, and Muslim world by Western nations who were riddled with guilt over their "indiscretion" in ignoring the Nazi extermination program. Nonetheless, as you develop your own informed opinion on this complex situation, please try to "walk a mile in the moccasins" of our interviewees, Jew, Christian, and Muslim, and sense how difficult it must be for them to sort out *proper patterns of action* in a land of intense ethical conflict.

Ethical Conflicts in Egypt; Interview with Reverend Menes Abdul Noor

In these two thematically-connected interviews, we move to the social environment of Cairo, Egypt. Reverend Menes Abdul Noor is a world renowned minister in the Protestant Evangelical branch of Christianity which, of course, is a minority religious group in predominantly Muslim Egypt. This great man exudes poise, peace, and compassion, but on the morning of our meeting he was reduced to tears of frustration by the pressure of ethical conflicts in Egypt. A young man who had recently converted from Islam to Christianity had been arrested at the Cairo airport. In the United States, a move from one religion to another would not raise an eyebrow; it is a matter of personal choice. But in Egypt, in the Islamic world, conversion from Islam to another religion is a crime punishable by death, at least according to religious law. Hopefully, Reverend Noor's poignant account of life as a "second class religious citizen" in Egypt will provide American students, particularly those who are Christian, with food for thought regarding the meaning and importance of religious freedom if diverse peoples are to live in a just and equatable society. Once again, we are witness to the corrupting influence of political power upon the ethical ideals of the world's great religions.

Sacred/Secular Tension in Egypt; Interview with Akmed, a Young Student in Cairo

Our interview with Akmed offers yet another look at this same issue. Recently, Egypt has been tormented by the rise of fundamentalist Islamic groups that are willing to use violence to prevent the further secularization of Egyptian society. The tourist trade is a major industry in Egypt, and terrorists have indiscriminately attacked and killed tourists in an effort to create social unrest and send a message to Muslims who adopt Western ways. Our stay in Egypt was, at best, difficult. The recent slaughter of tourists in Luxor had clearly diminished the tourist population and the monuments and museums were comparatively empty, giving the visitor a rather eerie feeling.

This observation touches on one of Akmed's most insightful comments. Into the complex mix of religion and politics, sacred and secular, goes a socioeconomic variable. The huge gap between the haves and have-nots in Cairo was glaringly evident. Mercedes limos with fully-stocked bars picked up wealthy patrons who enjoyed the disco at our hotel. But just around the corner, soldiers with machine guns shooed away the ragged poor who begged for coins to ease the constant sting of hunger. The "haves" in Egyptian society are willing to accept some compromises with the pleasures derived from Western secular ethical "patterns of action." Those who "have not" are becoming more radical in their shared demands to return Egypt to a political entity that is governed, theocratically, by traditional Muslim law. At some danger, Akmed shares this dilemma with us as he is clearly a young man caught in this religiopolitical web of ethical conflict.

Virginia's closing comment really sums up the theme of ethical conflicts. If people do not have rights, how are they to meet their ethical obligations? How are they to be responsible to the cherished ethical precepts of their chosen faith? In this kind of environment, patterns of action inevitably become patterns of despair. Harkening back to Professor Moore's vision for the 21st century, resolving these extended ethical conflicts peacefully, whether they emerge in Israel, the Balkans, Northern Ireland, Sri Lanka, or anywhere else in the world where the religious ego flourishes, is a primary challenge in the years ahead.

Videotape Graphics

At this stage we suggest you watch the videotape.
There are no graphics in this class segment.

Review Questions

Answering the following questions will help you review key class themes and prepare for the examinations.

1. What does the relationship between religion and politics in Israel teach us about ethical conflicts in general?

2. Provide some historical background on the Zionist movement and the creation of the State of Israel?

3. Sam, our Arab Christian guide, feels that he must leave his homeland. Why must he go, and how do the ethical interactions between Jews and Arabs reinforce his decision?

4. Considering, once again, that the ethical dimension defines *proper patterns of action*, how do religious tensions within Islam contribute to Akmed's *ethical dilemma* as he longs for "the good life" in the predominantly Muslim society of Cairo, Egypt?

Sources and Further Readings

Biale, David. "Zionism," *The Encyclopedia of Religion*, Mircea Eliade, ed., Vol. 15. NY: Macmillan, 1987.

Eliade, Mircea, ed. *The Encyclopedia of Religion*. Vol. 15 NY: McMillan, 1987. (Read David Biale's article, "Zionism.")

Smart, Ninian. *The World's Religions*. Englewood Cliffs, NJ: Prentice Hall, 1989, pp. 466-477.

BELIEFS AND BELIEVERS
Class 21 – Far East Religion

Introduction

Reflection: *If the link between the ethical dimension and the social dimension is about anything, it is about relationships. Twenty-five hundred years ago, a Chinese sage, K'ung-fu-tsu, sensed that social cohesion depended upon a refined set of ethical rules which would provide clear patterns of action to guide human beings in their interaction with each other. The religion he developed, which has come to be known as Confucianism, continues to influence the East Asian perspective on life to this day. As you view this segment, reflect on the important relationship between the ethical and social dimensions.*

As always in "Beliefs and Believers," when we encounter a new worldview, we never expect to fully grasp the subtleties of the religion we are studying. Rather, the religion can help us understand some important aspect of the dimension we are investigating, in this case, the *ethical dimension*. Certainly this is true of East Asian religions, including Confucianism, Taoism, Buddhism, Shintoism in Japan, along with a colorful mixture of ancient folk religious practices that emerged during prehistoric times.

In this class, we will primarily be focusing on Confucianism and Taoism. Like the mysterious and popular Yin-Yang symbol, these two major manifestations of Chinese religiosity, also shaped by centuries of Buddhist practice, represent complementary paths towards the same goal, that is, harmony or balance with the cosmos. Taoism is the tone-setter for the non-establishment side of Chinese religion with its rich mythology, colorful festivals, striking symbols and magical rituals. However, it is to Confucianism we turn to explore the ethical dimension because of its pervasive impact on *patterns of action* in day-to-day human relationships.

There are two primary reasons why we ask Confucianism to help us understand worldviews at this juncture in the course: a) Confucius' reflections on the ethical and social difficulties which plagued China during his lifetime sparked the insight out of which this major worldview grew; b) even our cursory exploration of Confucianism along with Taoism will tell us much about the differences between Eastern and Western ways of perceiving reality. One of the purposes of this class is to wake up to the fact that not all people see the world as we do. Hopefully it will become evident how the Eastern religious perspective generates a vastly different ethical and social experience than that produced by Western presuppositions about reality.

Before beginning our study of Confucianism and other East Asian religious expressions, it will be helpful to consider the relationship between religious ethics and social aesthetics. We don't often think of human action and interaction in terms of beauty – except perhaps while watching a ballet or gymnastic event. However, when you think about it, completely harmonious social relations – and we are speaking about the ideal – would be characterized by an ongoing, unbroken stream of perfectly executed interactions between people.

When you consider "the Good, the Beautiful, and the True," which Confucius certainly did, the question of relationship arises. Each of these ideals implies a knower and a known; a perceiver and that which is perceived. The profoundly religious insight which Confucius turned into a worldview was the perception of a pervasive cosmic harmony, displayed in the heavens and focused on Earth in human interaction, which human beings could aesthetically realize if they could but achieve perfect balance in the cosmic dance of *yin* and *yang*.

Both practitioners of Confucianism and Taoism, Confucianism's romantic and rebellious sister, strive to achieve an inner sense of balance which reverberates with the cosmic and ethical order of the universe – the *Tao*. In turn, the social dimension is transformed into an aesthetically-purified realm of human relationships. The ever-practical Confucius realized that the human tendency towards individualism, highly prized in our Western culture, was the culprit that disrupted social harmony. People who constantly think of themselves first are not mentally, emotionally, or spiritually equipped to behave towards one another in an aesthetically pleasing manner. Thus, Confucius proposed an educational system that served and supported a deliberate tradition designed to regulate human relationships. With the help of Reverend Wilson Lee, leader of the Chung Ching Taoist Association in San Francisco, James Miller of Boston University, and our guest expert, Dr. Glenn Shive, our exploration of the ethical and social dimensions, seen through the light of East Asian religion, is greatly enhanced.

Key Class Themes

This lesson focuses on the following themes:

1. The six dimensions of Chinese religion
2. The ethical and social dimensions in Confucianism
3. Taoism and balance in life
4. Relationships, East and West

Videotape Synopsis

- Class lecture/discussion
- Video interview with Mr. James Miller on the Yin Yang symbol
- Video interview with Reverend Wilson Lee at the Ching Chung Taoist Association, San Francisco
- Guest appearance and discussion with Dr. Glenn Shive

Videotape Commentary

I suggest you read this section before you watch the videotape. You will find that it will help you organize your thoughts so that when you watch the tape it will be more meaningful. When you have finished viewing the tape, you may want to read this section again.

We open our lecture/discussion section with the *Yin/Yang symbol*. Indeed, this visual expression of the *Tao*, the perfect balance between assertive and integrative forces in the universe, reflects the East Asian religious understanding of a universe that is *unitive*. While *Yang* is often associated with the masculine and *Yin* with the feminine, what we are really encountering in this symbol is the interconnectedness, the interrelationship, the indivisibility, the *oneness* of what we in Western culture perceive as *opposites,* and more precisely, opposites in competition or conflict: light and dark, good and evil, living and dying, joy and despair, moon and sun; the list is endless.

In Western religious systems, for the most part, the perspective is *dualistic*. The divine is separated from creation; the source of *being* is outside of human everyday experience. Often earthly existence is cast in a pessimistic light, nature is devalued, and the pain and suffering of our brief span of life on the planet is but a prelude to the more meaningful, eternal ontological sojourn in some distant, heavenly realm. In many Western religions, the Earth is merely a staging place for the ongoing cosmic battle between the forces of good and evil. Our quick look at conservative Christian Fundamentalism is illustrative of the *dualistic* view on life.

Most students taking "Beliefs and Believers" have, to some extent, incorporated a *dualistic* view of reality because it is pervasive in Western culture. If you are one of these students, now is the time to do some serious "moccasin walking." Imagine that the world is not divided in two, is not a place where opposites collide. The universe is a unified system, and there is no way, place or space where one can "opt out" of the system. There is no god or heaven outside the cosmic system of which we are a part here and now. In this unitive, monistic system, our focus is naturally turned to the world, a "this-worldly" focus that lends itself to understanding natural forces and achieving balance and harmony with "the way the universe really works." In other words, to know the *Tao* is to live the good life.

Ethical patterns of action are not just moral demands that when followed make you a "good person." The *ethical dimension* is the relational *microcosm* that on the human level reflects the universal *macrocosm*. All reality, from electrons to solar systems, is generated by the dynamic interaction between *Yin* and *Yang*. What the Chinese sages perceived in the balance of nature and the harmonious interaction of earthly elements is eminently applicable to the day-to-day interactions of human beings in society. Thus, the *Yin Yang* symbol becomes a mirror reflecting the *way the world really is!* As we move through the graphics and view East Asian religion through the aperture of the *six dimensions*, notice how each dimension intertwines and creates a strong exterior foundation for this interior understanding of the *oneness* of all creation.

Interview with Mr. James Miller

Mr. Miller's use of the "sun and shadow on the mountain" metaphor provides us with a wonderful entrance into the East Asian "garden of reality." One can almost imagine an ancient Chinese shepherd quietly tending his flocks in a mountain meadow as the sun moves slowly across the sky. Again, nature is the primary paradigm for the *Tao*. Mr. Miller again underscores the fact that Taoism seeks balance. The Tao has variously been described as the way of ultimate reality; the way of the universe; the way human beings should order their lives. The *Yin/Yang* symbol presents this ideal order as the balance or complement between all opposites. *Yin* is associated with such forces and qualities as earth, moon, night, winter, moisture, coolness, contraction, nurturing, mother and so on. *Yang* represents heaven, sun, day, summer, dryness, warmth, expansion, and aggression.

The tiny black dot in the white whoosh and the corresponding white dot in its black complement reveal, symbolically, that nothing is ever entirely *yin* or *yang*. The goal of life is to find balance between these two extreme poles in a single continuum. When perfect balance is achieved, one is in harmony with the *Tao* and, with *effortless effort*, all human relationships and activities are successful.

Interview at the Ching Chung Taoist Association in San Francisco

Our interview opens with Reverend Wilson Lee and his wife performing a chant designed to honor the ancestors and bring harmony to the temple grounds. The Ching Chung Taoist Association was founded in 1981 in Chinatown in San Francisco and primarily serves the Cantonese speaking population of the area. Notice the colorful symbolic decorations, typical of the Taoist perspective. This temple focuses its ritual practices on Lu Tung-pin, one of the Eight Immortals in Chinese mythology, part of the pantheon of Taoist spiritual ancestors who founded the *Tao* and achieved immortality and great spiritual powers during his lifetime.

The temple includes two main rooms. Reverend Lee speaks to us in front of the central altar in the room used for communal worship. We also get a glimpse of the chamber that houses ancestral shrines and shrines for special prayers. Worship services are regularly held throughout the year, usually on the weekends, new moon, full moon and festival days, but the temple is open daily for people to offer prayers. Thus, the Ching Chung Taoist temple reinforces the three identity-giving factors of family, ancestors, and sacred space.

When we arrived at the temple, we noticed about 30 "planet baskets" set out in order on the temple floor. Reverend Lee explains the symbolism of the objects in each basket. Notice how the most common objects – a ruler, candy, a pair of scissors, food for the family – reflect the order and harmony of the cosmos; hence, each member of the temple congregation has his or her own "planet basket" designed for this harmonizing ritual.

Interview and Class Discussion with Dr. Glenn Shive

Dr. Shive joins us as an expert on Chinese religious and political culture. Like many Westerners, he has been drawn to the *unitive* view of the world inherent in traditional Chinese religious expressions. In fact, in our class discussion, he notes that the famous Catholic writer, Pierre Teilhard de Chardin (1881-1955), developed his quasi-mystical theses on human spiritual evolution while living in China. Dr. Shive helps us understand Chinese religious culture by pointing out that Confucianism, Taoism and Buddhism have acted as three religions in one. In fact, a balanced life might reflect the ethical/ritual demands of Confucianism, the mystical flow of Taoism, and the meditative detachment of Buddhism. In his comments on family, patriarchal culture, and the socio-political changes China has endured under the Communist system, notice that we are clearly on track in our encounter with East Asian religion. The *ethical dimension*, or "how should we then live?" is key to understanding beliefs and believers in the Far East.

Videotape Graphics

At this stage we suggest you watch the videotape. The graphics you will see on the screen are reproduced below to save you the trouble of copying them down. You might like to add your own comments as you watch the tape.

Yin-Yang

Six Dimensions of East Asian Religion

Confucianism, Taoism, and Buddhism form a single, dynamic religious system

Six Dimensions of East Asian Religion

Experiential

Identity: the universe is ONE

Relationship: to live in harmony with the Tao, the way or principle through which nature works

Ch'i = material energy

Li = principle of spiritual energy

Ch'i + Li = essence of all that exists

Mythic

Confucius - born approx. 551 b.c.e.

Lao Tzu - born approx. 604 b.c.e.
 – wrote the Tao Te Ching

Tian = "heaven" – both place and power that rules, especially through the moral order

Yin and Yang = the female and male principles whose interplay forms the basis of all life

Ritual

Li = ritual, ceremonial behavior, propriety, a central concept in Confucian education

Ritual offerings to ancestors

Doctrinal

The teachings of Confucius, Lao Tzu, and classics mediated by the educational system

Ethical

Family relationships become the ground of ethical activity; observance of ancestral rites; honoring parents and meeting ethical obligations; *patterns of action correspond with the Tao*

Ren = virtue, high principle, living in harmony, love

Jun-zi = the superior person who embodies Ren

Social

Ideally, society mirrors the natural harmony and balance of the universe; macrocosm and microcosm are ONE

Importance of family, temples, monasteries, and the Taoist priesthood

Class 21

1. Using our six dimensions of worldviews as your organizational guide, describe the key elements in East Asian religion.

2. What does Confucianism teach us about the importance of the *ethical dimension* in the East Asian view of the world?

3. Describe the primary difference between the Eastern and Western ways of envisioning reality.

4. According to Mr. James Miller, what is the meaning of the *Yin/Yang* symbol?

Sources and Further Readings

Ellwood, Robert S. *Many Peoples, Many Faiths*, 5th ed. Upper Saddle River, NJ: Prentice Hall, 1996.

Smart, Ninian. *The World's Religions*. Englewood Cliffs, NJ: Prentice Hall, 1989.

Waley, Arthur. *The Analects of Confucius*. London: George Allen & Unwin, 1938.

BELIEFS AND BELIEVERS
Class 22 – Social Dimension: Religious Diversity

Introduction

Reflection: *Throughout this course, we have talked about a number of ways human beings relate to life and to each other. As we enter our final dimension, the social dimension, we want to focus on issues regarding religious diversity. For instance, how many different religious organizations can you name in your own community? Is there one dominant religion or does your community reflect the diversity we find on the national level in the United States? Do religion-based tensions exist in your town? Religious diversity also means that in a free society, we have new religious movements emerging all the time. What makes some spiritual movements successful and others fail? These are the kinds of issues we will be exploring as we move through the social dimension.*

Certainly any thinking, caring person is aware that learning to deal with difference is a top priority for the human race. In evolutionary terms, as we move into the first years of the 21st century, learning to handle differences in ethnicity, gender, race, sexual orientation, ableness and, yes, religion may represent a cultural hurdle for human beings on the scale of walking upright, developing language or learning to use tools. Unless we learn to live with our differences, even celebrate our diversity, it is unlikely that as a species we will successfully navigate the turbulent cultural waters ahead.

Unless you have recently emerged from a mountain cave where you have been meditating for the last 40 years or so, you know that the latter decades of the 20th century tossed the United States into the midst of this evolutionary fray. Racism, sexism, homophobia and prejudices of all kinds have attacked the body of our society like a vengeful cancer. Great organizations have emerged to tackle these problems in public programs with familiar titles: the Civil Rights movement, the Feminist movement, Gay and Lesbian Rights, and Multiculturalism, just to name a few. Our ongoing struggle to create a society with "liberty and justice for all" has been covered on TV, in newspapers, and in books to such an extent that the zeal needed to resolve these issues is in danger of degenerating into passive acceptance of the status quo – familiarity breeding indifference.

But what about religious diversity? Rarely do you read or hear about the struggle to overcome religious prejudice. It is only when something extraordinary happens – a religious sect shoots it out with government agents, then commits mass suicide – that the challenge of religious diversity hits the papers and the six o'clock news. Because of this lack of response, the *social dimension* section of "Beliefs and Believers" is designed to help you understand how religious institutions *work*. By understanding the inner workings of religious institutions, you will be better equipped to make sense of the *behavior* of believers who may belong to a religion quite different from your own. Using our unique "Beliefs and Believers" format, we will be investigating the cultural factors that create a fertile field for religious diversity in the United States, identifying the various types of religious institutions and exploring *institutional* dilemmas that religious organizations face, all for the purpose of developing neutral criteria for approaching then appreciating the social reality of religious diversity.

Class 22

Key Class Themes

This lesson focuses on the following themes:

1. Factors contributing to religious diversity
2. Religious ecology
3. Dilemmas of institutionalization
4. Religious ecology at Tabor Lutheran Church and Willow Creek Community Church

Videotape Synopsis

- Class discussion
- Interview with Dr. J. Gordon Melton on appreciating religious diversity
- Interviews with Reverend Robert Lowe and Reverend Cheryl Pero, Tabor Lutheran Church
- Video-roll-in at Willow Creek Community Church

Videotape Commentary

I suggest you read this section before you watch the videotape. You will find that it will help you organize your thoughts so that when you watch the tape it will be more meaningful. When you have finished viewing the tape, you may want to read this section again.

Video Interview with Dr. J. Gordon Melton

Dr. J. Gordon Melton, Director of the Institute for the Study of American Religion and author of the "Encyclopedia of American Religion," is eminently qualified to speak about appreciation of religious diversity. Though he is a devout Methodist and a minister in that faith, he has spent a lifetime chronicling religious diversity here in the United States. More recently, he has turned his attention to global religious diversity. In this short interview, Dr. Melton makes two extremely important points that cut to the core of our "Beliefs and Believers" journey: a) as we move into the early years of the 21st century, population growth and information technology will make human beings in all cultures more intensely aware of religious diversity; b) consequently, overcoming religious prejudices and learning to really appreciate religious diversity may make the difference between global harmony and social chaos. In other words, we are all going to have to get used to "walking a mile in those unfamiliar moccasins."

In the introduction to his "Encyclopedia of American Religion," Dr. Melton identifies four key factors which have contributed to religious diversity in the United States. They are religious freedom, immigration, prosyletization and denominationalism/voluntarism. Let's look at each factor in turn.

1. *Religious Freedom*

"Congress shall make no law respecting the establishment of religion or prohibiting the free exercise thereof. . ." The first Amendment to the United States Constitution begins with this short, 16-word, phrase. The social insight behind these words, however, is unparalleled in terms of the recognition of the power of religion. How interesting that the founders who conceived of and penned the Bill of Rights made the first freedom, religious freedom. Thomas Jefferson and his colleagues hereby receive a posthumous "A" in "Beliefs and Believers." Their understanding of religion as an *identity-forming* and *relationship-guiding* force led them to the societal step of separating religion from all institutions of government.

Now we might take for granted the protection against the establishment of religion and the guarantee of freedom to exercise our religious beliefs. But in the latter years of the 18th century, these concepts were radical! We sometimes refer to a *wall of separation* between church and state, though we have already seen that it functions more like a picket fence. In any event, as long as the minimally accepted mores of society are honored (people tend to frown on rituals like animal sacrifice), citizens of the United States are free to believe what they want, create religious communities and institutions to protect and further their beliefs, or to believe in no religion whatsoever.

2. *Immigration*

Most religious organizations that you might be able to identify arrived on this continent in the hearts and souls of believers who came from someplace else. For instance, French, Irish, Italians, Hispanic immigrants and others brought Roman Catholicism. English, Scotch, Dutch and German believers built a wide variety of Protestant Christian churches representing Methodism, Presbyterianism, Lutheranism, Baptist groups and others. Over time, people from Asia or the Middle East carried Buddhism, Hinduism, Chinese religions and Islam to the shores of America. Settlers from eastern European countries practice Orthodox Christianity. Jews have been in North America since colonial times.

3. *Proselytization*

When we think of proselytizing, an image comes to mind of opening the door to a couple of sincere Mormon missionaries or intense Jehovah's Witnesses. Though these groups may be the most visible in local communities, "evangelism," spreading the gospel whatever it might be, has been part of American culture from colonial times. From great orators like George Whitefield during the early 1700s to a Billy Graham revival in the Rose Bowl, religious people have exercised their right to religious freedom by successfully promoting their worldview and gaining new believers.

We have mentioned that religion is pervasive. The result of proselytizing activity is that a larger percentage of people belong to some religious organization now than at any other period in the nation's history, and with continued immigration, great missionary religions like Buddhism and Islam will, no doubt, attract even more adherents.

Because of religious freedom, people are free to convince other people that their religious perspective is the right one for all people. Sometimes religious zeal in proselytizing crosses the boundaries of free exercise when true believers attack another religion in order to promote their own. This leads to the importance of the next diversifying characteristic.

4. *Denominationalism/Voluntarism*

Denominationalism adds to a social environment characterized by religious pluralism. Religions are "relegated" to a one-among-many status. Denominationalism is a sociological description of how religious organizations have come to be organized in the United States. Unlike a dominant church, no one group takes precedence in a nation with over 1,500 different religious organizations. Given religious freedom, people have the right to *voluntarily* choose a denomination that appeals to them, move to another, create a new religious movement, or choose not to belong to any religious organization at all. Thus, while a group may be incredibly zealous in their beliefs, they cannot effectively upset the apple cart of religious freedom through proselytizing or any other method.

Religious Ecology; Interviews at Tabor Lutheran Church, Chicago and Willow Creek Community Church, South Barrington, Illinois

As you no doubt have realized by now, "Beliefs and Believers" takes the *anthropological approach* in our quest to understanding a wide range of worldviews. Instead of the more traditional theoretical methods available in religious studies, in each class we investigate religions as they exist in distinct communities. We talk to real believers who practice their chosen worldviews in social environments that, as we have found, can be incredibly diverse and complex.

The model or method we have been using is best described as *religious ecology*. Religious organizations in any cultural environment represent creative human activity that may contribute to or challenge the delicate balance between harmony and discord in a given community; *ecology* underscores this living, dynamic relationship between a religious organization and its immediate cultural setting.

Class 22

Put simply, religious organizations change communities; communities change religious organizations. We have also noticed that these organizations are made up of unique individuals. Certainly Buddhism, Christianity, Islam and so on are recognizable and describable religious phenomena. But in the day-to-day lives of human beings, there are no *pure form* Buddhists or Christians or Muslims. There are people practicing, say, Tibetan Buddhism, like Greg Conlee at the Dharmadatu Meditation Center, or Ramtha followers like Pavel Mickeloski, or African- American Muslims like Dr. Salaam. These people practice their religion within a distinct community and *ecological niche*, so to speak, that is affected by and affects religious expression in that community.

As part of our exploration of the *social dimension*, we want to develop this concept of *religious ecology*. In order to accomplish this task, we are fortunate to have three excellent examples of a successful, dynamic relationship between a religious organization and the community in which it arises: Tabor Lutheran Church in an African American community on the south side of Chicago and Willow Creek Community Church in the wealthy Chicago suburb of South Barrington.

Interview with Reverend Lowe, Tabor Lutheran Church

The moment you step into Tabor Lutheran Church you are swept up in the energy of the organization. Though the church edifice is not particularly large, every inch of space is put to use in the service of the surrounding community. The bulletin board is filled with signs advertising jobs, day care, educational and medical assistance programs, self-help programs and so on. Reverend Lowe even opens the church sanctuary to other religious groups in the community who are without a building. When we arrived for our interviews, a group of Haitian Seventh Day Adventists were holding services. The preacher spoke in English which was being translated by an interpreter into French!

Reverend Lowe's comments about the early years of his ministry certainly support our religious ecology theory. As neighborhoods change, churches need to meet the challenges those changes bring. The image he describes upon first visiting Tabor – 70-year-old white Swedes who had literally boarded up the windows to keep the surrounding neighborhood out – provides us with an excellent example of a religious organization pushed entirely into the private sphere. One might expect that when the last member of the predominantly white church died, the congregation would fold, and the church would be sold to some other group. Reverend Lowe, however, attacked those dilemmas of institutionalization with a vengeance, striking a working balance between secular and religious activities. As he says, the primary work of the church is evangelism, renewing the spiritual energy of the Christian believers who attend the church. All the rest of the week, in the name of Christ, the church takes over as a multi-institutional center, serving the worldly needs of all peoples in that particular *ecological niche* of south-side Chicago.

Interview with Reverend Cheryl Pero

Reverend Cheryl Pero underscores our religious ecology theme when she states that you need to have a handle on the cultural context of a congregation before you can begin to be an effective pastor. Just as Lithuanian Catholics and Hispanic Catholics have different styles of worship within the same religion, Swedish and African American Lutherans are going to demand different social responses from the leaders of their respective churches. Reverend Pero seems to be saying that once you establish a balance between spiritual aspiration and secular need, you can successfully proceed with the business of evangelism without hindrance. Or, as Reverend Lowe colorfully remarks, his church is successful because the believers know who they are; "We're black first, Christian second, and Lutheran third!" What does his comment tell us about the identity, community and the nature of successful religious organizations?

Religious Ecology; Willow Creek Community Church

A Saturday evening service at Willow Creek Community Church may be the best entertainment value in the entire Chicago area. Essentially, it is free, but the talent, the timing and the professional atmosphere would rival any dinner show in Las Vegas. Yet the Christian message is sincere and powerfully felt by those in attendance. If there ever were an example of a religious organization that successfully adapted to the pressures of secularization, it is Willow Creek Community Church.

The obvious visual proof of success was explained to us by Mark Mittelburg, head of evangelism at the church. About 20 years ago, Willow Creek's founder Reverend Bill Hybels, decided to establish a church that was relevant, entertaining, and spiritually authentic. Taking a page from the business community, he initiated a marketing program designed to see what keeps people from attending church. When he found that people considered the average church service to be boring or not relevant in helping individuals through life's challenges, he essentially melded ancient Christian doctrine to a sparkling, modern format of dance, music, drama and, of course, good Christian preaching.

While the cynic might suspect that the church was in it for the money, that is not the impression you get from speaking with church leaders or simply wandering around the halls of the massive, modern church edifice. Like Tabor Lutheran, Willow Creek acts as a multi-institutional center for the community. Through more than 90 different ministries – from food pantries to marriage counseling to spiritual direction – this religious organization responds to the needs of the people who, once again, populate the church's own *ecological niche*.

In addition, the show-business exterior hides a truly authentic Christian ministry. People may be initially attracted to the church because of the upbeat services, but their devotion to the organization through volunteer work and the joy that seems to accompany the entire effort indicates that something important is happening to them experientially, in this case, as Christians. The serious side of the ministry is demonstrated in the effort to challenge believers with intellectual questions and provide evidence for the truthfulness of Christianity. Here we have an interesting connection between the *doctrinal* and *social dimensions*.

If you reflect on the segment of Reverend Hybels' sermon which we were able to record, you find another example of the expert blend of the sacred and the secular, a religious organization and its community. We happened to visit at the beginning of a six week set of sermons on marriage. Obviously, family relationships present a major life challenge to members of the upscale communities that surround the church. Reverend Hybels reduces all of life's problems to the selection of a Master (in this case, Jesus Christ), a mate, and a mission (or purpose, career, occupation and so on). The primary thrust of the church is spiritual, but in a religiously ecological manner, the church offers a pathway to the holy that leads through the day-to-day challenges members meet in their lives. The path to the extraordinary leads through the ordinary.

In summary, we have seen two churches that have successfully bargained with the secular, overcome the dilemmas of institutionalization and entered into a balanced, productive relationship with the surrounding community. Religious ecology at work!

Videotape Graphics

 At this stage we suggest you watch the videotape. The graphics you will see on the screen are reproduced below to save you the trouble of copying them down. You might like to add your own comments as you watch the tape.

Religious Freedom in America

1st Amendment to the Constitution

"Congress shall make no law respecting the establishment of religion or prohibiting the free exercise thereof . . ."

Two clauses
– no establishment
– free exercise

Diversity in American Religion

Four factors contribute to a religiously diverse social environment

Religious Freedom
– 1st Amendment protection;
  "don't tread on me!"

Immigration
– I brought my religion with me!

Proselytization
– I'm free to knock on your door
  and spread "the faith"!

Denominationalism/Voluntarism
– Nobody's going to tell me where to
    worship; I can make my own choice,
    thank you!

Four Factors = a diverse religious ecology!

Religious Ecology

Examples

Tabor Lutheran Church =
Rev. Lowe and Rev. Cheryl Pero

Willow Creek Community Church =
Rev. Bill Hybels and Rev. Mark Mittelburg

Religious Ecology

Each religious organization is successful in
handling the "dilemmas of institutionalization"
by adapting to its respective cultural environments.

> **Dilemmas of Institutionalization**
> – mixed motivation of members over time
> – maintaining the vitality of the symbol
>   system (myth and ritual)
> – organizational elaboration vs.
>   movement effectiveness
> – need for concrete definition (doctrine)
>   vs. legalism
> – balancing power factions within and
>   without the organization

Review Questions

Answering the following questions will help you review key class themes and prepare
for examinations.

1. What are the four major factors that contribute to religious diversity in the social environment of the United States?

2. What is religious ecology? Provide some examples, other than the ones we use in this class, to illustrate the concept.

3. Identify the five dilemmas of institutionalization and describe their impact on a secular and a religious organization.

4. Do you think the style of worship at Willow Creek would work at Tabor Lutheran? If not, what does this tell us about the relationship between a religious organization and its immediate community?

Sources and Further Readings

McGuire, Meredith. *Religion: The Social Context,* 4th ed. Belmont, CA: Wadsworth, 1997.

BELIEFS AND BELIEVERS
Class 23 – Social Dimension: New Religious Movements

Introduction

Reflection: *In our previous lesson, we developed the concept of religious ecology. Religious organizations are part of a complex web of institutions, the totality of which make up a given sociocultural environment. We need to consider another interesting dilemma faced by religious organizations. Institutions, by nature, are secular; they function in the realm of the ordinary. Yet the religious impulse calls humans towards the sacred, the extraordinary. In terms of our religious ecology theme, what happens when a religious organization becomes too secular and no longer satisfies the spiritual needs of its adherents? We will be exploring a variety of scenarios that might occur in response to this rather common situation.*

Warning! Warning! This class may stimulate the *confusion centers* in your brain! And, as is so often the case when studying religion, *temporary confusion* is both appropriate and natural. What we will be attempting to do in our class on new religious movements is essentially impossible. We want to try to define different types of religious organizations so that we can develop a terminology or typology for new religious movements. In an academic atmosphere, this endeavor is also appropriate and natural. However, drawing on our *ecological* model, no religious movement exists as a discrete or separate organization apart from other institutions in society. What seems to be a *new religious movement* to outsiders may well be a re-discovery of ancient truths to those inside the movement. If you recall Cynthia Jones' description of Diana's Grove, that is exactly how she envisions the *new* spiritual movement she created.

Thus *churches* or *denominations*, the established-species in our ecological niche, are also linked to *sects* and *cults* in their own complex struggle to maintain supremacy in a limited spiritual food chain. What all of this means is that one person's *established religious organization* may well be another person's *cult*. As students attempting to develop a typology of religious organizations, which we are, the best we can hope for is a set of *neutral* terms that will help us distinguish between long-term, successful religious organizations that have weathered those pesky *dilemmas of institutionalization* and the *mutant-species* that inevitably break off from their parent organizations in the quest to find authentic spirituality.

Someone once defined a "cult" as any religious group another religious group doesn't happen to like. In fact, most people tend to use the term *cult* along with *sect* to identify a religious organization that is out of the mainstream, perhaps considered dangerous, certainly in tension with the more established institutions in society. For more than 100 years, sociologists of religion have tried to hammer out criteria for determining these types of religious organizations and basically have come up with two major defining characteristics.

In this class we try to make the case that sect and cult formation are a natural process within a dynamic, open ecological niche characteristic of a nation like the United States. In fact it is the process of secularization that contributes to emergent religious activity. Keep in mind as you work with this material, that we are talking about a process. For the sake of clarity and review, we might outline this process as follows:

Step one: all institutions face the dilemmas of institutionalization (see previous class).

Step two: in dealing with these dilemmas, religious organizations are forced into a more secular stance. They must spend more energy (time, money, human effort) dealing with worldly concerns rather than concentrating on the distinctly spiritual nature of their shared endeavor. Another way to put it is that organizational success increases secular concerns; a true dilemma!

Step three: members who no longer feel that their spiritual needs are being met will, in fact, leave the organization and start a new one which from the seeker's point of view is more spiritually authentic and less involved with ordinary, secular concerns.

Thus, the formation of sects and cults is not some kind of disruptive or devious activity but is part of the dynamic living ecological process that continuously transpires in the social dimension. For example, we have mentioned in class that there are over 1500 different varieties of religious organizations in the United States. When you consider that of this number 900 or so are varieties of Christianity, you get a sense of the pervasiveness of the sect-cult formation process.

Terms like cult and sect are culturally relative and can only be applied according to the new organization's relationship with the dominant religious organizations present in a particular society. For example, in the United States, the dominant religious organizations are Christian. A new religious organization that still makes claims to being Christian would be a sect. But if the leaders decided to form the same group in, say, a predominantly Hindu section of India, the lack of cultural connection would place the group in the cult category. Can you see how this method of applying these terms relieves us of pejorative connotations and more fairly describes the dynamics of religious organizations in society?

Another important point, from the perspective of religious ecology, is that we can detect a cyclic pattern in sect-cult formation. Yesterday's cults may well turn out to be tomorrow's established denominations. As we discuss in class, religious organizations may, over time, evolve through different stages from cult, to sect, to denomination. Mormonism provides an interesting example. Joseph Smith certainly felt he was restoring the true Christian church. In relation to the dominant Christian society, the early Mormon church could be defined as a sect. However, over the course of several years, some of Smith's unique revelations, such as the institution of polygamy, pushed the organization into a more cultic stance with the dominant culture. Today the Mormon church reflects a more denominational stance – one of many established groups that an American may voluntarily join. Yet, periodically, splinter groups will break off from the church as believers react to perceived secularization in Mormon institutions. Though the Latter Day Saints group is by far the largest, a recent perusal of the Encyclopedia of American Religion revealed over 40 existing groups that claim to be Mormon.

Another example; Christianity began as a Jewish sect. However, through the influence of St. Paul's progressively more radical interpretation of the life and teaching of Jesus, a new religious movement was born, Christianity. Christianity was a cult in its relation to other religious institutions in first century society. Today, of course, depending on the cultural context, you can identify Christian groups that might fit into each of our four categories, church, denomination, sect, and even cult.

Without the development of new religious movements, the world would never have known Buddhism, Christianity, Islam or the other great world traditions. Depending again on the cultural context, all the major religions were, at one time, a sect, a cult, or both. Consequently it is both inaccurate and unfair to use the terms as negative appellations for groups you don't happen to appreciate.

Key Class Themes

This lesson focuses on the following themes:

1. The *cultic impulse*
2. Secularization and religious organizations
3. Types of religious organizations
4. Baha'i World Faith

Videotape Synopsis

- Class discussion
- Video interview - Dr. J. Gordon Melton
- Video interview - Ronald Precht, Baha'i faith

Videotape Commentary

I suggest you read this section before you watch the videotape. You will find that it will help you organize your thoughts so that when you watch the tape it will be more meaningful. When you have finished viewing the tape, you may want to read this section again.

Class Discussion

Our opening class discussion extends our collective struggle with the same sociological quandary we wrestled with in Class 22. How does any religious organization strike a balance between social relevance and spiritual authenticity? Suzanne makes the case for social relevance in her interrupted story about the rich farmer who wanted to build bigger barns to hold all his grain. His motivation, at first, seems noble enough. The farmer wanted to invite all his friends over for a huge feast. But the hierophonic voice of God booms down upon him, condemning him as a fool who is doomed to die that very day. He should have shared his wealth with any human being who hungered not hoard his grain so his friends could be impressed by his material good fortune.

As Suzanne points out, the moral of the story, from the Christian perspective, is that we are not owners of what we receive, only stewards of the material rewards that come our way. Put another way, the farmer obviously missed one of the real fundamentals of Jesus' ministry; compassion, caring, and concern for all human beings not just friends or family. In essence, the farmer missed the social relevance dimension of his chosen faith. An ancient Eastern Orthodox Christian saying goes, "When you go to heaven, you go in community; when you go to Hell, you fall alone." Virginia underscored the importance of a religious organization being socially relevant with her contribution about the San Diego church that successfully ministers to an incredibly diverse constituency.

On the other hand, Janet's real life anecdote about the struggle for spiritual authenticity at a Thai Buddist Temple illustrates one of our key sociological factors. When a religious organization is overly attentive to worldly, secular concerns, members may be compelled to leave the group and form a new sect. In this instance, in response to what they considered excessive preoccupation with Thai culture, members of the organization left the Temple and formed a sect where the primary focus returned to meditation. Spiritual authenticity won out over social relevance. But what might happen several years down the pike when new members of this sect begin to be concerned about social conditions in the Thai community. Will they leave to form a new sect? Once again, the lively, effervescent world of religious ecology is evident! And this is exactly what we want to explore in Class 23.

Class 23

Interview with Dr. J. Gordon Melton

Dr. Melton returns to challenge the very practice of developing typologies for religious organizations. Please don't be overly confused by his claim that terms like sect and cult may no longer be relevant in a religious world that is increasingly pluralistic. If you listen carefully to what he says about religious diversity, he takes issue with the use of religious types if they continue to be used by members of the religious establishment to demean a minority religion in a given social environment. His point is well taken. During our class discussion, we wrestle with his provocative perspective on the sociological practice of typologizing religious organizations. There is no easy answer, but categories do help us understand diversity, if, once again, they are the categories that are not used to ostracize or criticize someone or some group that is different. What is your informed opinion now on the use of terms like sect and cult to define new religious movements?

Inteview with Ronald Precht, Baha'i World Faith

We purposely picked the Baha'i World Faith to illustrate how difficult it is to cast a new religious movement as a sect or a cult. You will notice in our interview with Ronald Precht that he backs away from our categories, preferring to see the emergence of the Baha'i faith as a completely new religious revelation with no connection to the culture from which it emerged. Well, you can't argue with a believer, but the historians and sociologists do recognize a distinct cultural environment, or ecological niche, that provided the necessary "gene pool" for the Baha'i religious species. Some historical background will help.

Since the roots of the Baha'i faith can be traced to 19th century Persia (Iran, today), we need to consider the development of this new religious movement in relation to the dominant Islamic society. Mirza Ali Muhammad (1820-50) was the first of two religious visionaries who ignited the movement. He declared himself to be the Bab or gate through whom people would know about the imminent coming of a messenger from God – a world redeemer who would teach the "true religion of God," relieve the sufferings of humanity, clear up all the mistakes made by previous religions, and initiate a new age characterized by world peace, justice, morality, and equality. Do you notice any similarities with the early Muslim mythos?

Soon the Bab had sufficient followers to make him a threat to the establishment, and he was accused by the Persian authorities of inciting political revolution and was executed. A follower, Mirza Husain Ali (1817-92), became convinced that he was the prophet foretold by the Bab. In 1863 he declared himself to be that manifestation of God come to Earth to redeem the world at the end of the age and interpret God's plan for a new era. He changed his name to Baha'u'llah, meaning "Glory of God," and claimed to be the fulfillment of the promises in all religions of a coming messiah who would bring about the long-awaited kingdom of God.

Though small at first, the Baha'i World Faith has continued to grow until, today, the movement is represented in over 70,000 centers located in Asia, Europe, Africa, and North and South America. The primary appeal of the Baha'i World Faith is its doctrinal and institutional universality which is reflected in the following eleven principles:

- the independent investigation of truth
- the oneness of the human race
- religion should be the cause of love and affection (not hate)
- the conformity of religion to science and reason
- the abolition of religious, racial, political, and patriotic prejudice
- the equal opportunity to the means of existence

- the equality of persons before the law

- universal peace

- the noninterference of religion in politics

- the equality of the sexes

- the power of the Holy Spirit as the means of spiritual development

When society is finally transformed according to God's will as revealed by Baha'u'llah, there will be one executive and legislative body, a universal language, a single currency, and a uniform system of justice. Baha'is see their religious services as a spiritual preparation for the social tasks that will bring about this global revolution. What a wonderful example of the relationship between the doctrinal, ethical, and social dimensions!

Mr. Precht makes a strong case for the uniqueness of the Baha'i faith. As you can imagine, he is responding to two counter-claims that Baha'is find offensive: a) the religion is a sect of Islam; b) the religion is an amalgam of other world traditions, constructed artificially from Islam, Christianity, and Eastern religion. While Baha'is see their worldview as a completely independent, revealed, new religious movement, in its relationship to other religious organizations within the global ecological niche, the Baha'i World Faith has moved and continues to move, as do all religious organizations, through the relational types we have discussed in the institutional quest to survive and prosper.

Videotape Graphics

At this stage we suggest you watch the videotape. The graphics you will see on the screen are reproduced below to save you the trouble of copying them down. You might like to add your own comments as you watch the tape.

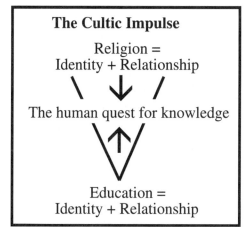

The Cultic Impulse

Religion =
Identity + Relationship

The human quest for knowledge

Education =
Identity + Relationship

Institutional Dilemma

Religion like *Education* is, at the same time, an institution of stability (control) and change (progress/evolution) in society

Cults and *Sects* are "institutional mutations," sometimes dangerous, often beneficial, but always part of the process in the religious ecology of a free society

The Formation of New Religious Movements

The dilemmas of institutionalization; all institutions in society face these dilemmas

The Formation of New Religious Movements

The Process of Secularization

– The dilemmas of institutionalization force religious organizations into a more secular stance
– They must spend more energy (time, money) dealing with worldly concerns rather than concentrating on religious concerns
– Occasionally, members who no longer feel that their spiritual needs are being met leave the religious organization and start a new religious movement

Sect = renews the true faith

Cult = innovative; does not share the symbol system of the dominant religions in a given social environment

Religious Organizations

Four types within the religious ecology of any culture
Established species:
Religious organizations that have successfully handled the dilemmas of institutionalization

Four Types:

Church
a dominant religious organization in a given society

Denomination
one of many religious organizations in a diverse social environment; voluntary attendance

Sect
a splinter group that forms to renew the true faith; breaks off from an "established species" but maintains the same symbol system
Example: Branch Davidians are a sect of the Christian Adventist groups

Cult
a splinter group that is innovative; a new religious movement that shares little symbolic connection to the "established species" of religion
Example: Ramtha or Cindy Jones' Diana's Grove

Review Questions

Answering the following questions will help you review key class themes and prepare for the examinations.

1. Define church, denomination, sect and cult. How do the dilemmas of institutionalization and secularization affect the formation of these different groups? Please use examples from our class materials to illustrate this process.

2. Describe the process of sect/cult formation in terms of our religious ecology theme. Why, in American society, would we expect to find more dynamic organizational activity on the religious front than in some less pluralistic social environment?

3. After listening to our representative from the Baha'i World Faith, would you describe the religion as a sect of Islam, a new religious movement (a cult, in our terminology), another denomination or all of the above? Please explain your perspective.

4. What social factors determine whether a new religious movement is considered a sect or a cult?

Sources and Further Readings

Elwood, Robert S. *Alternative Altars*. Chicago: University of Chicago Press, 1979.

Hathcer, William S. and J. Douglas Martin. *The Baha'i Faith*. San Francisco: Harper & Row, 1984.

Melton, J. Gordon. *The Encyclopedia of American Religions*. Detroit: Gale Research, 1989. (See the material on Baha'i World Faith).

Stark, Rodney and William Bainbridge. *The Future of Religion*. Berkeley, CA: University of California Press, 1985.

BELIEFS AND BELIEVERS
Class 24 – Social Dimension: New Directions

Introduction

Reflection: *As we come to the end of the course, we want to reflect on one of the most important questions we have addressed this semester. As society becomes increasingly religiously pluralistic, how are adherents of different worldviews going to respond? Time and time again, we have seen that true believers fervently wish to see their beliefs realized in the world around them. However, common sense tells us it is simply not going to be possible for society to be shaped by so many different perspectives. As you view this class, please keep this question in mind; given the variety of worldviews that compete for power in society, is pluralism possible? If it is not, then what is the alternative? As Professor Robert Moore so eloquently puts it in our accompanying interview, isn't it time for the religious leaders of the world to join forces in working for peace and a sustainable future for all species on this planet?*

Key Class Themes

This lesson focuses on the following themes:

1. Conventional and non-conventional religions
2. Conventionality in the United States
3. Criteria for conventionality
4. Summary remarks by the students

Videotape Synopsis

- Class discussion
- Video-interview; Dr. Keith Naylor, Occidental College, Los Angeles
- Video-interview; Dr. Robert Moore, President, The Institute for World Spirituality

Videotape Commentary

I suggest you read this section before you watch the videotape. You will find that it will help you organize your thoughts so that when you watch the tape it will be more meaningful. When you have finished viewing the tape, you may want to read this section again.

Class Discussion/Neutral Culture-Based Criteria That Determine Conventionality

The first question we should ask ourselves is why bother trying to create categories in which to place religious organizations? The simple answer is that the exercise brings order to our study of what is certainly a most complex social phenomenon. The factors we identified in Class 22 that contribute to religious diversity in the United States represent a living, active, dynamic process that generates a veritable plethora of worldviews. In sorting out groups along our church-denomination-sect-cult continuum, we not only learn something about the ecological patterns of religion in America, but, in addition, we might discover clues that will tell us how society can successfully deal with increasing religious pluralism.

201

In class discussion, the students do a good job of identifying commonsense, non-threatening reasons why a religious organization may be deemed conventional or non-conventional in the United States or in any ecological niche. Janet points out that a religious organization seems conventional if just about every town or city in a given social environment has one. That's the common sense dimension of these criteria. A religion is conventional if we don't notice it! During my weekly commutes from Macomb, Illinois up to the Chicago area, I regularly passed through many small towns with Methodist, Baptist, Lutheran, or Roman Catholic churches. Like most people, I hardly noticed them because I simply am used to seeing them within the social environment of Illinois.

But what if I'm cruising through the corn fields and, low and behold, I pass a traditional Hindu Temple. Inevitably, my cognitive faculties scream out, "Non-conventional alert!" In fact, this often happens near Aurora, Illinois where the Hindu community has built a beautiful temple just off of I-88. When driving that stretch of road, it's amusing to watch other travelers gawk at this non-conventional structure rising out of the corn fields. However, even the most predominant religious organization can take on non-conventional status given a change in social environment. As Lynne observes in her comment about the "Catholic settlement," it is ecological niche that defines conventionality. Roman Catholicism is the largest Christian denomination in America, but, in the small Methodist town Lynne visited, Catholics seemed so unconventional that they were seen to occupy their own "settlement," not unlike the Amish.

Barbara notes that religion and culture go hand in hand. A religion seems conventional if it reflects the traditions and values of a given culture. Accordingly, religious organizations that have been around longer are more likely to seem conventional. When people look out on the social horizon, they see familiar cultural contours when they encounter conventional religions. And, as Helen adds, conventionality has much to do with "making sense" to believers. Obviously, it is easier for a religion to "make sense," experientially, if it embraces familiar themes that touch on conventional traditions and values.

As we move through the graphics on the criteria of conventionality, see if you can remember any experiences you've had in which these criteria may have caused you to involuntarily deem a religion conventional or non-conventional. And notice how the following criteria can be applied to cultural phenomena other than religion, be it politics, fashion, economics, or education.

1. Longevity: anything, including a religious organization, seems more conventional if it has been around a given cultural environment longer.

2. Tradition: because they have been around longer, conventional religions tend to share and reflect the cultural *ambience* or have played an important part in shaping cultural traditions.

3. Reflection of prevailing values: conventional religions, especially in the ethical dimension, express and support the values and mores that most citizens embrace.

4. Numbers: conventional religions have more members and, consequently, influence society's perception of what is correct religious behavior in our B+B=B equation.

5. Tension: having met all of the above criteria, conventional religions blend in well with other institutions in the cultural landscape; they are in harmony with other institutions and social structures.

We have met a number of good, sincere people who happen to belong to a religious organization that is non-conventional according to our characteristics of conventionality within the cultural environment of the United States: Shankara, a devotee of the Krishna Consciousness movement, Cynthia Jones of Diana's Grove, JZ Knight who channels Ramtha, Kate Cogan, a witch, or Dr. Salaam, the African American Muslim. All are exceptional people who simply have chosen to express their religiosity in an institutional form that, for one reason or another, does not meet the criteria of conventionality in the dominant culture.

So how might we divide up religious organizations according to our conventional/non-conventional categories if we apply our neutral, culture-based criteria to the cultural environment of the United States? In this nation, we have a Judeo-Christian core and other religious organizations which, for one reason or another, are divergences from the core. Of course just as in our church-denomination-sect-cult typology, religious organizations can move from conventional to non-conventional, and back again within the religious ecology of the nation.

For example, Christian Science, the 19th century made-in-America religion we have discussed previously, has, for many years, functioned like a conventional religious denomination in American society. However, with the recent manslaughter conviction of Christian Science parents who sought to treat their child's illness with prayer – unsuccessfully – the organization is being pushed into a more non-conventional stance vis-a-vis the dominant society. In other words, an increase in tension between secular and sacred institutional expressions of healing makes an otherwise conventional denomination more sect-like.

During our class discussion of conventionality, Helen takes issue with my placement of Unitarian Universalists in the Middle Ground category between conventional and non-conventional. Helen identifies herself as a Unitarian, and proceeds to launch into a mini-lecture on the non-creedal, liberal traditions of Unitarian Universalists. Here is a case where a student in the class actually becomes data for the class, not unlike my negative teaching experience with the Nation of Islam student who attacked me in class for showing a traditional Muslim prayer service (see Class 18). Helen is a believer. Though she is, herself, a scholar and an intellectual, when it comes to her religion, she takes it personally and rises to defend what she considers to be a slight against her chosen religious path. Her reaction teaches us an important lesson. It is relatively easy to create categories for religious organizations, using scholarly methods in a detached and open-minded manner. It is not so easy to get believers to rest comfortably in those categories. Once again, we have evidence of the power of religious belief and the intense emotions religious beliefs can generate, even in a neutral classroom setting. In any event, thanks to Helen, we got to learn more about another important American religion, Unitarian Universalism, and I received a beautiful pin illustrating the sacred symbols of the world's great religions!

Returning to our investigation of conventionality in religious ecology of the United States, let's look at a rough breakdown of conventional and non-conventional groups. Of course the groups we identify are examples of a much wider range of religious organizations, be they conventional or non-conventional. Remember that there are over 1500 different religious organizations in the United States and of that number probably 900 consider themselves Christian.

Core Groups

Christian:
- Lutherans
- Roman Catholics
- Episcopalians
- Methodists
- Reformed-Presbyterians
- Baptists
- Independant Christian groups
- Eastern Orthodox Christianity

Judaism:
- Reformed
- Conservative
- Orthodox/Hasidism (possibly occupying the Middle Ground)

Middle Ground

Obviously, we have groups that occupy a middle ground between conventionality and non-conventionality in this categorization process because of differences on belief or behavior. Being a relatively new church, such as the Pentecostal Assembly of God, might place a group in this area. Mormons might be included because of doctrinal differences with the more established forms of Christianity. We have already mentioned the Christian Science Church due to its believers' clashes with the secular medical establishment. Jehovah's Witnesses occupy a middle ground because of their aggressive prosyletizing and refusal to acknowledge certain political patterns of action such as swearing the oath of allegiance to the Flag. My position on the Unitarian Universialists is they occupy a middle ground precisely because of their non-creedal, liberal, open-minded attitude towards religious expression. Though Helen might not agree, most established religious organizations would find it a bit "non-conventional" to legitimize a group of pagans at the national convention. More power to them and her! Yet all these groups are certainly established enough to reflect a guarded conventionality.

Non-Conventional Religions

We want to stress again that our criteria for determining conventionality or non-conventionality are neutral and culture-based. A Methodist church in Macomb, Illinois is conventional because, in that cultural setting or ecological niche, Methodism meets the criteria of conventionality. On the other hand, a Methodist church in Pakistan would be non-conventional according to those same neutral criteria. Non-conventionality has nothing whatsoever to do with a religion's truth, quality, or ability to satisfy the spiritual needs of adherents. It is only non-conventional for one or more of the reasons listed above. As we mention in class, Islam is conventional in Pakistan but non-conventional in Macomb, Illinois simply because Islam has not been in that particular cultural environment as long as, say, Methodists have. Nevertheless, as the country becomes increasingly more religiously diverse, Islam has passed Judaism as the "Number 2 faith" in the United States. While Buddists may be as rare as Tofu in Macomb, in parts of Los Angeles and San Francisco, there are more Buddhist temples than Methodist churches. In fact, some groups can be listed in all three areas which is helpful in understanding that this categorization process is, again, a dynamic, changing part of the religious ecology in any culture. Here would be some examples of non-conventionality in the United States.

Eastern traditions:
- Buddhism
- Hinduism
- East Asian religions

Middle Eastern traditions:
-Islam
-Baha'i faith

New Age Spirituality, Gnostic Spirituality:
- Ramtha School of Enlightenment
- Diana's Grove

Skeptics:
- Atheists
- Humanists

New Religious Movements:
- Unifications Church
- Scientology

Millennial Groups:
- Branch Davidians

Occult Traditions:
- Spiritualists
- psychics
- Tarot
- Wicca
- Kabbalists
- Theosophy
- Rosicrucianism
- UFO groups
- Ritual Magic
- Satanists

The point here is that there are over eight hundred religious organizations that are divergences from the core groups. It is possible, over time, for any one of them to move into the conventional category. For instance, in Dearborn, Michigan, some high schools have a Muslim population that exceeds one third of the students. In that community, it would be hard to say that Islam is non-conventional. Here we have another important lesson in religious ecology; you cannot really understand the presence and importance of a given worldview outside of the cultural environment in which it arises.

Video Interview with Dr. Keith Naylor

Religious diversity presents a challenge because, so often, tensions and prejudices that exist in the general culture spoil the relationship between different religious groups and distort the religious expressions in that culture. Several times throughout the semester, we have seen how patriarchal traditions in a given cultural setting have generated androcentric attitudes in religion. Dr. Naylor helps us out with another cultural disease that spreads dissonance in this culture, namely, racism. In the Los Angeles riots of the early '90s, Koreans and African Americans found themselves entangled in a web of distrust, hostility, and violence. From his own experience living in Los Angeles, Dr. Naylor shows how religious organizations, in this case, one Korean and one African American, can work together to overcome prejudice and, in doing so, create a more authentic spirituality within their respective churches. Not a bad paradigm to apply in easing social tensions around the nation!

Video Interview with Professor Robert Moore

Professor Moore, whom we met in a previous class, provides us with a fitting last interview. Perhaps our entrance into a new millennium, at least according to the Western calendar, has engendered a sense of urgency when it comes to healing ancient wounds and developing new, positive patterns of action on the global level. Dr. Moore, a practicing psychoanalyst, makes the astute observation that organizations who misuse their collective energy to exploit the natural environment and prey on other human beings seem to have no trouble coming together to further their negative goals. Why can't the religious leaders find common cause and join with other world leaders to work for peace and harmony and save the planet for our children's children?

At the Institute for World Spirituality which he heads, Dr. Moore works with other like-minded people to harness its energies for the construction and safeguarding of community. If we are, in fact, at a critical point in world history, a *kairos* as the famed theologian Paul Tillich calls it, then we need to rid ourselves of self-limiting attitudes and prejudices. For

Dr. Moore, the "Beliefs and Believers" goal of appreciating religious diversity is more than just an academic objective. The religious leaders of the world must tap into the spiritual current that links all authentic spiritual paths, then, in an atmosphere of communication and consensus, work together to create a peaceful, inclusive, sustaining global environment and, thus, save our species and all others on our beautiful, blue planet Earth.

Concluding Remarks

In the closing minutes of Class 24, Janet and Suzanne offer new insight into our quest to appreciate religious diversity. Janet asks us to look for commonality in religious expressions. She points out how often the believers we met during the semester made use of the most common elements on the planet to articulate or express their respective beliefs. That element is water. From Christians being baptized in the waters of the river Jordon to Dr. Davé's myth of the Ganges and on to Cynthia Jones' impromptu class ritual or the ascended master Ramtha toasting his followers, water, that life-giving substance that unites all the planet's continents and peoples, is, indeed, a wonderful symbol of commonality.

Suzanne asks us to take risks. Change is inevitable. As we move into a new millennium that surely will be characterized by increased diversity in all cultural experiences, we can either respond to change with fear and anxiety or we can risk letting go of old but comfortable prejudices and stereotypes. Taking a class like "Beliefs and Believers" is not particularly risky. Risk comes in when you leave the classroom and the course behind and begin to apply your newly-acquired worldview analysis skills in real life situations.

Class 24 marks the end of the "Beliefs and Believers" Teleclass, but for the student who wants to make the most of this unique educational experience, it is only the beginning. Now comes the fun part; applying your newly developed worldview analysis skills in the world around you. Over the semester, we've met many, many believers who have talked to us about what they believe, why they believe it, and how it affects their behavior. You've also gotten to know our wonderful students in the television classroom who have brought so much collective insight to our discussions. I've certainly learned a lot from them, and I hope you have.

I've taught this class more than a hundred times, yet each class brings new insights. I thought it appropriate to close out this "new and improved" edition of the Study Guide with a collection of special insights on the nature of religion and spirituality that have emerged in our class discussions, our interaction with class guests, as well as our reflections on video interviews with a diverse group of believers from around the globe. The following thoughts are not necessarily scholarly observations. Rather they embody the "spirit" of our educational journey together. Since you are now part of that journey, please feel free to add your own good thoughts, but most of all, pass them on to anyone you might meet as you continue to explore beliefs and believers. Enjoy the journey!!

Class Insights:

1. There is no such thing as religion. Only people, real human beings, practicing their faiths within a complex web of cultural, political, economic, and social institutions.

2. There are no true or false, good or bad religions. A religion is only as good and true as the person living it.

3. Killing in the name of religion always represents a failure of human spirituality.

4. Walk a mile in someone's moccasins before you judge him or her.

5. Human spiritual instinct precedes the institutional expression of the world's religions.

6. Religion and education suffer from similar dilemmas; they are at the same time institutions of stability (control) and change (evolution/transformation) in society.

7. In the foothills beneath the great mountain of human religiosity, believers might argue and fight over the truth or falsity of the world's religions. At the top of the mountain, conflicts evaporate in the bright sunshine of spiritual unity.

8. It takes a true spiritual leader to overcome cultural prejudices like racism and gender bias and create a religious expression that is inclusive of all peoples.

9. You can't talk to people about God if they're hungry. Invite everyone to the table, feed them, comfort them, meet their human needs, then they're ready to hear about God.

10. The world's great religious leaders need to cease squabbling over doctrinal differences and work with leaders of other institutions at the global level to assure a safe and sustainable future for all species on planet Earth.

Videotape Graphics

 At this stage we suggest you watch the videotape. The graphics you will see on the screen are reproduced below to save you the trouble of copying them down. You might like to add your own comments as you watch the tape.

Neutral Culture-Based Criteria that Determine Conventionality

– longevity
– tradition
– reflection of prevailing values
– numbers
– tension

Neutral Culture-Based Criteria that Determine Conventionality

Example

A Methodist church in Macomb is conventional because, in this culture, it meets the criteria; a Methodist church in Pakistan would be non-conventional according to the same neutral criteria

---

Conventional Religions

Examples of core groups in the USA

Christian
– Lutherans
– Roman Catholics
– Episcopalians
– Methodists
– Reformed Presbyterians
– Baptists
– Independent Christian
– Eastern Orthodox Christian

Judaism
– Reformed
– Conservative
– Orthodox/Hasidic

Class 24

```
Middle Ground

Groups that because of differences of belief
or behavior may occupy middle ground between
conventionality and non-conventionality

Examples
– Adventists including Jehovah's Witnesses
– Mormons
– Christian Scientists
– Unitarian-Universalists
– certain Fundamentalist Christians
– ultra-orthodox Jews
```

```
Non-Conventional Religions

Examples
– Eastern traditions; Buddhism, Hinduism,
   Chinese and Japanese traditions
– Middle Eastern traditions; Islam, Baha'i
– New Age spirituality; Ramtha, Edge of Perception
– Skeptics, atheists, humanists
– New revelations; Unification Church, Scientology
– Millennial groups; Branch Davidians
– Occultists; spiritualists, psychics, ritual magic,
   Theosophy, Wicca, Tarot, Gnostics
```

Review Questions

Answering the following questions will help you review key class themes and prepare
for the examinations.

1. Identify an example of a conventional religion and explain why it is considered as such in
   American society.

2. Do the same for a non-conventional religion.

3. Do you agree with Professor Moore's assessment of the world's critical situation and his solution for it?

4. In the opening section of the first class, you were asked to jot down what "religion" meant to you. Has the concept of "religion" changed for you after participating in "Beliefs and Believers?" If so, how?

Class 24

Sources and Further Readings

Melton, Gordon. *The Encyclopedia of American Religions*. Detroit: Gale Research, 1989.

Institute for World Spirituality
The Chicago Theological Seminary
5757 S. University
Chicago, IL 60637-1507

kairos@worldspirit.org

http://www.worldspirit.org

TELECLASS PRODUCTION

Executive Producer ....David Ainsworth

Producer/Director .... Jon M. Tullos

Instructional Developer ....David Ainsworth

Assistant Producer .... Denise Graham Zahn

Assistant Directors ....Mike Griffith

Mark Traverso

Production Secretary... Sharon Browne

Editors: .... Mark Traverso

Jon M. Tullos

Audio .... Mark Burda

Jack Mulder

Video Engineers .... Ed Flowers

Barbara McLennan

Tom Sauch

Wally Strine

Electronic Graphics ....Jacquie Hemingway

Leone Middleton

Print Graphics ....Jacquie Hemingway

Still Photography .... Dick Burd

Production Assistants .... Nick Capodice

Tim Finchum

Chuck Klaas

Mark Kundla

Rudy Mendoza

Amy Sorenson

Svend Tranberg

Sohhyun Yi

Produced by Communications Services .... David Ainsworth, Acting Director
A division of the Center for Extended Learning and Communications Services

211